# Alienated

# CRITICAL AMERICA

General Editors: Richard Delgado and Jean Stefancic

# Alienated

*Immigrant Rights,*
*the Constitution, and*
*Equality in America*

Victor C. Romero

NEW YORK UNIVERSITY PRESS
*New York and London*

NEW YORK UNIVERSITY PRESS
New York and London
www.nyupress.org

Library of Congress Cataloging-in-Publication Data
Romero, Victor C.
Alienated : immigrant rights, the constitution,
and equality in America / Victor C. Romero.
p. cm. — (Critical America)
Includes bibliographical references and index.
ISBN 0-8147-7568-3 (cloth : alk. paper)
1. Emigration and immigration law—United States.
2. Constitutional law—United States.
I. Title.  II. Series.
KF4819.R66     2004
342.7308'2—dc22          2004015756

New York University Press books are printed on acid-free paper,
and their binding materials are chosen for strength and durability.

Manufactured in the United States of America
10 9 8 7 6 5 4 3 2 1

*To Corie, Ryan, and Julia*

We must delight in each other, make others' conditions our own, rejoyce together, mourn together, labor and suffer together, always having before our eyes our community as members of the same body.

—Governor John Winthrop, Massachusetts Bay Colony

# Contents

# Acknowledgments

I have been blessed with the support of many wonderful colleagues, friends, and family.

Thanks first to Richard Delgado and Jean Stefancic for suggesting that I might write a book for their Critical America series, and to Debbie Gershenowitz at NYU Press, whose vision helped provide shape and substance to the manuscript. Two anonymous readers provided useful and encouraging feedback.

For their willingness to read and comment on a full draft of the manuscript, I am grateful to Raquel Aldana-Pindell, Barb Brunner, Jen DeMichael, Julie Goldscheid, Tristan Loanzon, Alex Miller, and Metty Vithayathil.

I have been fortunate to have the encouragement of deans Peter Glenn and Phil McConnaughay, as well as my many colleagues at Penn State's Dickinson School of Law. Equally important has been the mentoring and friendship provided by the community of immigration scholars around the country. I want to especially acknowledge Jack Chin, Kevin Johnson, Steve Legomsky, Hiroshi Motomura, and Michael Olivas for their assistance over the years.

Research assistants past and present, including Vinny Avagliano, Barb Brunner, Jen DeMichael, Bill Dorgan, Matt Hughson, Gwenn McCollum, Amy Phillips, Penny Rebert, Raphael Sanchez, and Jeff Wong, contributed to the law review articles that formed the backbone of the manuscript.

For their unwavering support throughout, I have my family in the Philippines to thank: my parents, Roberta and Roel Romero; siblings, Georgy, Ben, Bets, and Billy; and the first person who talked to me about the law and lawyering, my late grandfather, Judge Francisco Carreon, Sr.

But most of all, I have my wonderful wife and best friend, Corie Phillips Romero, and my children-who-are-growing-up-too-fast, Ryan and Julia. Thank you for your patience, your laughter, and your unconditional love. It is to them that I dedicate this book.

Thanks as well to the many law review editors and associations who gave me permission to build upon my prior work in an attempt to capture my ideas in book form. Many of the ideas and significant portions of several chapters in this book first appeared in the following articles and essays:

Romero, Victor C. 1998. "Broadening Our World: Citizens and Immigrants of Color in America." *Capital University Law Review* 27 (Fall): 13–31.

———. 1998. "Expanding the Circle of Membership by Reconstructing the 'Alien': Lessons from Social Psychology and the 'Promise Enforcement' Cases." *University of Michigan Journal of Law Reform* 32: 1–47.

———. 2000. "Aren't You a Latino? Building Bridges upon Common Misperceptions." *University of California at Davis Law Review* 33: 837–49.

———. 2000. "The Domestic Fourth Amendment Rights of Undocumented Immigrants: On Guitterez and the Tort Law-Immigration Law Parallel." *Harvard Civil Rights–Civil Liberties Law Review* 35: 57–101.

———. 2000–01. "On Élian and Aliens: A Political Solution to the Plenary Power Problem." *NYU Journal of Legislation and Public Policy* 4: 343–86.

———. 2002. "Devolution and Discrimination." *NYU Annual Survey of American Law* 58: 377–86.

———. 2002. "Postsecondary Education for Undocumented Immigrants: Promises and Pitfalls." *North Carolina Journal of International and Commercial Regulation* 27 (Spring): 393–418.

———. 2002. "The Selective Deportation of Same-Gender Partners: In Search of the Rara Avis." *University of Miami Law Review* 56: 537–600.

———. 2003. "The Child Citizenship Act and the Family Reunification Act: Valuing the Citizen Child as Well as the Citizen Parent." *Florida Law Review* 55 (January): 489–509.

———. 2003. "Decoupling 'Terrorist' from 'Immigrant': An Enhanced Role for the Federal Courts Post-9/11." *Journal of Gender, Race and Justice* 7 (Spring): 201–11.

———. 2003. "Noncitizen Students and Immigration Policy Post-9/11." *Georgetown Immigration Law Journal* 17 (Spring): 357–66.

———. 2003. "Proxies for Loyalty in Constitutional Immigration Law: Citizenship and Race after September 11." *DePaul Law Review* 52: 871–91.

Finally, I thank Hap Palmer for permission to print part of the lyrics of "We Are All Alike" from the CD *Can Cockatoos Count by Twos?* Words and Music by Hap Palmer, © Hap-Pal Music, www.happalmer.com.

# Alienated

# Introduction

## *The Constitutional Immigration Law Paradox: How Do We Make Unequals Equal?*

*An Approach to the Constitutional Immigration Law Paradox:*
*Lessons from a Kids' Video and a Racist Encounter*

I study the intersection of American immigration and constitutional law, two fields that, by themselves, create enough problems for the average seeker, but when combined in the growing field of "constitutional immigration law" raise particularly perplexing issues. Put simply, immigration law divides people into citizens of the United States and others, between those who can claim legal status as full members of this republic, and those who cannot. While the Constitution recognizes this distinction, it simultaneously aspires to provide due process and equal protection of the laws to all persons, regardless of citizenship. So here is the dilemma: to what extent should the Constitution protect noncitizens—immigrants, undocumented persons, tourists, foreign students—in the United States?[1]

Living in multicultural America, our children learn early on to appreciate differences. My kids, ages three and five, have a favorite video of children's songs that they do not seem to tire of watching. One of the songs is entitled, "We Are All Alike,"[2] and opens this way: "Like each flake of snow falling from the sky, we are all unique, we are all alike. Take a look around, you will see it's true: you're a lot like me, I'm a lot like you." As a Filipino immigrant married to a Caucasian U.S.-born wife living in rural Pennsylvania, I like this song quite a bit. It teaches my children that even though they might look different from most of their friends, they really are very much the same: everyone has skin and eyes, the song continues, even though they may be of different shades and

1

shapes. It concludes by noting that "a common bond goes on and on, we're people one and all."

It's a great message, although it falls short of fully capturing twenty-first-century American life in at least two important ways. First, even if two children have the same color skin and the same shaped eyes, the U.S. Constitution explicitly allows our government to distinguish between them (which it does) based on whether they are citizens of the United States or not. Article I, Section 8, clause 4 grants Congress the power to establish "an uniform rule of naturalization," while the Fourteenth Amendment grants citizenship to those born or naturalized in the United States. Second, sometimes two children who have different skin tones and eye shapes are treated differently because society assumes that one of them is not a citizen of the United States, which is exacerbated by the lines the government is permitted to draw. As historian Philip Gleason has observed, America has long had "a latent disposition toward an ethnically defined concept of nationality."[3]

The following story from my first year of law teaching illustrates these two points more fully:

The fall of 1995 saw my wife's and my return to Pennsylvania after many years, when I was fortunate to be offered a job teaching at the Dickinson School of Law in Carlisle, just twenty minutes outside of Harrisburg, the state capital. Needless to say, we were both thrilled: Corie because she would be closer to her family after having spent a good bit of time in California, and me because of the opportunity to teach law. Having had our fill of Los Angeles, we were both excited to be moving to peaceful, rural south-central Pennsylvania. We gladly gave up our hour-long commutes in exchange for smog-free walks to the law school. And we settled into Carlisle nicely: on a handshake (our wonderful landlady did not believe in leases), we rented the ground floor of a quaint Victorian home in the town's historic district and looked forward to quickly assimilating into the culture of small-town life. We do not miss big city life. We have settled comfortably into our new roles, she as a graduate student and I as a law teacher, and we have come to fully appreciate the tranquility rural Pennsylvania has to offer. In a year's time, we have become small-town folk and have enjoyed the transformation along the way.

However, unlike probably 90 percent of Carlisle's married couples, we have an interracial marriage. Corie traces her Caucasian roots to Europe, while I came to the United States from the Philippines in 1984. And while 99 percent of the time Corie and I are never reminded of this difference by others, when we are, it can sometimes be a painful and frightening experience. On a balmy May evening in 1996, Corie and I decided to take a walk around the neighborhood, something which we have enjoyed on many an afternoon. As we crossed Willow heading south on West Street, we noticed a pick-up truck whose occupants began to whistle wolf-calls and shout lewd remarks. Naively, my first thought was that these words were being directed at others around us or at occupants of another vehicle. It soon became clear that we were the target of these obscenities:

"Hey, you Japanese sonofabitch! Why don't you fuck her? I have!"

That said, the truck slowly approached the next intersection, more obscenities coming from within. At the time, I remember trying to decide where we should run should these people come after us. Corie related to me later that a part of her wanted to grab me and kiss me passionately, proclaiming to our assaulters and the rest of the world that we were not ashamed of our relationship. After several tense moments, we were relieved to see the truck pull away as it rounded the corner. As a last show of power, one of the occupants extended his white arm and thrust his fist into the night air while simultaneously letting out a taunting laugh.

As the truck left our view, Corie and I abandoned our walk and hurried home. Surprisingly, the primary emotion we felt was not anger, but hurt and sadness. Hurt, because we felt that it was unfair that we could no longer enjoy walking around our neighborhood at night; sadness, because here we were in 1996, in what was otherwise an idyllic community, and we had to endure the kind of racist remarks many people only read about in books. Indeed, Corie told me later that evening, "For the first time, I experienced what it is like to be a minority."

Recall my opening point: Even if two individuals appear to be of the same physical makeup, the Constitution permits the government to draw distinctions between them based on their citizenship. Had I been white, Corie and I would probably not have been harassed. The truckers would probably have seen us as no different from them—same color skin, same shaped eyes—and would have looked for another target. But even if I had been physically white, the government could have treated me as if I was not, and indeed, it formerly did so by way of the immigration laws.[4] For example, in 1924, Congress passed a law limiting immigration from southern and eastern Europe.[5] While few (including our harassers) would consider an Italian or Hungarian "nonwhite" today, the federal government, representing the people of the United States, saw fit to limit the influx of otherwise "white" southern and eastern Europeans because of their narrow, Anglocentric view of whiteness. But the intersection of race and immigration still finds its way into contemporary legislation, resulting in the 1990 creation of an immigrant visa lottery that, in operation, favors the Irish above all groups.[6]

The narrative illustrates the second point even more vividly. Where individuals appear to be different, society sometimes assumes them to be foreigners, influenced in part by the government's decision to draw lines based on citizenship. Because I have almond-shaped eyes and brown skin, our harassers decided to use the slur "Jap." Although they may not have consciously gone through this analysis, their decision to use that term highlighted not only the *racial* differences between Corie and me, but also implied my *foreignness,* a sense that I did not belong, and could not be trusted, either with my "American" wife or in the United States. It is difficult to ignore the role law has played in equating race with foreignness, adding a normative dimension to what should be a legal status only. In *Korematsu v. United States,*[7] the U.S. Supreme Court upheld the federal government's wartime decision to establish internment camps for citizens and noncitizens of Japanese ancestry, deferring to the military's assessment of the dangers posed to the West Coast following the Pearl Harbor attack. The Court relied heavily on the testimony of General John L. Dewitt, who, interestingly enough, chose the same slur that our friends did when he told a congressional panel that, regardless of citizenship, "a Jap's a Jap."[8]

As critical race theorist Neil Gotanda explains, "The evacuated Japanese-Americans, including U.S. citizens, were presumed to be sufficiently foreign for an inference by the military that such racial-foreigners must be disloyal. Japanese Americans were therefore characterized as different from the African-American racial minority. With the presence of racial foreignness, a presumption of disloyalty was reasonable and natural."[9] More recently, while the Bush administration has publicly condemned vigilante attacks against Arab and Muslim populations following the September 11 tragedy, it has simultaneously given wide latitude to Attorney General John Ashcroft to use minor immigration violations as the pretext to round up many Arabs and Muslims for possible links to terrorism.

So I return to the question: To what extent should the Constitution protect noncitizens in the United States? In my view, the best reading of the Constitution is one that provides as much parity as possible between citizen and noncitizen, regardless of formal immigration status. Throughout American history, the government has used U.S. citizenship and immigration law to protect privileged groups from less privileged ones, using citizenship as a "legitimate" proxy for otherwise invidious, and often unconstitutional, discrimination on the basis of race. While governmental racial discrimination is rarely constitutionally acceptable today, profiling on the basis of citizenship is still largely unchecked. I suggest that "we, the people" should be concerned about the possible abuse of this government power, and provide theoretical and practical alternatives to the status quo.

I base this reading of the Constitution on two tenets of critical race scholarship: "antiessentialism" and "antisubordination."[10] "Antiessentialism" dictates that the Constitution should be read so as not to assume that all people are alike just because they look alike. Thus, no one would argue that Microsoft billionaire Bill Gates and the "American Taliban" John Walker Lindh enjoy the same privileges or perceive the world in the same way simply because they are both white males. Put differently, one cannot divine the shared characteristics of a group based on a single real or perceived trait like race or gender (think especially of the difficulties endured by biracial or mixed-race individuals!).[11] The danger of antiessentialism, however, is that it might be used to perpetuate an oppressive status quo—if immigrants do not want to be treated as a group but as individuals, shouldn't the government eliminate all categories that divide on the basis of group characteristics, such as affirmative action programs for racial minorities? In response, the "antisubordination" principle asks whether the challenged government action works to further the oppressive status quo or undermine it (and would therefore argue in favor of affirmative action). Hence, an "antisubordination" reading of the Constitution would work to protect foreign nationals who, because of their citizenship status, already enjoy fewer rights than their U.S. citizen counterparts. Finding lawful ways to give more rights to noncitizens helps level a playing field that the Constitution allows Congress to create unevenly. These two principles find expression in my critique of my children's music video: even those who appear alike in terms of race and gender might not necessarily be treated alike by the government because of their citizenship (antiessentialism); and those who are perceived as different (because of race or gender, say) may be more likely to be treated differently by a government that uses citizenship as a proxy, therefore cautioning special vigilance under the Constitution's equality principle (antisubordination).

This book will advance a multidimensional, interdisciplinary analysis of constitutional immigration law that supports an equality-based reading of the Constitution; apply this multifaceted approach to several pressing immigrant rights issues of the day; and articulate an alternative theoretical and practical vision to the status quo, one that more fully preserves the personhood of noncitizens in the United States.[12] I explore each of these three goals in greater detail below.

First, I employ a multidimensional, critical analysis of constitutional immigration law that supports an equality-based reading of the Constitution, drawing liberally from three sources aside from the tools of traditional constitutional interpretation: (1) my own experiences as an adult immigrant and naturalized U.S. citizen from the Philippines; (2) areas of the law outside constitutional immigration law, such as tort theory; and (3) nonlegal perspectives such as history and social psychology. Too often, conventional constitutional law is more concerned with theories of interpreting the text (or history or structure or precedent) that fail to truly consider the effects such interpretations have on those subject to the Constitution. By resorting to personal narrative, nonconstitutional immigration law, and nonlegal sources, I hope to provide another side to the story in a way that gives meaning to the law's effect on the average noncitizen. More specifically, I believe this interdisciplinary approach provides a more nuanced and accurate analysis of immigrant rights issues when compared with the current system, which often privileges government power to the detriment of substantial and important human rights concerns. Chapter 1 illustrates this multidimensional analysis by briefly reviewing the Supreme Court's constitutional immigration law jurisprudence, paying attention to the themes of antiessentialism and antisubordination I have outlined above.

My second goal is to apply this multidimensional analysis to various problems in constitutional immigration law, starting first with a brief look at the post-9/11 climate in chapter 2, placing the terrorist tragedy in a larger interdisciplinary context before focusing on specific issues related to immigration. I discuss the federal government's immigration enforcement response to the 9/11 tragedy by examining citizenship and race as proxies for (dis)loyalty, both in a historical and contemporary setting, drawing upon insights from disciplines outside the law such as history and criminal sociology. From this broad, interdisciplinary discussion, I narrow the focus a bit to explore the government's use of immigration law as a vehicle for combating terrorism. As the war against terrorism continues to be a likely emphasis, rightly or wrongly, of our immigration policy, chapter 2 urges that Congress and the president continue to explore reasonable solutions that further the ends of equal and fair treatment for noncitizens.

It seems the 9/11 tragedy made nearly every noncitizen (and a few U.S. citizens) a potential terrorist suspect. As 9/11 fades from view, and as the federal government is better able to balance its immigration needs and its national security interests, state and federal governments will turn more of their attention to the treatment of ordinary, nonterrorist noncitizens living in the United States.

Chapter 3 examines the tension between two long-held values in immigration policy: family unification and the deportation of criminal noncitizens. Put simply, the issue is this, should the government be allowed to deport a noncitizen for criminal activity even when that means separating her from her family?

Chapter 4 explores the Constitution's Fourth Amendment right to be free from unreasonable searches and seizures, paying particular attention to recent Court decisions suggesting that perhaps certain undocumented migrants may not constitute "the People" the text describes as enjoying the right. I critique these decisions for failing to understand that whether one is "undocumented" is less a question of morality than of immigration policy.

Chapter 5 explores a possible "ceiling" of rights for the undocumented migrant by focusing on the issue of subsidized access to public postsecondary education. A growing immigrant rights concern is the extent to which many public colleges and universities preclude undocumented persons from obtaining financial aid to attend, despite being among the most qualified. Chapter 5 surveys the federal and state landscape, noting a growing number of states that are beginning to provide tuition subsidies for the undocumented; interestingly, most approved this legislation after 9/11. I conclude, however, that the greatest chance for true equality for undocumented students lies in federal protection, most likely through the passage of legislation designed to adjust students' immigration status while simultaneously providing financial aid for college.

Chapter 6 analyzes the extent to which the Supreme Court's gay rights and immigrant rights cases since the 1980s might provide insight into the government's practice of selectively deporting certain groups of noncitizens—to wit, would the Supreme Court find constitutional the deportation of a foreigner wed to a U.S. citizen in a same-gender marriage ceremony performed in Massachusetts? This question brings together two civil rights issues likely to be of paramount concern in the coming years: gay rights and immigrant rights. Although most commentators believe that selective deportation based on race would be outrageous, no one has explored the contours of the test as applied to same-gender binational partnerships.

My third goal for this book is to outline a pragmatic strategy for securing greater protection for noncitizens. To this end, chapter 7 will offer both theoretical alternatives and practical solutions to those wishing to secure greater rights for noncitizens. Despite the popular conception (and the legacy of *Marbury v. Madison*) that the Supreme Court is the final arbiter of the Constitution, I subscribe to the view[13] that legislators at the state and local levels are also entrusted with constitutional interpretation and can be, in some instances, more effective in securing rights for noncitizens than their federal counterparts in the judiciary or Congress might be. I argue that preserving personhood in the face of constitutionally permissible discrimination against noncitizens is paramount to upholding the equality norms of antiessentialism and antisubordination. I also consider whether it would benefit certain noncitizen out-groups to have states gain more control over immigration policy. I contend that while immigration devolution might not have positive effects on race relations, it might improve the prospects of gay and lesbian noncitizens, especially in the context of their binational relationships with U.S. citizens as discussed in chapter 6.

Finally, I turn to the nuts and bolts of implementing a more immigrant-friendly political agenda. While I have contended throughout that federal legislative and judicial efforts are most likely to effect widespread relief for noncitizens, I argue that immigrant rights advocates should not neglect state and local initiatives aimed at benefiting noncitizens. State and local initiatives might sometimes work better than federal ones because interested citizens are more likely to know the benefactors of their largesse as people first, rather than as noncitizens of the United States. Put simply, it's easier to sympathize with one's neighbor than it is with some unnamed individual across the country. Although immigration law reform can only be effected at the federal level, improving the lives of noncitizens among us can be done in our own communities every day.

# 1

# Equality for All as a Constitutional Mandate (Noncitizens Included!)

In this brief chapter, I combine a traditional analysis of constitutional immigration law with the multidimensional approach I described earlier—merging personal narrative, other legal sources, and nonlegal sources—in support of my thesis that the best reading of the Constitution is one that maximizes parity between the U.S. citizen and noncitizen, regardless of the latter's formal immigration status.

## First Things First: Examining the Constitution's Text

A traditional legal analysis of American "constitutional immigration law" would likely begin by asking to which government—federal or state—the Constitution grants power over immigration policy, which dictates the flow of noncitizens in and out of the United States. After all, the founding of the federal republic succeeded the establishment of the thirteen states, and it is therefore generally understood that the federal government is one of limited powers. By default, then, the individual states should have power over immigration unless the Constitution says otherwise.

One traditional approach to this dispute is to look at the text of the U.S. Constitution, which purports to allocate powers between these entities. Unfortunately, the word "immigration" appears nowhere in the Constitution.[1] The terms "naturalization,"[2] "commerce with foreign nations,"[3] and the congressional power "to declare war"[4] have all been raised as possible textual foundations for the federal immigration authority,[5] although none specifically use the term. Immigration scholar

Steve Legomsky has raised the question whether immigration might be a "necessary and proper"[6] derivative of the federal government's naturalization power.[7]

## A Contextual Analysis of Precedent: The Noncitizen Outsiders (Shoved?) behind the Plenary Power Doctrine

In the absence of specific textual support, lawyers rely on judicial precedents to support constitutional claims. In that vein, the U.S. Supreme Court has long found the immigration power to reside in the federal government, and not among the states. Specifically, the Court has consistently affirmed, explicitly and implicitly, Congress's power to enact legislation requiring the exclusion or expulsion of various noncitizens based on the federal legislature's and executive's best judgment as to the proper balance between these foreigners' desire to remain as our guests and the nation's interest in denying them access. At one level of logic and law, such judicial deference to the political branches makes sense. If Congress believes that a noncitizen poses a national security risk, then the Supreme Court should not stand in the way of the executive branch enforcing Congress's conclusion arrived at for the benefit of the United States and its citizens.

But there are, of course, other sides to this story. Against the apparently logical exposition of constitutional text and precedent described above, we should examine the context in which the political branches chose to exclude or expel the noncitizens in those cases brought before the Supreme Court. A great many of them were brought by noncitizen plaintiffs who were societal outsiders, such as the turn-of-the-twentieth century Chinese in *Chae Chan Ping*[8] and *Fong Yue Ting*,[9] communist sympathizers in the 1950s trilogy of *Knauff*,[10] *Harisiades*,[11] and *Mezei*,[12] and alleged terrorists of the 1990s in *Reno v. AADC*.[13] These cases are worth a closer look.

The genesis of the plenary power doctrine lies in the infamous 1889 *Chinese Exclusion Case* entitled *Chae Chan Ping v. United States*.[14] The Supreme Court upheld congressional revocation of entry permits to Chae Chan Ping, a Chinese laborer who had temporarily left the United States in reliance on these reentry documents. After recognizing that the power to exclude noncitizens is incidental to national sovereignty, the Court concluded that "[w]hatever license, therefore, Chinese laborers may have obtained, previous to the act of October 1, 1888, to return to the United States after their departure, is held at the will of the government, revocable at any time, at its pleasure."[15] The Court further noted that it could not second-guess Congress's decision to enact a race-based exclusionary policy, stating that such "determination is conclusive upon the judiciary."[16]

*Chae Chan Ping* is an especially important case because just three years prior, the Court had recognized that the Chinese could avail themselves of the Constitution's Equal Protection Clause to protect themselves against invidious racial discrimination. In *Yick Wo v. Hopkins*,[17] the Court overturned the conviction of a Chinese national for violating a San Francisco safety ordinance regulating the operation of laundries. The evidence clearly showed that variances were granted to all but one of the non-Chinese operators, while all the Chinese-run laundries had been ordered closed.

Read together, *Chae Chan Ping* and *Yick Wo* indicate that the Court was willing to defer to legislative and executive action in the realm of immigration policy, but not outside it. Because *Yick Wo* focused on nonimmigration issues, the Court was free to develop the plenary power doctrine in immigration law as it saw fit. In its 1893 decision in *Fong Yue Ting v. United States*,[18] the Court built upon the foundation laid in *Chae Chan Ping* by upholding a congressional statute requiring Chinese nationals (and only Chinese nationals)[19] to register with the federal government or face deportation. While recognizing the constitutional limits placed on government conduct by cases such as *Yick Wo*, the Court quickly added that because "they continue to be aliens, . . . [the Chinese respondents] remain subject to the power of Congress to expel them, or to order them to be removed and deported from the country, whenever in its judgment their removal is necessary or expedient for the public interest."[20]

While these race-based exclusionary rules generally abated from the late 1800s through World War II,[21] the 1950s saw the return of the plenary power doctrine in three decisions that squarely pitted individual claims to both procedural and substantive constitutional rights against Congress's plenary power over immigration. This time, racial prejudice was not the underlying reason for individual exclusion; instead, the fear of communism drove congressional action.

In the first case, *United States ex rel. Knauff v. Shaughnessy*,[22] the noncitizen wife of a U.S. citizen was barred entry into the United States based on classified information obtained by the government, which, it was later revealed, suggested that she had communist affiliations. Knauff argued before the Supreme Court that exclusion without a hearing compromised her due process rights. In rejecting this argument and reaffirming Congress's plenary power over immigration matters, the Court issued a chilling pronouncement: "Whatever the procedure authorized by Congress is, it is due process as far as an alien denied entry is concerned."[23] Even considering the country's anticommunist mood at the time, the extent to which the Court was willing to defer to Congress in *Knauff* was noteworthy, if not surprising. Knauff, the noncitizen spouse of a U.S. citizen, only wanted an opportunity to be heard, yet the Court was unwilling to grant even that.

Nonetheless, supporters of individual rights could have taken solace in *Knauff*'s limited impact. First, *Knauff* did not endorse the abrogation of any *substantive* constitutional rights, only *procedural* ones. If the *Knauff* court had dealt with Knauff's claim that she had been deprived of her First Amendment right to free speech, for example, it would have presumably given greater weight to that substantive claim than to her procedural assertion that she was not granted an opportunity to be heard. Indeed, after the Supreme Court rendered its decision, administrative hearings were held and eventually the Board of Immigration Appeals found Knauff admissible on the merits.[24] Second, the *Knauff* opinion upholding the denial of a hearing might arguably have applied only to first-time entrants to the United States. For instance, one might argue that a longtime resident of the United States who returns from a temporary trip abroad should be entitled to greater procedural rights than Knauff, a person seeking entry into the country for the first time.

However, in the three years following *Knauff,* the Court expanded Congress's plenary power in two important cases. In *Harisiades v. Shaughnessy,*[25] the Court filled the *Knauff* gap between procedural and substantive rights by denying noncitizens' claims on substantive constitutional law grounds. A year later, in *Shaughnessy v. U.S. ex rel. Mezei,*[26] the Court extended its *Knauff* holding to deny the procedural due process claim of a long-time U.S. resident seeking reentry.

In *Harisiades,* the Court approved the removal[27] of three former Communist Party members who were rendered deportable under a recently enacted congressional act. Passed after the petitioners had quit the Communist Party, the statute made deportable any individual who had ever advocated the violent overthrow of the U.S. government. The petitioners did not dispute the government's assertion that the Communist Party adhered to that belief, and they were accordingly adjudged deportable. The petitioners' citations of the Due Process Clause, the First Amendment, and the Ex Post Facto Clause notwithstanding, the Court upheld the law, finding violations of none of these three substantive constitutional provisions.[28]

*Harisiades* thus appeared to preclude substantive constitutional rights claims left open by the *Knauff* Court's procedural approach. After *Harisiades,* not only could Congress deny an individual noncitizen the right to a hearing, but it could also retroactively apply a new deportation law to remove a noncitizen whose affiliation with the offending organization had already ended! In language tracking that seen in other plenary power cases, the *Harisiades* Court justified this abrogation of the petitioner's substantive rights by stating that it was not its role to formulate immigration policy, that this was the role of the political branches, and, therefore, any grievances arising out of such policy should be addressed to those bodies:

> We think that, in the present state of the world, it would be rash and irresponsible to reinterpret our fundamental law to deny or qualify the Government's power of deportation. However desirable world-wide amelioration of the lot of aliens, we think it is peculiarly a subject for international diplomacy. . . . Reform in this field must be entrusted to the branches of the Government in control of our international relations and treaty-making powers.[29]

Just as the Court extended the plenary power doctrine to reach substantive claims in *Harisiades,* it also broadened the *Knauff* holding in *Mezei* by curtailing procedural due process for a longtime U.S. resident.[30] Mezei, a U.S. resident for twenty-five years, was denied readmission into the country after leaving temporarily to visit his ailing mother in Romania. Upon his return, he was detained on Ellis Island as excludable, ostensibly for national security reasons, and therefore sought admission elsewhere. After he was denied entry in over a dozen countries, Mezei advised the INS that he would no longer seek to depart. He then challenged his confinement on Ellis Island without a hearing as a denial of due process.[31]

The District Court and Court of Appeals granted Mezei's request for a hearing, perhaps signaling limits on Congress's heretofore plenary power over immigration or, alternatively, the decline of the "red scare."[32] In addition, these decisions renewed the hope that some constitutional individual rights claims could survive *Knauff* and *Harisiades*.

However, upon appeal to the Supreme Court, *Mezei* followed precedent, and the Court overturned the lower courts' decisions. After the Court recited the facts, its first statement was a reaffirmation of the plenary power of Congress followed by a citation of the four cases described above—*Chae Chan Ping, Fong Yue Ting, Knauff,* and *Harisiades*: "Courts have long recognized the power to expel or exclude aliens as a fundamental sovereign attribute exercised by the Government's political departments largely immune from judicial control."[33] While acknowledging that departing noncitizens may avail themselves of procedural due process protections, the Court appeared to characterize Mezei not as a returning twenty-five-year resident, but as "an alien on the threshold of initial entry."[34] As such, *Knauff*'s deferential standard of judicial review applied to the Attorney General's actions here: "Whatever the procedure authorized by Congress is, it is due process as far as an alien denied entry is concerned."[35] Despite the attempts by Justices Jackson and Black in dissents to distinguish *Knauff* by emphasizing that, unlike Knauff, Mezei was actually detained at Ellis Island and therefore deserved at least a hearing on the merits,[36] the Court would not be dissuaded. As in the two other "anticommunist" era cases—*Knauff* and *Harisiades*—the stigma attached to suspected Communist Party affiliations played an apparent role in the Court's findings. For example, in distinguishing Mezei's case from *Kwong Hai Chew v. Colding,*[37] which had recognized that lawful permanent residents deserved due process protection when returning from a temporary sojourn abroad, the Court specifically mentioned Mezei's nineteen months behind the "Iron Curtain" as cause for suspicion.[38] Just as *Chae Chan Ping* and *Fong Yue Ting* appeared to have been driven by nativistic sentiments fueled by race prejudice against the Chinese,[39] *Knauff, Harisiades,* and *Mezei* were decided under the specter of the burgeoning Cold War, when allegations of Communist Party affiliation were, for noncitizens, scarlet letters that could lead to summary exclusion.

Just as it upheld the immigration powers of Congress and the executive against the asserted rights of Chinese nationals in the 1880–90s and foreign communist sympathizers in the 1950s, the Supreme Court has continued this trend against suspected terrorists in the late 1990s. In *Reno v. American-Arab Anti-Discrimination Committee,*[40] the Court stated that noncitizens could not defend against an otherwise valid deportation order by claiming that their First Amendment associational rights had been violated. The Immigration and Naturalization Service (INS) had sought to deport eight noncitizens (two of whom were permanent residents) because of their affiliation with the Popular Front for the Liberation of Palestine (PFLP), which the government described as a terrorist organization.

In response to the First Amendment defense, the government contended that while the freedom to associate would protect the rights of U.S. citizens to affiliate with groups such as the PFLP, the same protection does not extend to noncitizens. The lower courts agreed with the noncitizens that the First Amendment required that they not be selectively targeted for deportation solely because of their political affiliations.

The Justice Department pursued an appeal to the Supreme Court. Although the case was resolved on statutory grounds, the Court nonetheless ruled on the selective prosecution argument, siding with the government and noting that the First Amendment typically did not prevent the INS from choosing whom to deport among noncitizens illegally present: "[A]n alien unlawfully in this country has no constitutional right to assert selective enforcement as a defense against his deportation."[41] The Court reasoned that allowing such claims would unnecessarily hamper the operations of the executive branch as it seeks to merely enforce the immigration rules set by Congress. Without specifying a concrete example, the Court did note, however, that rare cases may arise in which the alleged basis of discrimination is so outrageous that the balance tipped in the noncitizen's favor.

While not specifically mentioned, the plenary power doctrine underlies the Court's argument here as well. Congress has the power to determine the terms and conditions of a noncitizen's presence in the United States and has vested in the Attorney General the power to enforce such provisions; therefore, it is not for the Court to second-guess the other branches' actions in the typical deportation case except when their conduct is constitutionally outrageous. Thus, *Reno v. AADC* has both a positive and a negative message for noncitizen constitutional claimants in the immigration context. The good news is that the Court has left open the possibility that the government is precluded from engaging in discriminatory conduct so egregious as to rise to the level of a constitutional offense. The bad news is that the Court views such a possibility as arising in the "rare case"[42] and that, otherwise, the Court should defer to the political

branches' expertise in immigration matters even if an analogous prosecution of citizens based on their group affiliations would raise a valid constitutional claim.

Further, the Court's deference to a Congress and executive bent on
combating "terrorism" is reminiscent of the prejudice against the Chinese
underlying *Chae Chan Ping* and *Fong Yue Ting*, or the "red scare" that
likely influenced the *Knauff, Harisiades,* and *Mezei* decisions. While race
relations have improved in the years since *Chae Chan Ping* and the end
of the Cold War will preclude a reprise of *Knauff,* these precedents are
still cited to justify the denial of noncitizens' constitutional claims in the
name of congressional plenary power over immigration, this time against
alleged terrorist supporters, which will be of continuing, sustained concern in post-9/11 America.[43] Perhaps even more interesting will be the extent to which other out-groups find themselves collaterally affected by
stricter immigration norms justified ostensibly by national security concerns. Might undocumented immigration, for example, resurface as a federal concern as it did during the Depression and post–World War II years,
this time recast not as a mere border control concern but as an antiterrorism issue? Conservative journalist Michelle Malkin (herself a first-gen-
eration Filipino American) argues vehemently that halting undocumented
immigration should be considered a national security concern and advocates broad reforms, citing, among other things, reports that al-Qaeda
operatives obtained false immigration documents from Mexican smug-
glers.[44] To the extent the American public and its government representatives subscribe to Malkin's views on immigration, there might be many
more groups other than suspected terrorists who might fit her so-called
"immigrant profil[e]."[45]

## Narratives and Extralegal Perspectives: Why Upholding Equal Treatment Is Important

Despite its problematic treatment of racial and political outsiders, the traditional legal analysis of constitutional immigration law yields a logical
policy argument in favor of strong federal congressional and executive
power over immigration, supported by the Constitution's text and the
Supreme Court's precedent. When placed into actual context, however,
another side of the story is revealed. In the preceding section, I questioned
the wisdom of deferring to federal political branches whose view of the

dangerous or undesirable foreigner may be based less on reality than on false perception.

Regardless of how one answers the foregoing question, I suggest that the Constitution generally requires the protection of those most vulnerable to unfair treatment. The equal protection guarantees of the Fifth and Fourteenth Amendments[46] require the government to treat all "persons," not just citizens, equally. The plenary power cases described above teach us that we should be skeptical about how the political branches characterize threats by others, especially noncitizens, whom they deem to be different. The federal courts were created to provide a check on the actions of political majorities, especially when they appear to be acting arbitrarily against vulnerable minorities.[47]

Nevertheless, a strong disconnect exists between people's perceptions of how immigration law operates and how it works in fact. The following personal narratives illustrate how we who live in America (whether citizen or not) perceive and expect immigration law and policy to treat noncitizens more fairly than it does. This gap between perception and reality suggests that legal actors, whether the judiciary checking the political branches or the political branches creating immigration policy, should strive for parity and equality between the rights of citizens and noncitizens living in the United States. While it is true that for many laypersons, laws and legal institutions of any kind are puzzling, immigration and nationality laws present a particularly difficult challenge because they often operate contrary to the way many Americans assume they should.

I arrived in the United States as a foreign student in 1984. After graduating from college and completing a year as a litigation paralegal at a law firm on the east coast, I moved to Los Angeles to begin law school in the fall of 1988. Since I had not been back to visit my family in Manila for a few years, my mother was anxious to have me return during the semester break in December. Because my original student visa had expired, I consulted with the International Students Office (ISO) at my university, who gave me updated paperwork that they said I should show to the U.S. Embassy in Manila while I was home. I asked the ISO personnel whether they thought my lapsed visa would raise red flags and they assured me it would not because I was legitimately enrolled in a graduate program.

After enjoying the holidays with family and friends, I dutifully appeared at the U.S. Embassy to renew my student visa. At the interview, the consul asked me what I planned to do with my U.S. law degree, since I would not be able to practice law either in America (I would need a different visa for that) or the Philippines (which requires that one complete law school there). Naively, but in all sincerity, I responded that I had not thought that one through, but in the meantime I found valuable the education I was receiving. At the end of the interview, she told me that she was denying my application. I cannot recall whether she gave me the reasons for her denial, but I surmise now that she did not believe I intended to return to the Philippines because I was studying American law, which would not allow me to practice law back home; the implication is that I, like many Filipinos, was intending to stay beyond graduate school—in immigration parlance, to "overstay." I objected that had I known that my visa would be denied, I would have not invested the time, money, and effort to move to Los Angeles to begin my graduate studies, but would have returned to Manila instead. I believe she said she was sorry, but she stood firmly behind her decision. I asked for her name and how I could appeal the decision. She said it was not the Embassy's policy to give out names, but that I could file an appeal with her supervisor, which I did, to no avail.

Like Chae Chan Ping and his counterparts in *The Chinese Exclusion Case,* even though I had a certificate to return, the Consular Officer had the discretion to deny me that opportunity if she thought I was an overstay risk. Yet the assumptions that I made and that were made by other nonlawyers around me about how the immigration system *would* work suggests that I and others expected better treatment from the law and its enforcers—that I would be treated as an individual and not as an overstay risk simply because I was a Filipino national seeking a visa to continue his legal studies in the United States. First, I assumed that because my undergraduate school had complied with INS regulations regarding my enrollment, my graduate school would have as well. I mistakenly believed that by disclosing my citizenship status on my graduate school application, such information would be shared with the federal government so that I would enjoy the same privileges as my citizen classmates.[48] Second, I assumed that when an International Students Office, which is dedicated to normalizing the school experiences of foreign and citizen students, renders immigration advice, such advice is trustworthy and reliable. Third, I assumed that the Consular Office in Manila would be able to fairly balance the equities and treat my case on an individual basis. I thought that my many years as a student legally in the United States and the fact that I had already begun my law school studies would have outweighed my inadvertent overstay.

Fourth, and perhaps most telling, my law school classmates assumed that if I had been treated unfairly, it was not the American government's doing. When word got back to campus that I had taken a leave of absence, my classmates uniformly assumed that it was because the Philippine government would not let me leave, not that the U.S. government would not let me return. My classmates, like many in the public, were under the mistaken assumption that it was (and is) fairly easy to lawfully enter the United States. With few exceptions, there are but four ways a noncitizen can immigrate to the United States—that is, make America her permanent home—namely, through a close family relationship, through an employment opportunity, by winning the immigration "diversity" lottery, or by qualifying as a refugee. I became an American not because of my achievements in college or law school, but because my wife happens to be an American citizen.

I suspect that some readers (especially immigration lawyers and scholars) may find the foregoing narrative unconvincing on the merits. After all, I have provided reasons for why the Consular Officer acted within her discretion: I was an overstay, I was from the Philippines, I was pursuing a law degree which was of no real use to me back in Manila. Of course, I have also offered an alternative analysis: I did not intend to overstay, I had lived in the United States for several years without incident, I valued the education I was receiving for its own sake.

But to me, the most interesting question is whether it was permissible for the Consular Officer to use my Philippine citizenship as a factor in determining whether I was an overstay risk (again, since she did not provide me the reasons for her decision, I am speculating here, but at least one U.S. consulate was found in court to have explicitly engaged in racial and ethnic profiling).[49] Writer Dinesh D'Souza would argue that it was reasonable for the Consular Officer to rely on my being Filipino as one factor in her determination, even if others might object to it as racist. In *The End of Racism,* D'Souza relates the story of Michelle Joo, an Asian American shopkeeper in Washington, D.C., who discriminates on the basis of race in deciding whether or not to let prospective patrons into her jewelry and cosmetics store.[50] "Young black men are kept out if they seem rowdy, Joo says."[51] This theory suggests that, in order to protect property, it is rational to discriminate against racial groups; the color of their skin and the allegedly high statistical correlation between race and crime make race relevant. D'Souza calls this "rational racism."[52] Others might agree with D'Souza, but for different reasons. Peter Schuck has noted that discriminating on the basis of national origin is not the same as race-based discrimination—he cites the statistic that half of all immigrants from Africa are white, not all black as some might presume.[53] Hence, Schuck might argue that if the Consular Officer based her decision partly on my Filipino citizenship, then that was based on my national origin, not my race.

Whether one describes this as rational racism or national origin discrimination, I respond by returning to the first principles of antiessentialism and antisubordination. As Steven Pinker reminds us, statistical correlations based on racial stereotypes might be rational, but they violate the moral imperative of treating individuals as individuals, and not as group members. Moreover, while national origin and race are not synonymous, we should be more skeptical of their intersectionality when used by the government to perpetuate subordination. Thus, U.S. Consular Officers should not favor Filipino *mestizos* (usually fairer-skinned persons of Spanish or American heritage) over Filipinos of aboriginal, Malayo-Polynesian, or Chinese stock. A legacy of European colonialism, favoritism for "whiter" individuals of the same race or citizenship is common among peoples as diverse as African Americans, Filipinos, and Latin Americans. Indeed, Michael Lind has argued that with the growing number of interracial marriages between Caucasians and Latino/as *and* Caucasians and Asians, as compared with fewer marriages between Caucasians and African Americans, America may soon find that the racial divide will play along shades of brown, much like it does among communities of color around the world.[54]

Another important lesson to be drawn from antiessentialism is that citizens of color are not immune from alienage discrimination, as this second narrative about my U.S. citizenship interview demonstrates. After having received my citizenship interview notice in the mail, I carefully gathered and reviewed the documents the INS requested that I bring and went to the local office in downtown Los Angeles for my interview, the last step before actually being sworn in as a citizen. I handed my papers to the clerk and took a seat among the many others—the white, black, brown, and yellow faces, some with lawyers, some without—waiting patiently for their names to be called. When I got up to stretch my legs, I overheard one of the INS clerks say to another in disgust, "Can you read this? Can you believe some of these names?" implying that it would have been much easier if everyone had an "American" name like "Mike

Smith" or "John Jones," rather than "Guillermo Rodriguez" or "Lee Jee Yoon."[55]

Finally, my name was called (and pronounced correctly) and I was led in to talk to an INS officer, who I believed was Latina. After I had completed the citizenship test, the examiner reviewed the documents I had. Because I had obtained my immigrant status through my marriage to a U.S. citizen, the papers I brought were supposed to show that we were still legally married. I had also brought copies of my bank account statements and other documents the INS notice requested. The Latina officer took one quick look at my papers and said, "None of these show that you are married to your wife *today*. Do you have any documentation to prove that you are married to her *today*?" I told her that I had brought what the notice said I should but that I could very easily call my wife and ask her to come over because her office was only a few minutes away. "No," she replied, rejecting my suggestion with a huff, "we will not do that." Trying to keep my composure, I searched my wallet desperately for some piece of information that might satisfy the officer. I produced a State Farm auto insurance card with both my wife's and my name on it and feebly handed it over to the officer. "This will work," she said. Before I knew it, she turned to me with a smile and said, "Congratulations!" as if nothing had happened. As I left the INS office in a daze, my citizenship certificate in hand, I thought to myself sarcastically, "Well, Victor, welcome to America!"

Looking back at that experience, why could not that Latina INS officer have been more sympathetic to me? Why could she not have thought about her own ancestors and many of her Latino/a brothers and sisters, who like me have to deal with "La Migra"[56] every day, often under much more stressful and unpleasant circumstances? Why would she treat me as the "other" after I had played by all the rules, after I had carefully reviewed the documents her agency had required of me and had brought them to the interview? Did she take steps to make sure that the other clerks did not look down upon those with "foreign-sounding names"[57] but instead tried to help them understand that America should be a celebration of different names, cultures, and peoples? This narrative is a cautionary tale of how my essentialist assumptions about this person (i.e., "she'll be sympathetic; she's Latina") were sorely misguided, and how multiculturalism (here, the hiring of a Latina to serve as an INS officer) can be coopted by the dominant power to perpetuate, rather than dismantle, subordination. Political historian Angela Dillard documents the rise of what she calls "multicultural conservatism" in her book, *Guess Who's Coming to Dinner* Now? Dillard points to the Bush administration's multicultural cabinet as an example of the conservative right coopting affirmative action by exploiting essentialist thinking in the service of the status quo. While Bush has appointed more people of color to cabinet positions than even Bill Clinton, he has chosen conservatives—Condoleeza Rice and Colin Powell, among others—to fill these positions, not unlike the way his father tapped Clarence Thomas to fill the "black slot" vacated by Justice Thurgood Marshall.[58] As another example of multicultural conservatism that is more to the point, 25 percent of those who self-identified as Latino/a voted for Proposition 187, the California initiative that sought to deny certain public benefits to undocumented migrants.[59]

From a lawyer's perspective, there might be a plausible, race-neutral explanation for the INS officer's behavior. Perhaps she thought she was just doing her job, which I had made more difficult by not following the rules as she interpreted them. The INS officer was not really going to deny me citizenship, but was just testing me to see whether I was credible, given that I had not brought my wife—the "source" of my U.S. citizenship—to the interview. Perhaps she was having a bad day. Perhaps she resented a wife who chose not to play the role of Tammy Wynette and "stand by her man" if it meant taking a measly hour out of her workday to accompany him for this important interview. Perhaps I was more naive than I thought: I assumed that I would be treated fairly if I acted in good faith by bringing the documents the Service requested and passed the written and oral literacy/civics test that would be administered to me. I did not expect that the last step before citizenship would be fraught with proverbial land mines, real or imagined. A "citizen-in-waiting"[60] should not be treated that way, thought I and everyone to whom I have told the story.

Yet, I am lucky because I am now a privileged U.S. citizen. As I write this, federal courts around the country are debating whether criminal misdemeanors (i.e., less serious crimes) can be considered "aggravated felonies" (i.e., very serious crimes) for purposes of deportation, reaching various, and sometimes inconsistent, results. While the idea that a minor crime can be elevated to a serious one in order to render someone deportable would not likely pass the "snicker" test in a public poll ("Whaddya mean a misdemeanor can be an aggravated felony??"), this very issue is being litigated by noncitizens' counsel and government attorneys around the country. Like the assumption that it is easy to immigrate to the United States, like the myth that my failure to return to the United States in 1988 was really the Philippines' doing, not America's, and like my mistaken belief that the Latina INS officer would be sympathetic, the already complex rules governing noncitizens and immigration are rendered even more difficult by the even more complex interplay of race and privilege in American society.

Thus, the question we started with remains: How does one ensure that the equality principle enshrined in the Constitution applies to noncitizens the same Constitution has created? As I hope to explore in the remaining chapters, where the government is constitutionally allowed to draw lines between U.S. citizens and others, it should ensure that the borders it decides to establish simultaneously secure the rights of each individual to be treated fairly under the law.

# 2

# Immigrants and the
# War on Terrorism after 9/11

One of the first acts of government profiling following the September 11, 2001 terrorist attacks was conducted not against people, but against cargo. As he watched the pillars of smoke billow from the World Trade Center towers from his office across the river, Kevin McCabe, Chief Inspector of the Contraband Enforcement Team of the U.S. Customs Service, determined he needed to take action: "I figured . . . that we were under attack, probably from some group in the Middle East, and I had no way of knowing what was in any of those containers," a reference to the seven thousand–odd truck-sized cargo containers that had just arrived at port in the last twenty-four hours. McCabe then decided to subject each of the six hundred containers that had originated in or stopped at ports in the Middle East or North Africa to the kind of scrutiny usually reserved for cargo suspected of containing illicit drugs. Upon reflection, McCabe admitted that his decision was "as much an emotional reaction as a practical one. We felt we had to do something." It soon became clear that, as a practical matter, McCabe's proposed solution was flawed in two key respects: first, at best, U.S. Customs had the capacity to inspect no more than 2 to 3 percent of the seven to nine thousand containers they received daily; and second, Customs needed a plan to actually prevent the arrival of a terrorist package—discovering a nuclear or biological weapon among the containers already at port might be a case of "too little, too late."[1]

McCabe's predicament that fateful morning parallels the complexity the federal government has faced in finding ways to deploy its immigration power in the post-9/11 war on terrorism. In the three sections that follow, I examine several of the government's responses, from its initial decision to engage in national origin profiling, to its use of the immigration power to enhance its investigatory might, to its more nuanced approach toward admitting commuting students at the border. I assess the promises and pitfalls of each response, measured against the twin principles of antiessentialism and antisubordination. My goal is not to offer a comprehensive treatment of the government's entire post-9/11 immigration response—legal scholar David Cole has recently provided an excellent evaluation of just that.[2] Rather, I use the three sections to move from a bird's-eye view of post-9/11 immigration policy, situating it in the broader context of history, sociology, and psychology, to a microanalysis of specific legislation the government has enacted, outlining how it can (and has) reacted appropriately in seeking a fair balance between the rights and responsibilities of noncitizens.

And so I offer three observations here, which I explain further in the sections below: first, because of the high correlation between national origin and racial, ethnic, and religious profiling, the federal government should be wary about using such accidents of birth and culture as proxies for disloyalty, especially when such profiling promotes essentialist stereotyping and subordination without the promise of enhanced security. Second, while using its civil immigration laws to detain violators and investigate possible terrorist cells enhances the government's criminal enforcement power, deportation (the preferred immigration remedy) risks the release of a terrorist who then is free to strike another day. Put differently, the government should not be able to use its civil immigration authority as a bootstrap to deny due process to suspected terrorists it has no real intention of deporting, but should rather detain and prosecute criminally. And third, the government should resist the temptation to pass legislation like the USA-PATRIOT Act as an emotional reaction to 9/11, when it is also capable of enacting more reasonable laws like the less well-known, but more effective, Border Commuter Student Act of 2002, which grants student visas to Mexican and Canadian nationals who commute to schools in the United States. That the Border Commuter Student Act was enacted only a year after the terrorist attacks suggests that the federal government can use its immigration power to effectively separate the "terrorist" from the "immigrant" or "noncitizen" without relying on stereotypes or proxies for disloyalty.

*Proxies for (Dis)Loyalty in Constitutional Immigration Law: Citizenship and Race after September 11*

## 1. Proxies for Disloyalty: Muslim and Arab Noncitizens Post-9/11

The *American Heritage Dictionary* defines "loyal" as "steadfast in allegiance to one's homeland, government, or sovereign."[3] As with any vague and ambiguous term, "loyal" might be best understood by way of example: The president of a nation is expected to be "loyal" to that nation; a terrorist, in contrast, is not. Post–September 11, we have been duly concerned with the second, negative example—with those who might be dangerously disloyal, those willing to give up their own lives in order to harm the United States and things "American."

This search for the next terrorist has affected many of us most profoundly in the context of airport security. In an ideal world, perhaps, there would be a "terrorist screening device" through which all airport passengers would have to pass; it would search not only the person's belongings for potentially dangerous weapons, but would also unerringly read the passenger's mind to determine whether he or she plans to hijack the next flight—a souped-up "lie-detector test," if you will.

Despite our twenty-first-century advances, we have no such gadget (nor is any looming on the technological horizon)[4] and we often settle for second-best solutions such as using race and citizenship as proxies for (dis)loyalty. When we use race and citizenship this way, we ask whether there is a particular kind of person who is disloyal, or a "disloyal type." In considering the utility of these factors, it might be helpful to look at analogous efforts by criminologists and sociologists to determine whether there is a classifiable "criminal type."

According to sociologist Jessica Mitford, prior to the end of the nineteenth century people believed that the devil was the cause of crime.[5] She explains, however, that in the late 1800s Cesare Lombroso, an Italian criminologist, insisted that criminals were born and could be identified by distinct physical and mental characteristics.[6] Lombroso contended that "criminals have long, large, protruding ears, abundant hair, thin beard, prominent frontal sinuses, protruding chin, large cheekbones."[7] Mitford asserts that during the twentieth century efforts to identify the criminal type persisted, but with bewildering results.[8]

Mitford argues that obtaining a more realistic view of the criminal type requires examining the composition of the prison population.[9] She explains that "[t]oday the prisons are filled with the young, the poor white, the black, the Chicano, [and] the Puerto Rican."[10] Mitford opines that the reason certain groups are disproportionately represented in prisons and jails is that the only crimes available to the poor are those that are easily detected, such as theft, robbery, and purse snatching.[11] She also points to psychologist Theodore Sarbin's suggestion that the police are conditioned to treat certain classes of people—currently people of color, but formerly immigrants—as more potentially dangerous than others.[12] She contends that in the American criminal justice system a white person is more likely to be dismissed with a warning, but an African American is more likely to be arrested and imprisoned.[13] Mitford concludes, "Thus it seems safe to assert that there is indeed a criminal type—but he is not a biological, anatomical, phrenological, or anthropological type; rather, he is a social creation, etched by the dominant class and ethnic prejudices of a given society."[14]

Mitford's analysis rings true when we examine the less-than-careful finger-pointing that ensued during the war on terrorism recently launched. In the days and weeks following 9/11, both the public and pundits alike approved of profiling airport passengers based on immutable characteristics such as race and national origin.[15] A *Time*/CNN poll from fall 2001 revealed that 57 percent of all Americans were willing to allow the government to discriminate on the basis of race, gender, and age during airport searches.[16] And the government has breathed life into this sentiment. As immigration scholars Susan Akram and Kevin Johnson carefully detail,[17] thousands of Muslim and Arab immigrants have been detained and questioned by federal authorities, all without producing any direct evidence of their terrorist affiliation. Even those skeptical that race and citizenship profiling might work have argued that, on balance, it should be used discreetly. As Michael Kinsley, editor of the cyberzine *Slate,* contends: "But assuming [racial profiling works], it's hard to argue that helping to avoid another September 11 is not worth the imposition, which is pretty small: inconvenience and embarrassment, as opposed to losing a job or getting lynched."[18] *Newsweek* columnist Stuart Taylor adds that while he generally believes racial profiling to be deplorable, "I think people getting on airliners [is] a very special case. Unless you can thoroughly search everyone, which would be great, but it would take hours and hours and hours, it makes sense to search with special care those people who look like all of the mass murder suicide hijackers who did the deeds on September 11th."[19]

Supporters of this view believe this to be an objective cost-benefit analysis. There is great benefit to preventing another terrorist attack and the cost to the innocent individual is minuscule, and certainly not the same as losing a job or getting lynched. Or being interned in a wartime camp. In *United States v. Korematsu,* a majority of the Supreme Court upheld the internment of mostly U.S. citizens of Japanese descent, partly for the reasons that Mr. Taylor articulates. The Court was unwilling to substitute its judgment for the military's about the possibility of a West Coast invasion by Japan.[20] But as Justice Murphy pointed out in dissent, the underlying rhetoric employed by the internment camps' chief enforcer, General DeWitt, was based more on stereotypical conceptions of who might be disloyal than on statistical fact:

> Further evidence of the Commanding General's attitude toward individuals of Japanese ancestry is revealed in his voluntary testimony on April 13, 1943, in San Francisco before the House Naval Affairs Subcommittee to Investigate Congested Areas[:] "I don't want any of them (persons of Japanese ancestry) here. They are a dangerous element. There is no way to determine their loyalty. The west coast contains too many vital installations essential to the defense of the country to allow any Japanese on this coast. . . . The danger of the Japanese was, and is now—if they are permitted to come back—espionage and sabotage. It makes no difference whether he is an American citizen, he is still a Japanese. American citizenship does not necessarily determine loyalty. . . . But we must worry about the Japanese all the time until he is wiped off the map. Sabotage and espionage will make problems as long as he is allowed in this area."[21]

While interning Japanese Americans is admittedly not the same as asking Arab citizens more questions at the airport, the underlying rhetoric is surprisingly similar. During World War II, as now, the public and government were willing to use proxies for disloyalty as a means of safeguarding national security, despite the cost to innocent persons swept into the dragnet.

And, as Akram and Johnson contend, the government has gone beyond airport profiling to arrest and detain many Muslims in a sweep reminiscent of the Japanese internment. Akram and Johnson report that in the weeks following the attack on the World Trade Center, the U.S. government arrested and detained roughly one thousand noncitizens, with

Pakistanis and Egyptians most heavily represented. This dragnet, however, apparently did not reveal any direct links to the terrorist acts. Undeterred, the Justice Department sought interviews with an additional five thousand men, most of whom were Muslims between the ages of eighteen and thirty-three, who had come to the United States on nonimmigrant visas since January 1, 2000. Akram and Johnson maintain that no evidence existed that any of those men were involved in terrorist activities. They conclude, therefore, that "the legal measures taken by the federal government reinforce deeply-held negative stereotypes—foreignness and possibly disloyalty—about Arabs and Muslims."[22]

The psychological costs of race- and citizenship-based suspicion should not be underestimated. Social psychologists and critical race theorists have long documented the damage done by prejudice administered in small doses—microaggressions, as they are called.[23] Just as the exclusion of those of Japanese ancestry signaled their outsider status in a physical way, the targeting of Muslim and Arab immigrants post–September 11 sends the same message, albeit in psychological form. As lawyers and law students know from first-year Torts, and as laypeople and common sense bear out, emotional distress may be just as harmful as physical injury.[24] Indeed, as many critical scholars have demonstrated,[25] stereotypes of foreignness seem to follow racial patterns: Latinas and Asians are perpetually foreign; European and African Americans are not.

But what of the claim that there is a rationality to racial and citizenship profiling?[26] That is, doesn't it make sense to stop all Muslim and Arab immigrants because all the 9/11 terrorists were Muslim and Arab? There are at least four responses to this point: first, as David Harris documents in *Profiles in Injustice*,[27] federal and state officials who have studied racial profiling conclude that it does not lead to better law enforcement. For example, a General Accounting Office report of U.S. Customs Service procedures in 1997 and 1998 revealed that customs officers were less effective when they relied on race and gender profiles in conducting searches for contraband than when they did not, prompting Customs to require better oversight of officer actions.[28]

Second, even assuming that racial profiling is marginally effective, shouldn't we expand our profiles to target non-Arab terrorist types as well? We know, for instance, that the Abu Sayyaf group in the southern Philippines has links to al-Qaeda, hence America's military involvement in that country's affairs.[29] Should we begin profiling Filipino and Filipino-looking individuals at airports? After all, our terrorist profiles should be inclusive, not exclusive. Ironically, focusing excessively on a "foreign terrorist" profile might be exactly what al-Qaeda wants: Osama bin Laden aide Abu Zubaydah has apparently instructed terror recruits to "shave their beards, adopt Western clothing and 'do whatever it takes to avoid detection and see their missions through.'"[30] Indeed, one of the few individuals with proven, established links to terrorism is John Walker Lindh, a European American—not an Arab, and not a noncitizen.[31]

Third, given the importance of profiling in the war against terrorism, shouldn't we advocate profiles in other law enforcement contexts, which would require us to strictly scrutinize white, rural schoolchildren in the school shooting (a.k.a. Columbine) context; rich, white males for white-collar crimes such as embezzling and corporate fraud (think: Enron); and disenfranchised white male spies like Aldrich Ames in the counterespionage game?[32] To the extent that disloyalty encompasses a general disrespect for our criminal laws, racial profiling of whites should occur if the statistics suggest links between ethnicity and specific crimes.

Fourth and finally, the next successful terrorist will likely thwart any profile we create. While I have no problem using specific, accurate information—including race and citizenship—to find a suspect accused of a crime,[33] as was done to eventually apprehend the Unabomber, as a practical matter, profiles will not capture the next successful terrorist because he or she will thwart the profile.[34] Indeed, the next terrorist might not even know she is one. Case in point: in 1986, Israeli officials found a bomb hidden in the luggage of an Irish woman who reported that her significant other was Jordanian.[35]

My preference would be for the U.S. government to do what Philippine officials appear to do at the Ninoy Aquino International Airport in Manila. Before I board my Northwest Airlines flight to Detroit, my luggage is inspected several times, including once just before we board. At the boarding gate, all hand-carried items are subject to a thorough search and each individual is frisked and a metal detector is employed. Once cleared, anyone who leaves the secured area (to get something to eat or to use the bathroom) must undergo a full inspection to reenter. To many Americans, this may seem like an extraordinary inconvenience. To a certain extent, it is. We are required to be at the airport at least three to four hours before departure, unlike the customary one-and-a-half to two hours required in the United States. However, when I board that plane, I do so in the belief that every one of us and our belongings has been inspected multiple times, and that no one appears to have been singled out for special treatment based on national origin, religion, race, ethnicity, or citizenship.

Admittedly, the United States is a much larger nation with much busier airports, such that labor-intensive, manual inspections of every passenger and her luggage might not be possible. But the equality principles of the Constitution should prompt the government to try harder. Indeed, there are signs of progress. As of January 1, 2003, all U.S. airports are required to electronically screen all checked luggage, which has, perhaps counter-intuitively, not slowed things down as some had feared.[36] Perhaps with more advances in technology under way, the government will be able to finally let go of race and citizenship profiling as tools in the war against terrorism.

## 2. Proxies for Loyalty: The Presidential Eligibility Clause and the Immigrant Founder Exception

Now that we've explored one extreme on the "(dis)loyalty" spectrum, let's examine the other: what it means to be "loyal." The issue here is the opposite of the terrorism question. If we believe that the paradigm example of loyalty should be the president, the question becomes, "What qualities must a president possess to demonstrate loyalty to her nation?" The Founders contemplated this exact question by passing the following resolution on July 26, 1787:

> Resolved That it be an instruction to the Committee to whom were referred the proceedings of the Convention for the establishment of a national government, to receive a clause or clauses, requiring certain qualifications of landed property and *citizenship in the United States for the Executive,* the Judiciary, and the Members of both branches of the Legislature of the United States[.][37]

Just as we have no technology for divining the next terrorist, nor do we have a device for helping us select the most loyal person for president. As in our terrorism calculus, we rely on proxies for loyalty. In the context of the presidency, Article 2, Section 1, Clause 5 of our Constitution[38] requires that the president be a natural-born citizen or a citizen of the United States at the time of the adoption of the Constitution. So, while naturalized citizens were originally eligible for this highest executive office, this provision was intended to specifically reward those Founders who were immigrants. Indeed, in its initial draft, the conventioneers drew no distinction between "natural born" and "naturalized," using the single term "citizen."[39] That they changed the text to differentiate between the two suggests that natural-born citizens were more presumptively loyal that naturalized ones.

This interpretation is supported by Justice Joseph Story in his famous commentaries on the Constitution. Story noted in 1833 that this "immigrant Founder" exception was

> doubtless introduced (for it has now become by lapse of time merely nominal, and will soon become wholly extinct) out of respect to those distinguished revolutionary patriots, who were born in a foreign land, and yet had entitled themselves to high honours in their adopted country. A positive exclusion would have been unjust to their merits, and painful to their sensibilities. But the general propriety of the exclusion of foreigners, in common cases, will scarcely be doubted by any statesman. It cuts off all chances for ambitious foreigners, who might otherwise be intriguing for office; and interposes a barrier against those corrupt interferences of foreign governments in executive elections, which have inflicted the most serious evils upon the elective monarchies of Europe.[40]

Specifically, Story referred to the nations of Germany and Poland as examples of executive governments unduly influenced by foreign forces.

Story's rhetoric shares a striking similarity to General DeWitt's. Both describe the need to distinguish the loyal from the disloyal—DeWitt suggested that the Japanese be "wiped off the map," while Story advocated the establishment of a "barrier" against foreign influence. Both acknowledged the permanency of foreignness—DeWitt argued that a Japanese person would always be disloyal even if a naturalized citizen, while Story draws no clear distinction between naturalized citizen and foreigner, stating only that he believes that the immigrant Founders had earned the designation "loyal," rendering them fit to be president, in what Story believed to be a narrow exception to the general rule.

But perhaps the most telling feature of Story's commentary is his remark that to not exempt the immigrant Founders would have been "unjust to their merits, and painful to their sensibilities." Put another way, the immigrant Founders had demonstrated that, even though they were presumptively disloyal and foreign, they were actually good Americans worthy of being president. Contrast this observation with Michael Kinsley's earlier evaluation that the harm visited upon innocent victims of post–September 11 airport race profiling was "pretty small: inconvenience and embarrassment, as opposed to losing a job or getting lynched." It seems to me that one could easily imagine switching Story's and Kinsley's rationales to argue *for* not exempting naturalized citizens at the time of the nation's founding, on the one hand, and to argue *against* racial profiling, on the other. Paraphrasing Story, post–September 11 racial profiling is "unjust to [the] merits" of Muslim and Arab peoples and "painful to their sensibilities." Citing Kinsley, excluding the immigrant Founders from the presidency visits a harm that is "pretty small: inconvenience and embarrassment, as opposed to losing a job or getting lynched."

Yet most people's reactions are similar to Story's and Kinsley's, rather than the other way around. Even though most agree that race and citizenship are, at best, imperfect proxies for loyalty, many are willing to tolerate post–September 11 terrorist profiling on the basis of race while not too many get excited about amending the Constitution to rid it of the birthright-naturalized citizen distinction in the Presidential Eligibility Clause. In a well-known law review symposium on the stupidest provisions of the Constitution, two leading legal scholars—Randall Kennedy and Robert Post—independently selected the natural-born citizenship clause as the worst.[41] Aside from the clause's inability to accurately measure loyalty, it disproportionately precludes persons of color from the presidency, since most naturalized citizens today are from Asia and Latin America. Indeed, the clause's effect on naturalized citizens of color is not unlike the disparate effect of the disenfranchisement of felons on the African American community. Yet, when I ask my students whether they think a constitutional amendment to get rid of the birthright-naturalized citizenship distinction would pass, they are uniformly pessimistic about such a project.

I am troubled by what such indifference suggests about America's priorities when we are quick to racially profile post–September 11 despite its inaccuracy, and yet are unwilling to eliminate the birthright citizenship distinction in the Presidential Eligibility Clause despite its inanity. In a sense, I am speaking out of self-interest as one of many naturalized citizens of color who would theoretically fit the prosubordination, essentialist stereotypes in both the terrorism and presidential eligibility contexts. Being Filipino by national origin and ethnicity, I fit the Abu Sayyaf terrorist racial profile, and being a naturalized citizen (but not an immigrant

Founder) I am presumptively disloyal and therefore ineligible for the presidency. But I do not think of myself as anything but a loyal American. While my parents and siblings still live in the Philippines, I thought long and hard about where my loyalties lay when I took my U.S. citizenship oath in 1995. I took seriously the charge that I disavow allegiance to any foreign potentate. In the unlikely event that the Abu Sayyaf take over the Philippines and the United States declares war, I am ready to serve in the U.S. armed forces, if conscripted (which, by the way, naturalized citizens and immigrants are subject to under federal law).[42] Yet, somehow these reassurances do not rebut the presumption of my disloyalty to qualify me for the presidency.

Although, fortunately for my wife and kids, I do not aspire to be either a terrorist or U.S. president, the question remains: why are most Americans willing to tolerate race and citizenship profiling in the contexts of battling terrorism and determining presidential eligibility, despite an acknowledgment by most that both are far from perfect proxies for loyalty? Not surprisingly, critical race theorists and social psychologists teach us that we tend to think of those who are different—that is, racial and noncitizen outsiders—as disloyal. Hence those who are nonwhite and noncitizens are presumptively suspect. Conversely, we believe that those who are similar to us are more loyal and hence less suspect. As psychologist Gordon Allport explained in his path-breaking work, *The Nature of Prejudice,* every individual draws distinctions between in-groups and out-groups for survival: "[In-group] memberships constitute a web of habits. When we encounter an outsider who follows different customs we unconsciously say, 'He breaks my habits.' Habit-breaking is unpleasant. We prefer the familiar. We cannot help but feel a bit on guard when other people seem to threaten or even question habits."[43] Allport contends, however, that in-groups can be cohesive without being antagonistic toward out-groups: "Narrow circles can, without conflict, be supplemented by larger circles of loyalty."[44] Hence the presidency of the United States should be open to both birthright and naturalized citizens (a larger circle of citizenship), even though immigration and nationality law distinguishes between U.S. citizens and noncitizens (a narrower circle). Similarly, airport security burdens should be visited upon all airline passengers (a larger circle of travelers) rather than only upon Muslims and Arabs (a smaller racial and religious circle).

But how do we convince the 57 percent of Americans[45] who were in favor of profiling following the 9/11 attacks and the many more who are disinclined to eliminate the Presidential Eligibility Clause's birthright-naturalized citizen distinction that drawing large circles of loyalty makes sense? The answer is that these citizenship and race distinctions are irrational proxies for loyalty. I contend that, even within the contexts of the "disloyal terrorist" and the "loyal president," relying on race and citizenship as proxies for loyalty are so inaccurate that they are unnecessarily antagonistic to those in the racial and citizenship out-group. My suspicion is that those who fancy themselves loyal believe that there is a group of readily identifiable "disloyalists" whose racial and citizenship characteristics are different from theirs. Hence, the Arab or Muslim naturalized citizen is more likely a terrorist and least likely qualified to be president of the United States than the average white Anglo-Saxon birthright citizen.

The reality, of course, is that terrorists and presidents come in all citizenships and colors (remember President Alberto Fujimori, a Peruvian of Japanese descent?), and indeed, the danger of assuming that the terrorist is someone who belongs to one group overlooks the possibility that the terrorist could come from the so-called nonterrorist group. Two examples are worth noting: after the Oklahoma City bombing, many terrorist experts immediately suspected Arab terrorists to be at fault, only to discover that the crime was perpetrated by two white men with links to racist hate groups.[46] Following September 11, deaths by anthrax led many to wonder whether al-Qaeda had struck again; some believe that the killers are probably domestic, right-wing extremists.[47] The lesson here is that the enemy—especially the terrorist enemy—can very easily be a member of the in-group capitalizing on public scrutiny of out-group behavior.

## *Decoupling "Terrorist" from "Immigrant": An Enhanced Role for the Courts*

Immigration law is traditionally understood to encompass the rules that govern foreign citizens' entry into and departure from the United States, and may therefore be seen as an important domestic arm of the nation's foreign policy power. Immigration law is the exclusive purview of the federal government. While there are times when federal law might have unintended effects upon noncitizens, as a vehicle for effectuating foreign policy immigration law can serve as an effective complement. For example, if the United States declares war on Iran, it might make sense to exclude all Iranian citizens from immigrating to the United States, not just for our own citizens' security, but for theirs as well.

But what should our immigration laws say when the object of our foreign policy is not another nation, but a multinational guerrilla movement such as al-Qaeda? How does the United States balance its national security concerns against fair treatment of the individual noncitizens affected by its immigration laws? In 2002, Congress passed a law requiring greater scrutiny of visa applications from nationals of countries that sponsor terrorist activity. Clearly, not every visa applicant from North Korea is a terrorist, and yet it would be imprudent not to consider North Korea's past practices in ruling upon the application. On the other hand, is it fair to subject every single person from North Korea to increased scrutiny in the name of fighting terrorism when we are not (nor will we likely be) at war with North Korea? And what of North Koreans who might already be in this country? Should they all be deported; detained and screened for possible deportation; or interrogated about their links to terrorism?

In what ways may our immigration laws requiring the exclusion or removal of noncitizens assist in the war on terrorism? Even if technological advances permitted us to infallibly determine whether a noncitizen was a terrorist or not, would immigration law be used to either exclude that individual at the border or remove her from the country? In close cases, the answer is probably "no." On the one hand, ridding the nation of a dangerous individual prevents her from directly threatening the country; on the other, deporting the terrorist means she is still at large, allowing her to strike another day either directly (by entering without authorization across the border) or indirectly (by abetting a plan to be carried out by associates). Indeed, our government is even willing to go beyond our borders to capture alleged terrorists who were never subject to our immigration controls in the first place. The government's obsession with capturing Osama bin Laden as well as arrests of alleged al-Qaeda henchmen in venues as distant as Singapore, Indonesia, and Pakistan are examples of the lengths to which the government will go in striving to secure peace. In perhaps a less well-known example, the *Washington Post* reported that in 2001 the government had interrogated a noncitizen who, they later discovered, was an al-Qaeda operative, long after he had left the United States.[48] Thus, as a theoretical matter, if the government discovers a particularly dangerous terrorist among the noncitizens it is investigating, it will likely invoke its criminal laws to prosecute the person for treason or subversion, rather than its immigration powers to deport or exclude.

Why then has Attorney General Ashcroft used immigration proceedings to seek out terrorists? As mentioned earlier, following the September 11 attacks, the INS arrested and detained approximately one thousand mostly Arab and Muslim noncitizens for immigration code violations in an effort to uncover possible terrorists among them.

Notwithstanding the questionable desirability of deporting a known terrorist, using immigration rather than criminal proceedings to screen persons makes sense from the government's perspective. First, the process gives the government the greatest number of remedial options: if it decides a noncitizen is not a terrorist, it can deport her; if she is a terrorist, it can charge her criminally. In addition, the government is able to take advantage of the administrative and civil nature of immigration proceedings to aggressively prosecute its claims without providing as much due process protection to the individuals charged. For example, because attorneys are not automatically provided to noncitizens in deportation proceedings,[49] the government is at a distinct advantage in investigating possible terrorist links in the context of deportation than it would be if it had to proceed in a criminal court. Second, given its limited resources and the similar profiles of the 9/11 bombers (all young, male Middle Eastern nationals), focusing government efforts on immigration violators provides it with a legitimate method for killing two birds with one stone: the government is able to enforce our immigration laws while simultaneously enhancing our national security (or at least attempting to do so).[50] Third, the government implicitly knows that by targeting immigration violators only,[51] it likely has the support of the majority of the public still grieving after 9/11[52] and the backing of constitutional immigration law, which has left decisions regarding the ingress and egress of noncitizens to the political branches.

Despite the arguable efficiency of the Ashcroft plan, there are similarly strong reasons to be skeptical about immigration law's ultimate effectiveness as an antiterrorist device. Assuming that political support remains high, once Ashcroft is done focusing on Arab and Muslim immigration violators, he may set his sights on other high-priority deportees such as aggravated felons, and so on down the government's list. Even if the government was able to rid the nation of all immigration violators, it might do so at the risk of not as actively combating citizen terrorism because of the added constitutional and criminal law safeguards afforded U.S. nationals. John Walker Lindh ("the American Taliban") and Jose Padilla ("the Dirty Bomber") are but two examples of alleged U.S. citizen terrorists. While these two have received much press,[53] little is known in the general public about the government's efforts to investigate U.S. *citizen* (as opposed to noncitizen) terrorist cells, except perhaps for the hounding of Dr. Steven Hatfill in connection with the anthrax attacks of 2002.[54] In contrast, the continued detention and investigation of immigration violators for possible terrorist links has received unending press coverage since 9/11.[55] Moreover, one should not underestimate the emotional, economic, and psychological toll placed on anyone subject to intense government scrutiny, especially upon persons like immigrants who, by law, already receive fewer statutory and constitutional protections than U.S. citizens.

In response, the government might argue that its efforts, despite their sometimes great costs to individual noncitizens, redound to the benefit of the country writ large. The sacrifice of the few is worth the well-being of the many. Of course, this argument would be more persuasive if the government could show definitively that the terms "terrorist" and "immigration violator" are synonymous, or that there is a sufficiently high correlation between the two. As the Lindh and Padilla cases remind us, the government's case is based, at best, on educated guesses and statistical probabilities, and at worst on stereotypical presumptions.

On the latter point, Ashcroft's Arab-Muslim immigration dragnet exacerbates racial, religious, and gender stereotypes. As many have documented, exclusively targeting certain groups, even among noncitizens, is unacceptably both over- and under-inclusive.[56] As mentioned earlier in this chapter, targeting certain groups is overinclusive because interrogating and detaining thousands of noncitizens based on accidents of birth offends our notions of liberal equality and individual civil rights. It is also underinclusive because, as mentioned before, there are U.S. citizens and other foreign nationals who may also be terrorist threats.

As a final rejoinder, the government might respond that in enacting and enforcing general immigration policy, it has no choice but to paint wide brush strokes. Congressional statutes are inherently broad so as to be of sufficiently general applicability. Executive enforcement strategies are equally so in order to provide sufficient flexibility to personnel. Indeed, our constitutional immigration law sanctions such extensive power, understanding that the political branches have the institutional competence to best engage in foreign relations, to which immigration law is linked through its regulation of migrants. Moreover, there are no significant signs that the public is willing to shelve immigration policy as a weapon in the war against terrorism, and thus we cannot expect that the political branches will either. And perhaps that is as it should be. Our national policies, for better or worse, are determined by our representative government, duly elected by our voting public, and in theory they try to capture majoritarian sentiment. If, despite the apparent flaws in implementation, most of the public feels comfortable using immigration law to combat terrorism, then our republican democracy should support that.

More interestingly, the support for Ashcroft's anti-immigrant, profile-charged dragnet may have a broader base than simply among middle-class white American voters. While most post-1965 immigration has come from Asia and Latin America, and while racial profiling has been roundly denounced by many in the African American and Latino/a American communities, immigration policy has long been a contested playing field. Thus, it may very well be that the much touted demographic "browning" of America may not lead to better treatment of noncitizens, especially post-9/11, for a number of reasons. First, as I noted in the first chapter, Angela Dillard has documented the growth of a multicultural conservative movement exemplified most visibly perhaps by several of Bush's key cabinet members—Colin Powell (Secretary of State), Condoleeza Rice (National Security Adviser), and Norman Mineta (Secretary of Transportation)—that might, at the margin, be more sympathetic to national security concerns linked to restricting immigration than to more traditional egalitarian principles. Second, both lawful and undocumented immigration will likely continue to be wedge issues among and within communities of color. Many African Americans oppose even lawful immigration on the grounds that it affects native blacks' employment prospects,[57] while recent immigrants from Asia and Latin America are often unsympathetic to civil rights claims by undocumented immigrants[58] (hence the popularity of California's Proposition 187 eliminating many public benefits for undocumented persons during the early 1990s). Following 9/11, *Time* magazine reported undocumented Mexican laborers upset at the enhanced border security wrought by the terrorist attacks, blaming the situation on the "damn Arabs."[59] And even on the issue of racial profiling, some African Americans who resent being subjected to pretextual traffic stops find themselves conflicted over the issue of more stringent law enforcement against those who appear to be Arab or Middle Eastern. As African American writer Eric Hinton of the progressive web magazine, *DiversityInc.*, admitted,

> On my next flight, when someone of Middle Eastern descent who is much more likely to be my neighbor than a terrorist sits next to me, what will my reaction be? Will I sit back and enjoy my ride? Will I want to signal for a flight attendant and demand this person be removed from the airplane because there's something "wrong" with him? Will I want to do something as harmless, but still insulting, as changing my seat? I don't know. And that troubles me.[60]

Thus, Ashcroft will find some unlikely allies even among citizens and immigrants of color.

Despite the likelihood that vigilant immigration enforcement continues to be the majority's will, our country also subscribes to an equality principle designed to protect the least powerful among us. The underpolicing of U.S. citizen terrorists and the perpetuation of invidious stereotypes evident in our current immigration policy undermine equality in two ways. First, because immigration law is premised on the unequal status of U.S. citizens and noncitizens, broad policies that apply only to noncitizens, even those enacted in the name of national security, are likely to widen the citizen-noncitizen divide and enhance tensions between the two groups.[61] Second, to the extent that most U.S. immigrants today are people of color from Asia and Latin America, the unintended burden of stringent immigration enforcement will fall upon racial outsiders, exacerbating tensions between whites and nonwhites.[62] Taken together, these two reasons further perpetuate essentialist notions of the nonwhite, disloyalist foreigner, while simultaneously strengthening the oppressive status quo.

Fortunately, there is an integral institution in our democracy designed and particularly well-suited to protect individual claimants—the federal courts. While they have long deferred to Congress and the executive in setting immigration policy, the courts have not shied away from providing needed checks and balances in instances in which the political branch has overreached. Most recently, some courts have curbed executive zealotry by slowing down the juggernaut, forcing the Attorney General to follow time-honored due process procedures. First, the federal Foreign Intelligence Surveillance Court chided the FBI for misleading the court in seventy-five alleged terrorism cases, all of which involved noncitizens.[63] Second, the Sixth Circuit Court of Appeals upheld a lower court decision opening immigration proceedings to the public and press unless the INS could prove specific threats to national security.[64] It is fitting that in the second case, *Detroit Free Press v. Ashcroft,* the opinion was penned by Sixth Circuit Judge Damon Keith, an African American jurist long supportive of civil rights. And most recently, the Supreme Court ruled that foreign citizens in Guantanamo Bay, Cuba, held indefinitely without being charged with any crime, could sue the federal government over their detention.[65] As Congress and the executive branch continue to experiment with how to prudently and effectively use their immigration power in the war against terrorism,[66] it will be up to the federal courts to ensure that individual noncitizens are provided sufficient protection in this post-9/11 world.

The federal courts have at least four good reasons to be skeptical of the federal political branches, especially during times of real or perceived crisis. First, while the legitimate goal of immigration law enforcement is deportation, Ashcroft's true objective in targeting noncitizens appears to be criminal prosecution for terrorism and subversion. After all, why would the INS risk letting a terrorist get away—which is what the deportation remedy would be[67]—rather than prosecuting him with the goal of life imprisonment or the death penalty? Thus, the constitutional defense of political plenary power is even less persuasive, especially when, as here, the foreign threat comes not from another nation (thus justifying the political branches' plenary international relations power), but instead from a multinational, multiethnic guerilla force that uses unconventional methods of attack, as it did on 9/11.

Second, we can well expect that Ashcroft will dispatch criminal law enforcement and immigration agents that might be tempted, at the margin, to play fast and loose with suspects' civil liberties, as evidenced by the FBI's deceptive practices in over seventy-five post-9/11 cases. I do not mean to suggest bad faith on the agents' part; I understand that if one believes that one is restoring "the rule of law to the immigration law,"[68] as Assistant Attorney General Viet Dinh has stated, one's noble ends might justify a liberal interpretation of otherwise suspect governmental means. Indeed, the decision to split the service and enforcement functions of the INS was prompted in part by the desire to ensure that civil servants long bent on enforcement do not end up in the petition processing section looking for ways to deny admission to family members of lawful permanent residents. It is the role of impartial courts to ensure that the twin constitutional equality principles of antiessentialism and anti-subordination are not unduly compromised.

Third, history is replete with examples of federal government zealotry, and the federal courts would do well not to bow to majority sentiment especially when racial, ethnic, religious, gender, and age stereotypes are reinforced at the expense of the egalitarian ideal. The legacy of *Brown v. Board of Education* should be that the Supreme Court will never reaffirm *Korematsu*'s principles.

And fourth, controlling political overreaching enhances our standing abroad. As I noted at the very beginning of this section, domestic immigration policy and international relations are interrelated, and as such, if we value human rights at home, our ambassadors abroad will have a stronger case when they accuse other nations of transgressing civil liberties. Nicholas Kristof, describing the nearly monthlong detention without charge or cause of a Yemeni "material witness" married to a U.S. citizen, summarized the argument thus: "Imprisoning a Yemeni because he is a Yemeni will not destroy our freedoms. But it undermines our ability to project our values abroad."[69]

## Noncitizen Students and Immigration Policy Post-9/11

In continuing my analysis from broad to specific, this last section describes the post-9/11 world for noncitizen students and scholars in light of recent federal legislation, focusing on two laws: the USA-PATRIOT (Uniting and Strengthening America by Providing Appropriate Tools Required to Intercept and Obstruct Terrorism) Act of 2001 and the Border Commuter Student Act of 2002. In both, Congress has tried to walk the fine line between providing fair access to postsecondary education to noncitizen students and guarding against the possibility that such institutions are being used as a springboard for terrorist activity. In my view, the USA-PATRIOT Act errs too much on the side of favoring national security at the expense of individual rights, while the Border Commuter Student Act strikes just the right balance between these important, yet competing, claims. Although I focus here on two specific laws, the lessons of balancing equality norms against competing national security and immigration concerns are timeless, and they provide a practical application for the more theoretical themes I discussed earlier in this chapter.

## 1. The USA-PATRIOT Act of 2001

The USA-PATRIOT Act of 2001 has been reviewed in the literature primarily for its expansion of the Attorney General's powers to detain and investigate alleged terrorists, both citizen and noncitizen.[70] It has received much less attention from legal scholars for its effects on U.S. colleges and universities. Apparently concerned that six of the nineteen 9/11 terrorists were believed to have studied at flight schools in the United States, Congress included within the PATRIOT Act several provisions designed to facilitate government access to information on possible terrorist activity on campus. Although provisions involving government monitoring of on-campus use of information technology and laboratories for possible biological and environmental hazards affect both citizens and noncitizens, my focus is on two provisions that are most likely to impact international students: Section 507, which allows the government access to student records in certain situations,[71] and Section 416, which requires schools to monitor more closely certain foreign students.

Section 507 amends the Family Educational Rights and Privacy Act of 1974 (FERPA),[72] a law that generally withholds federal funding from educational institutions that disclose a student's education record without either the student's or parent's[73] consent. FERPA does, however, allow disclosure under certain circumstances, for example in the case of a health or medical emergency.[74] Section 507 of the PATRIOT Act provides another exception to FERPA by allowing the Attorney General or his designee access to student records pursuant to an *ex parte* court order in connection with a terrorism investigation.[75] In addition, educational institutions complying with such orders need not record this disclosure, nor may they be held liable for records produced in good faith compliance with such orders.[76]

Although this provision could potentially affect both foreign and U.S. students, the FBI, both before and after enactment of the PATRIOT Act, sought information on international students only. In the weeks following the 9/11 attacks, the FBI asked colleges and universities for information on their foreign students, with about two hundred of those institutions choosing to comply.[77]

Some in Congress believe that Section 507 was specifically written to require the FBI to first seek a court order before approaching universities with such a request. Apparently, the FBI did not get that message. Section 507 notwithstanding, the *Washington Post* reported in December 2002 that the FBI had issued a new request for personal information on all foreign students and faculty at colleges and universities nationwide. The request asked for the "names, addresses, telephone numbers, citizenship information, places of birth, dates of birth and any foreign contact information" for all teachers and students who are non-U.S. citizens. The FBI plans to compare any information collected with the Justice Department's Foreign Terrorist Tracking Task Force database.

Needless to say, the legality of the FBI's request has been questioned. In a letter to Attorney General John Ashcroft, senators Ted Kennedy and Patrick Leahy questioned whether the request complied with the PATRIOT Act, since it was not pursuant to a court order in connection with a terrorism investigation. In response to the request, the Association of American College Registrars and Admissions Officers advised its ten thousand members that they might be legally liable if they disclosed information not pursuant to a valid court order or subpoena. The FBI's position is that the agency may request the information, but that colleges need not comply with the request.

The international reaction to the December 2002 FBI request is mixed. Malaysia's largest student organization decried the request as another example of the American government's post-9/11 antiterrorism paranoia; the president of the organization suggested that the United States contact the Malaysian embassy directly should it find evidence of individual wrongdoing rather than issuing a blanket request.[78] In contrast, Malaysia's Education Bureau chief Dr. Adham Baba found the creation of an FBI database useful so that the home authorities would be able to track their students abroad. In addition, Dr. Baba was surprised at the students' objection to such a request given that they were required to reveal such information to the U.S. State Department when applying for their visas in the first instance. This seemingly cavalier attitude toward potential privacy breaches is shared by some international students hailing from nations where such information is generally known by law enforcement agencies.[79] Other students, however, have expressed genuine fear that any follow-up questioning by U.S. authorities based on the information gathered might lead to their permanent detention, conjuring up stories of not-so-benign "visits" by police in their home countries.[80]

As a former foreign student from the Philippines who is currently a naturalized U.S. citizen, my sympathies lie with the Malaysian students and not with either the FBI or the Malaysian government. True, the information requested has already been disclosed to the State Department, but then why not have the FBI ask the State Department, another federal entity, for this material rather than from either state or private educational institutions? The best reading of Section 507 focuses on maintaining, rather than eroding, the strict division between "noncitizen" (in this case, "foreign student") and "terrorist" by requiring judicial scrutiny of federal requests for student information. Like the Ashcroft plan to use immigration law violations to further its terrorism investigations, the FBI's decision to request this information from educational institutions rather than from another federal agency perpetuates the "noncitizen as terrorist" stereotype. Furthermore, as the General Accounting Office reported in May 2003, the federal government should be working harder to establish not only better information-sharing policies within its many agencies, but to also explore ways by which it can both develop such relationships with state and local governments, as well as provide incentives for private institutions (such as many colleges and universities) to share information as well.[81]

This need to maintain an effective check on government overreaching to ensure fair and equal treatment of noncitizen students suggests a stricter interpretation of the PATRIOT Act's disclosure provisions than that proffered by the FBI. While nothing in Section 507 explicitly prevents the FBI from asking for a voluntary disclosure of student record information, FERPA also likely creates liability for disclosures obtained without consent. Notwithstanding foreign students' differing opinions on the privacy rights issues involved, colleges and universities should be concerned about losing federal funding should they violate FERPA by disclosing student information without first obtaining student consent or requiring a court order. While some institutions might understandably be sympathetic to the FBI's concerns about maintaining accurate databases on foreign students in light of the ongoing war against terrorism, they should also realize that improper disclosures might lead to losses in federal funding. (Of course, there is the genuine possibility that the loss of federal funding might not materialize if those enforcing that provision find the current war on terrorism a sufficient justification to trump the privacy rights of noncitizens.)

Unlike their disclosures to the FBI, colleges and universities obtain the consent of all students holding F-1 (academic), J-1 (exchange), and M-1 (vocational) visas to disclose to the State Department certain immigration-related information upon application.[82] For example, the I-20 form signed by F-1 students contains the following consent notice: "I authorize the named school to release any information from my records which is needed by the INS pursuant to 8 C.F.R. § 214.3(g) to determine my non-immigrant status."[83] Moreover, under Section 641 of the Illegal Immigration Reform and Immigrant Responsibility Act of 1996 (IIRAIRA),[84] the Attorney General, in consultation with the State and Education Departments, is authorized to collect information from colleges and universities on all foreign students.[85] Failure to comply forfeits a school's ability to further enroll international students.[86] Prior to September 11, the federal government did not concern itself much with these education provisions of the IIRAIRA, focusing instead on the legislature's delegation of broader deportation grounds to the executive branch via an expanded definition of "aggravated felony," for example.[87]

Section 416 of the PATRIOT Act was enacted to fill in the gaps left open by previous legislation by: (1) requiring that IIRAIRA's monitoring system be fully funded and operational by January 1, 2003; (2) collecting specific information on the date and port of entry of all foreign students and scholars; and (3) expanding the types of schools subject to this monitoring system to include air flight schools, language training schools, and other vocational institutions.[88]

On December 11, 2002, the INS[89] issued its final rule implementing SEVIS, the Student and Exchange Visitor Information System designed to put Section 416 into action.[90] The primary innovation behind SEVIS is that it is an Internet-based system which allows U.S. educational institutions and exchange program sponsors the opportunity to share information about international students, exchange visitors, and their dependents.[91] The final rule requires that schools keep records for the following visa holder categories and their dependents: F-1 (academic students), M-1 (vocational students), and J-1 (exchange students and faculty).[92] In the fact sheet accompanying the issuance of its final SEVIS rule, the INS touted the following as improved measures to maintain updated information on foreign students and scholars: (1) schools will be required to report a student's failure to enroll; (2) SEVIS will allow for electronic transmission and exchange of information; and (3) SEVIS will facilitate the creation of a more accurate database through the expedient release of requirement changes, better dissemination of student information updates, closer monitoring of schools, and the like.[93]

In contrast with the FBI's access to student information, few are bothered by the INS's (now ICE's) access to similar information, to the extent that such information has already been voluntarily disclosed by the international student upon applying for the relevant visa. A larger concern is how this information might be used. While no one quibbles with the idea that the INS should be able to strictly enforce the terms of a foreign student's stay, news reports alleging INS abuse suggest that some vigilance and oversight might be appropriate. On December 27, 2002, the Associated Press reported that, although finally released on bond, at least six Middle Eastern students were detained for up to forty-eight hours because they were not taking enough college credits, which was a violation of their student visas.[94] According to a University of Colorado official, one of their students was jailed because he was one hour shy of a full course load after the college had permitted him to drop a course. None of the students were charged with any other offense. The INS found out about these students' course loads when the students registered pursuant to the December 16 deadline imposed upon all males sixteen or older holding nonimmigrant visas from Iraq, Iran, Syria, Libya, and Sudan.[95] In response, Colorado State University decided to hold classes run by an immigration lawyer to apprise international students of the law.[96] Other reports of similar abuses in the implementation of the special registration program prompted at least one class action lawsuit,[97] as well as a joint letter from Senator Russell Feingold, Senator Ted Kennedy, and Representative John Conyers describing the program as an apparent "component of a second wave of roundups and detentions of Arab and Muslim males disguised as a perfunctory registration requirement."[98]

While the foregoing might more appropriately be a criticism of the special registration laws than of SEVIS, and while it would be unfair to fault the entire immigration service for the acts of a few agents, these arrests should cause some concern over the way the government plans to use the wealth of information it has available via the SEVIS network. One positive development in this area has been the Department of Homeland Security's decision to dispense with the special registration program in favor of a new technology-based entry-exit system.[99] The U.S. Visitor and Immigrant Status Indication Technology System (U.S. VISIT) plans to employ at least two biometric identifiers, such as photographs, fingerprints, or iris scans, to help build an electronic entry-exit system for all nonimmigrant students, workers, and other visitors.[100] If implemented with care, this system holds out the promise of a fairer balance between maintaining national security and providing equal treatment to all noncitizens, regardless of race, gender, or national origin.

## 2. The Border Commuter Student Act of 2002

One group of students that is not subject to the SEVIS final reporting and compliance rule are part-time border commuter students.[101] Unlike F-1 academic students who live across either the Mexican or Canadian borders and are pursuing their studies full-time at U.S. colleges and universities, *part-time* border students are not eligible for regular student visas.[102] Approximately 2,300 such part-timers attended three Texas schools along the Mexican border—El Paso Community College, New Mexico State University, and the University of Texas at El Paso (UTEP)—at the time enforcement was discussed, affecting not just the students but certain university departments as well.[103] UTEP spokeswoman Christian Clarke-Casarez estimated that their Mechanical and Electrical Engineering Department would suffer greatly, as it attracts many working professionals from nearby Juarez, Mexico.[104] In his floor speech before the House, Texas Representative Ciro Rodriguez affirmed that the law's benefits would accrue not just to the commuters and their institutions, but to the communities on either side of the U.S.-Mexico divide as well: "The border economies of Texas and Mexico gain from the improvement of skills and education among border residents. The enactment of partnerships among these two communities will enrich the quality of lives for all of the residents in South Texas and in our entire country."[105] Not only in Texas, but American universities bordering Canada such as Michigan's Wayne State University were expected to be adversely affected as well.[106]

In response, Congress passed and President Bush signed the Border Commuter Student Act of 2002[107] which created new F-3 and M-3 categories of student visa holders, permitting them to take college courses part-time without having to enroll in a full degree program. Specifically, only Canadian or Mexican nationals who reside in their home country and commute to a U.S. school for full- or part-time course work are eligible.[108]

Unlike the privacy and enforcement concerns over the PATRIOT Act's provisions, the Border Commuter Student Act is a practical, workable, and narrow exception to the existing student visa categories that strikes a fair balance between welcoming foreign students and maintaining national security. Moreover, the Border Commuter Student Act furthers the twin principles of antiessentialism and antisubordination. First, it helps dismantle the myth of the Mexican "illegal alien," and indeed, affirms the notion that many laypersons understand intellectually but fail to embrace emotionally, namely, that our institutions (here, U.S. colleges and universities) stand to benefit from procedures that treat all part-time commuting students, foreign and domestic, equally. And second, by helping part-time students continue their education, it helps them gain parity with those who have the luxury of pursuing their studies full-time. As the Act demonstrates, this can be achieved without sacrificing our nation's commitment to border security.

I take the passage of the Border Commuter Student Act as a healthy sign that we are beginning to understand the danger in the equation "foreign student equals international terrorist." Yet I remain wary of the abuse of executive power that might follow the acquisition of information about international students and scholars endorsed by the PATRIOT Act, especially in light of the December 2002 news reports from Colorado and Washington, D.C., hinting at the same. Hopefully, as the executive branch phases out its monitoring and registration requirements in favor of the technologically superior U.S. VISIT system, it will be better able to guard against further overreaching. In the meantime, I hope that others— such as the educational institutions, advocacy groups, federal legislators, and state governments who work with noncitizen students—continue to explore creative ways to balance the need for national security against this nation's role as a world leader in university education.

Often forgotten in this post-9/11 era are nonterrorist noncitizens—foreign nationals not considered to be national security threats, but deemed undesirable nonetheless. In the next four chapters, I focus on three categories of noncitizen "others": binational parent-child families, undocumented immigrants, and foreign same-gender partners of U.S. citizens, respectively. The chapters that follow explore the complex relationship of each of these groups to the United States, and how our federal constitutional and statutory law often fails to provide equal treatment to them because of their "otherness." Specifically, I examine whether our policies toward these noncitizens further the equality principles of antiessentialism and antisubordination by looking at three questions: first, should our immigration and nationality law treat noncitizen *children* of U.S. citizens differently from noncitizen *parents* of U.S. citizens? Second, what basic constitutional and statutory rights afforded U.S. citizens should noncitizens enjoy even if they are not here lawfully? And third, should our immigration law recognize state-sanctioned marriages performed in the

United States between binational gay or lesbian partners, one of whom is a U.S. citizen and the other of whom is not?

Just as chapter 2 highlighted the delicate balance the nation has been forced to seek between national security and noncitizens' rights post-9/11, the next four chapters weigh other national concerns—law enforcement and majoritarian moral norms—against the rights of noncitizens to be treated as individuals first, irrespective of their immigration status. Indeed, as time marches further and further away from 9/11/2001 and as America's demographics inch forward to a new immigrant nation of largely Latino/a Americans and Asian Americans, we will likely see the issues discussed in the next few chapters gain even greater prominence and currency in both academic and popular debate.

# 3

## Automatic Citizens, Automatic Deportees
### Parents, Children, and Crimes

My wife, Corie, and I have been blessed with two wonderful children, Ryan and Julia, whom we adopted from the Philippines, my place of birth. Corie had dreamed about adopting since she was in middle school. For me, the idea of adopting from the Philippines appealed as a way of further strengthening my cultural ties with my native land, and with my family and friends who still live there. While there is certainly something wonderfully romantic about the notion of adopting internationally, reality is a bit more sobering. Aside from the emotional uncertainty attending any adoption process, the international dimension dictates that the adoptive parents comply with all applicable national and foreign laws governing the procedure. For Corie and me, this meant following the laws of Pennsylvania, the United States, and the Philippines. (Fortunately, our experienced adoption agent and attorney helped us negotiate this maze rather nicely.)

It was through our adoption agent that I first learned about the Child Citizenship Act of 2000 (CCA). For U.S. citizen adoptive parents like us, the most noticeable advantage of the CCA is that it saves having to file yet one more piece of paper. Before the CCA, adoptive parents of foreign-born children had to undergo a two-step process in order to ensure that their children were also U.S. citizens: first, they had to complete their home state's legal requirements to finalize the adoption. Once the adoption was finalized, they needed to apply to the INS (now U.S. Citizenship and Immigration Services) to have the child naturalized as a citizen of the United States. In contrast, the CCA automatically bestows U.S. citizenship upon foreign-born adoptees upon finalization of the adoption, thus saving parents from having to complete that second step.

Because of the way our immigration law works, however, the benefits to the parent (and child) extend far beyond the time and expense saved. Our immigration law states that noncitizens convicted of certain crimes may be deported to their home countries. In theory, this makes much sense. If Jack the Ripper perpetrated any of his heinous crimes in the United States, not many would defend his right to stay. More pointedly, Jack would have about as much of a right to remain in the United States as Osama bin Laden—deporting criminals promotes national security perhaps even more than deporting terrorists (for the reasons I discussed in chapter 2). But what of Jill, the foreign-born adoptee whose parents never filed for naturalization pre-CCA, who then is convicted of a minor drug offense, say, possessing a small amount of marijuana,[1] during her college years? Since the government may not deport U.S. citizens, Jill's roommate and cohort in crime, Amy, is not sent to a country to which she has no real ties. But Jill, the noncitizen, is. Sympathetic members of Congress, some of whom were either adoptive parents themselves or had relatives who had adopted internationally, passed the CCA in record time.

Once I learned more about the CCA, I started to think about why this bill was so popular, especially at a time when immigration and nationality laws are being so fiercely contested both in the political and public arenas. I wanted to know what lessons could be learned from the swift passage of this bill, and what these lessons might mean for future proimmigrant legislation. In this chapter, I have chosen to compare the CCA with the Family Reunification Act of 2001 (FRA), which was first introduced by Representative Barney Frank in 1999, reintroduced in 2001, and then again in 2003. I examine the 2001 version of the bill because of the significant Committee changes that led to the omission of key language promoting family unity in the 2003 proposal. The evolution of the FRA provides a unique vehicle for examining some of the unspoken assumptions that might have been at work during the passage of the CCA, since both purport to maintain family unity. I hope this analysis provides some insight into the biases that perpetuate subordination and underlie our immigration policy based on society's essentialist notions of how race, gender, and class are constructed.

## Family Unity, the CCA, and the FRA

In April 2001, Cecilia Muñoz, Vice President of the National Council of La Raza, and Karen Narasaki, President and Executive Director of the National Asian Pacific American Legal Consortium, presented their respective constituencies' priority lists on immigration and naturalization before the U.S. Senate Subcommittee on Immigration and Claims.[2] Not surprisingly, while "INS reform" was specifically highlighted in both women's remarks, the idea of family reunification was also an important underlying issue. Ms. Muñoz talked about the need to allow Latino/a guest workers and farmworkers the ability to adjust their statuses to permanent residence, so that they might be able to reunite with their families. She also mentioned the disruption of family lives wrought by the infamous 1996 immigration reform laws, leading to the mandatory deportation of certain noncitizens. Similarly, Ms. Narasaki lamented the serious visa processing backlog that is disrupting strong Asian family relationships, which include the care of aging parents, child care by grandparents, and the pooling of resources by siblings to start family businesses or to purchase homes.

Thus, it appears that in both the Latino/a American and Asian American communities, keeping families intact continues to be a high priority and an issue that should have national and natural appeal beyond these two groups. After all, family immigration is a cornerstone of modern immigration law for which Congress has allotted at least 226,000 visas per year.[3] As Alex Aleinikoff, David Martin, and Hiroshi Motomura have noted, "The dominant feature of current arrangements for permanent immigration to the United States is family reunification."[4] This emphasis on family unity has been a staple of immigration law since the first comprehensive family-based set of preferences were established in 1952.[5] It would seem that any federal bill that would advocate family reunification would appear to have at least a fighting chance for passage.

Indeed, the Child Citizenship Act of 2000 or CCA, which conferred automatic citizenship status upon certain foreign-born children of U.S. citizen parents, was brought before both congressional chambers and signed by then President Clinton in a little over a month's time; it became effective on February 27, 2001. The CCA enjoyed broad bipartisan support chiefly because it helped bridge the still existing psychological gap between adopted and biological children, at no apparent cost to the government. In addition, by conferring U.S. citizenship upon a foreign-born adopted child when she enters the United States in the legal custody of her parents, Congress ensured that this legal permanent resident (LPR) turned citizen could never be deported. The law virtually guaranteed that the child would never be forced to live outside the United States. Thus, the CCA achieves two forms of family unity: psychological, by equalizing the citizenship status of the biological and adopted child; and physical, by removing the threat of deportation from the former LPR's life.

Following the triumph of the CCA came a second family unification bill: on April 4, 2001, Representative Barney Frank of Massachusetts introduced the Family Reunification Act or FRA, which was amended and then reported out of the House Judiciary Committee in November 2002.[6] The first Family Reunification Act was introduced by Barney in 1999; after that failed to pass, the 2001 version was proposed. Despite the Judiciary Committee's changes, this later version also failed to pass, and indeed, was reintroduced as the FRA of 2003.

In one sense, the FRA looks at the flipside of the family relationship examined in the CCA. Instead of focusing on the noncitizen child, the FRA's provisions hope to ensure that the noncitizen parent is not separated from her child, who may, in many instances, be a U.S. citizen himself. Because it takes, in many cases, both the parent and child to form a family relationship, one might suspect that if Congress welcomed the idea of strengthening the U.S. citizen parent-noncitizen child bond through the CCA, it might also embrace the inverse by approving the FRA's provisions to reunite the noncitizen parent and the U.S. citizen child. After all, it should not matter whether the child or the parent is the U.S. citizen if one of the underlying objectives of both the CCA and the FRA is to keep families together.

The rest of this chapter examines that hypothesis and unfolds as follows. The next section probes the CCA in more depth, concluding that, despite its promise of permanently uniting citizen parents and noncitizen children, it does not protect an important group of noncitizen children from deportation: those who, as adults, have committed crimes. I then apply the CCA analysis to the FRA bill and argue that, despite its stated goal of reuniting families, the FRA bill—in any version from its 1999 incarnation to its 2003 reintroduction—faces a steep uphill battle because it aims to provide relief to individuals who were specifically left out of the CCA, namely, criminal adult noncitizens. Next, I attempt to explain the reasons for this apparent disconnect, relying on outsider scholarship's emphasis on antisubordination to unmask the biases inherent in the passage of the CCA that might preclude broad support for the FRA bill. For instance, empirical evidence suggests that the racial makeup of the U.S. citizen parent-noncitizen child would likely be white-nonwhite, while the racial makeup of the noncitizen child-noncitizen parent would likely be monoracial, specifically nonwhite-nonwhite. Also at play is class bias: most native-born U.S. residents are of higher socioeconomic standing than foreign-born residents. These racial and class biases might explain why many of Congress's members, who share the same race and class as the U.S. citizen parents to be benefited by the CCA, viewed the bill favorably; however, these same biases may preclude them from passing the FRA. This section will also address possible responses to my bias arguments.

The concluding section argues that, even if much of the FRA is rejected (which I do not think it should be), at the very least the "humanitarian waiver" provision included in the original bills of 1999 and 2001 should be approved by Congress. Unlike the CCA, this provision does not provide a blanket citizenship remedy for those aggrieved, but instead allows for the weighing of humanitarian concerns, including family unity, against the noncitizen parent's deportability grounds. Much of current immigration law allows for such waivers. They would go a long way toward achieving parity by celebrating the parent-child bond, regardless of who is the citizen and who is the parent.

## The Child Citizenship Act of 2000

On February 27, 2001, seventy to seventy-five thousand foreign-born adopted children became automatic U.S. citizens thanks to the Child Citizenship Act of 2000. In an era when congressional politics has been notoriously partisan, the CCA enjoyed swift and easy passage. Introduced in September 21, 1999 as the "Adopted Orphans Citizenship Act," it was later revised to cover certain foreign-born biological children as well, hence its eventually more sweeping title. Following a single hearing held five months after its introduction, the bill was considered and unanimously passed by both chambers of Congress; then President Clinton signed the Act into law on October 30, 2000.

Two key provisions of the CCA are relevant to maintaining family unity—an "automatic citizenship" provision and a "deportation relief" provision. First, the law automatically confers U.S. citizenship upon bio-logical and adopted foreign-born children who are: (1) under eighteen years old; (2) admitted to the United States as an LPR; and (3) in the legal and physical custody of at least one U.S. citizen parent. And second, it provides instant relief from deportation and criminal prosecution for those LPR children who are eighteen years or older and who innocently voted in an election.

During the passage of the House bill, the "automatic citizenship" pro-vision was widely praised by various representatives for essentially four reasons. First, and as mentioned earlier, it cut back on the amount of pa-perwork U.S. citizen parents had to complete in the two-step adoption and citizenship process. Prior to the law, parents had to first petition their foreign-born children to become LPRs and enter the United States as im-migrants. After their children entered the United States, the parents had to file a second application for the naturalization of these LPR children, using virtually identical paperwork. The CCA makes these LPR children automatic citizens once their adoptions are final, thus getting rid of that last administrative barrier to citizenship.

The second reason follows from the first: because one bureaucratic layer has been eliminated, U.S. citizen parents now do not have to wait interminably long for the U.S. Citizenship and Immigration Service (USCIS, formerly part of the INS) to process these naturalization appli-cations, some of which historically took up to two years to complete.

Third, the automatic citizenship provision bridges the gap between foreign-born adoptees and their native-born biological siblings. By elimi-nating the need for their parents to file for naturalization, both foreign-born adoptees and their native-born biological siblings enjoy the same rights of citizenship, acting to further blur distinctions between adopted and biological children in the United States.

And fourth, because foreign-born LPR children automatically become citizens upon completion of their adoptions, they become immune from deportation. Tragically, adopted LPR children whose parents never filed for naturalization have been subject to deportation, often for minor crimes, including petty drug offenses. The automatic citizenship provi-sion acts as a preventative bar to future deportation for foreign-born adoptees. To deport a person to another country to which she has no ties struck some of the representatives as a disproportionately harsh punish-ment for relatively minor crimes.

Remarks directed to the "deportation relief" provision also stressed the importance of ensuring that deportation was an appropriate sanction for certain conduct. While fraudulently casting a vote in an election should be a deportable offense, exercising the franchise on the mistaken assumption that one is a U.S. citizen should not, nor should it be grounds for criminal prosecution or a bar to naturalization.[7] Related to this notion is the argument that children should not be punished for their parents' failure to file for naturalization, an idea that undergirds the "automatic citizenship" provision as well.[8] In sum, both the "automatic citizenship" and "deportation relief" provisions of the CCA work toward keeping LPR children united with their U.S. citizen parents, despite the citizen parents' failure to comply with the current law.

As we shall see below, the proposed Family Reunification Act of 2001 also works toward keeping families together, but acts to provide relief to the noncitizen parent rather than the noncitizen child, who is the CCA's focus.

## The Proposed Family Reunification Act of 2001

The proposed FRA was introduced in the House of Representatives on April 4, 2001 and was immediately referred to the House Committee on the Judiciary, which reported on an amended version to the House in November 2002. The primary thrust of both the original and amended bills is that it restores discretion to the Attorney General (now the Secretary of Homeland Security) by eliminating certain mandatory deportation rules.[9] Specifically, the amended 2001 bill restored discretion with respect to: (1) canceling removal for LPRs with less serious aggravated felony sentences (e.g., nonviolent offenses, single offense with a sentence of four years or less, etc.); (2) release from detention; and (3) eliminating the automatic bar for certain returning LPRs.

There are two important ways in which the arguments used to support the CCA, which won wide bipartisan support, could be made for the FRA. First, like the CCA, the FRA aims to ensure that deportation is an appropriate consequence of certain undesirable conduct. Just as the CCA sought to prevent the deportation of innocent LPR voters, the FRA of 2001 reserved deportation for only the most serious offenders. As part of the 1996 amendments to the Immigration and Nationality Act, AEDPA (the Antiterrorism and Effective Death Penalty Act of 1996)[10] and IIRAIRA expanded the definition of crimes for which one might be held deportable, including the list of potential "aggravated felonies." More pointedly, the definition of "aggravated felony," which began as one paragraph in 1988, now contains twenty-one paragraphs with many subsections. And, not surprisingly, "aggravated felons" are not just the hardened criminals of the world but include many convicted of minor offenses. Consider the following story from legal scholar Nancy Morawetz:

> Jose Velasquez, for example, was at a party when a friend approached him looking to buy drugs. Velasquez told the person that he did not sell drugs, but he identified someone else who might. He was arrested and later pled guilty to drug conspiracy, even though he had no financial connection to the person that he had suspected was selling drugs. The court imposed a fine and placed Velasquez on probation. Velasquez's conviction is treated as an aggravated felony, and Velasquez, who has lived in the United States for thirty-nine years as a legal resident, now faces mandatory deportation.[11]

Just as it would be unfair to send adopted children who have grown up in the United States to foreign lands, it would be just as unfair to deport Mr. Velasquez, who has lived in the United States for an even longer period of time. To use Connecticut Representative Gejdenson's words in support of the CCA, such deportation would be "needlessly cruel."[12]

But second, and more important, is the similarity in purpose between the CCA and proposed FRA which is to unify families, a touchstone of our immigration policy. Indeed, the CCA and the FRA are two sides of the same coin of family unity: the CCA focuses on keeping the noncitizen child with the citizen parent, while the FRA aims to keep the noncitizen parent with the (often citizen) child. The FRA's proposed restoration of administrative discretion, judicial review, and the removal of mandatory provisions that disproportionately disadvantage noncitizens operate in concert to keep the parent with the child, just as the CCA works to keep the child with the parent.

During the House Committee on the Judiciary's final discussion of the amended bill in July 2002, both conservative Chairman George Sensenbrenner and liberal representative Barney Frank noted the FRA's commitment to family unity. Sensenbrenner decried the current state of affairs:

[A] disturbing number of cases have arisen where permanent resident aliens have been deported for offenses which many feel do not merit such a penalty. . . . Many of these aliens have fully reformed, raised families, and become productive members of their communities in the ensuing years.[13]

Frank focused on the urgent need to pass the FRA:

Someone gets in trouble at 19 to 20. Eight, 9, 10 years later, having straightened out his life, having started a family, has a couple of kids, he's working, all of a sudden, he's deported. And I'm talking now about people in that category who were deported who cannot now come back to this country unless we pass this bill.[14]

As the next section suggests, however, the "family unity" theme that undergirds both the CCA and the FRA collapses under the gaze of critical scrutiny, revealing race, gender, and class bias that might make the FRA difficult to pass.

## Unmasking the CCA and the FRA

Taking a closer look at both the CCA and the FRA, it is highly unlikely that the FRA (or any legislation like it) will receive the same broad bipartisan support that the CCA did, because the CCA leaves out precisely the kind of person the FRA aims to protect—criminal adult noncitizens. I plan to demonstrate how certain persons left uncovered by the CCA will remind Congress of those likely to be protected by the FRA and how race, gender, and class privilege operate to support my analysis here.

While the CCA protects foreign-born adopted children under eighteen years of age by granting them automatic citizenship, it does nothing to protect those sons and daughters of U.S. citizens who have already been convicted of minor offenses, but have been subjected to deportation orders under the 1996 immigration reform bills.

Consider the following two stories of foreign-born adoptees who have been deported:[15]

In one well-known case, John Gaul[16] was adopted by a Florida family at the age of four. Though born in Thailand, he speaks no Thai, has no

Thai relatives, knows nothing of Thai culture and had never been back to Thailand—until the U.S. government deported him last year as a criminal alien at the age of 25. The Gauls had obtained an American birth certificate for John shortly after adopting him, and didn't realize until he applied for a passport at age 17 that he had never been naturalized. They immediately filed the papers, but due to INS delays his application wasn't processed before he turned 18. An immigration judge ruled that the agency had taken too long to process the application, but that the 1996 law allowed him no discretion to halt the deportation.

In another recent instance, Joao Herbert,[17] a 22-year-old Ohioan adopted as a young boy from Brazil, was ordered deported because he had sold 7.5 ounces of marijuana while in his teens. It was his first criminal offense, for which he was sentenced only to probation and community treatment. But because he had never been naturalized, he was considered an aggravated felon subject to deportation.

Herbert has been in detention for a year-and-a-half because the Brazilians consider his adoption irrevocable and refuse to accept him. Were they to do so, it is unclear how he would manage—he knows no one in his native country and no longer understands his native tongue.

Both these stories come from the press release issued by Congressman Delahunt, a key sponsor of the CCA.[18] The release also quotes the congressman as saying, "No one condones criminal acts, [b]ut the terrible price these young people and their families have paid is out of all proportion to their misdeeds. Whatever they did, they should be treated like any other American kid."[19] Interestingly, Delahunt's initial bill would have applied to children over eighteen, but he could not get it approved by his colleagues.

Except for innocent noncitizen voters over eighteen, no other deportable foreign-born adoptees are provided relief by the CCA. This fact does not bode well for the FRA, whose provisions specifically contemplate providing relief to adult noncitizens convicted of crimes. My sense is that societal race, gender, and class narratives influenced Congress's CCA deliberations, privileging U.S. citizen parents in the mixed-status family but not noncitizen adults, and therefore, not noncitizen parents/adults in the FRA debate. More specifically, the "citizen householder family" is more likely to be white and of a higher socioeconomic status than the "immigrant householder family," thereby prompting legislators to view the CCA more favorably than the FRA. In addition, race, gender, and class bias with respect to crime might explain the CCA exception precluding criminal adult offspring from receiving automatic citizenship and relief from deportation.

The key to the CCA was the notion that foreign-born adoptive children should be granted U.S. citizenship as efficiently as possible as a way to establish parity between adopted and biological children and to eliminate the possibility of deportation in the future. Most adults wanting to adopt in the United States are white, and most children waiting to be adopted, both domestically and internationally, are nonwhite.[20] Thus, many adoptive American families are likely to be ones in which the parents are white and the adopted children are nonwhite. Viewed from this perspective, it is easy to see why the CCA was so positively received. Many of the white senators and representatives[21] easily identified with the white U.S. citizen parents who wanted to make sure their nonwhite adopted children were U.S. citizens.

While the ensuing law included a provision to ensure that biological foreign-born children were treated in the same manner as adoptees, the CCA was originally named the "Adopted Orphans Citizenship Act." Indeed, one of the major sponsors of the CCA, Congressman Delahunt, adopted a child from Vietnam;[22] another, Representative Schakowsky, has two adopted relatives from Korea.[23] During the floor speeches, references were made to these personal connections, surely making the identification process even easier for their colleagues in the room.[24]

In contrast to the adoptive citizen family experience, most immigrant families are likely to have large, single-race homes, most of which are nonwhite. Family immigration from Asia and Latin America comprises the bulk of immigration to the United States post-1965,[25] and many Asian and Latino/a immigrants have more children than native-born families (whether white or nonwhite).[26] Furthermore, immigrant families usually do not have the financial wherewithal[27] or the cultural affinity for nonrelative adoptions (although relative adoptions are more common)[28] that many native-born Americans do.[29]

These facts suggest that most congresspersons probably have different narrative pictures of the "citizen householder family" and the "immigrant householder family": a "citizen" family is one headed by a middle-class, white U.S. citizen regardless of the color of the children, while an "immigrant" family is one headed by a poor, brown or yellow noncitizen, regardless of the color of the children. If this racial and class divide along citizenship lines underscores the CCA narrative, it makes sense that these privileged lawmakers would be able to more easily identify with the U.S. citizen parents than with the immigrants, and therefore be easily persuaded of the CCA's merits.

A further, more subtle, stereotype might also be at work here. I suspect that we tend to ascribe the parent's citizenship status to the child. After all, our immigration law allows for precisely that: a parent may confer citizenship status on a child, but not the other way around. Hence, the CCA is attractive because it reinforces that belief by making it easier for citizen parents to confer their status upon their noncitizen children. Thus, Congress may have viewed the collapsing together of LPR and citizenship status for foreign adoptees as noncontroversial because it appealed to their normative sense that children should have the same citizen status as their parents, even though the bill clearly showed that there were families for whom this was not true.

In addition, a race, gender, and class narrative may also explain the "criminal adult" exception built into the CCA. To the extent that the experiences of John Gaul and Joao Herbert, both male and both people of color, one Asian (Thai) and one Latino (Brazilian), were both raised on the House floor as examples of children deported under the 1996 acts, that may have unintentionally convinced many that the exception was well founded. Instead of engendering sympathy for these two men, Congressman Delahunt may have inadvertently reinforced the stereotype that young, male, noncitizen people of color are more likely to commit crime. In some persons' minds, Herbert and Gaul, because of their race, gender, class, and citizenship, might have crossed the line from child to criminal.[30] These status-based (as opposed to behavior-based) conclusions run afoul of antiessentialism by suggesting that criminality can be linked to specific physical traits, reminiscent of the work of Jessica Mitford on the so-called "criminal type," described at the beginning of chapter 2.

Should Congress view the FRA through the same race- and class-tinted lenses described above, even the watered-down 2003 version will likely stand little chance of passing (indeed, a bare majority of the Committee— eighteen to fifteen—voted in favor of the *compromise* 2001 bill).[31] From this perspective, the immigrant householder who might benefit from the FRA will probably not be as sympathetic a figure as the citizen householder favored in the CCA. It will be harder for a middle-class, white congressman to empathize with the plight of a poor, nonwhite noncitizen than to understand the hardships faced by a middle-class, white U.S. citizen parent.

Moreover, the CCA itself did not provide full relief to the citizen householder. As mentioned earlier, the CCA does not cover foreign-born children such as John Gaul and Joao Herbert who are older than eighteen years of age. If Congress was unwilling to protect adult offspring of U.S. citizens from deportation, why should it view other adult noncitizens more favorably, especially those of a different race, gender, and class?

The racial and class divide that separates the "immigrant householder family" and the "citizen householder family" may be overcome by two important facts. First, nearly one out of ten families with children in the United States is a mixed-immigration status family: that is, at least one of the parents is a noncitizen and at least one of the children is a citizen.[32] This suggests that, contrary to what some may surmise, many parents and children do not share the same immigration status. Indeed, if the CCA was meant to address the citizenship divide between U.S. citizen parents and their noncitizen children, then it makes sense that there would be families that fall into the other mixed-status category of U.S. citizen child and noncitizen parent.

But second, and more importantly, 89 percent of children in mixed-status families are citizens.[33] This fact suggests that family unification among "immigrant householder families"—those who would benefit from the FRA—is just as important as among "citizen householder families"—those who will benefit from the CCA. Put differently, if family unification is an important immigration policy, then both adults and children who are U.S. citizens should benefit. The CCA was successful because legislators could identify with the U.S. citizen parents who wanted to keep their children from being deported. The FRA's proponents may stand a chance if they can persuade Congress that the beneficiaries of the bill will not be the noncitizen parents, but their citizen children.

Even if Congress were to shift its focus from the noncitizen parent to the citizen child in considering the FRA, one might argue that Congress's desire to be tough on crime precluded it from giving citizen parents an unqualified right in the CCA to be united with their foreign-born adoptees. After all, the citizen parents of John Gaul and Joao Herbert saw both their sons deported when it appeared that Congress would not go forward on Representative Delahunt's original suggestion that the bill apply to all offspring, even those eighteen and older. In addition, one might contend that the whole idea of race, gender, and class being underlying reasons for the exception is overwrought. The real divide is between child and adult—adults deserve less protection than children, regardless of their race, and both Gaul and Herbert are now adults. As Representative Lamar Smith opined in Committee:

> If you invited a guest to your home, and that guest stole your jewelry, or used your child in pornography, or gave drugs to your teenager, you would ask them to leave. That is why we should continue to do so with criminal aliens who have been convicted of serious crimes.[34]

There are at least four responses to this objection. The first is an appeal to family unity, which underlies both the CCA and the FRA. While it certainly would have been better for the Herbert and Gaul families not to see their sons deported, both offspring were young adults at the time of their deportation and apparently are coping well in their new environs. Many citizen children adversely affected by a parent's deportation are likely to be younger: a comparison of age groups between native- and foreign-born Americans shows that a greater percentage of native-born persons are ages eighteen and younger because most of the children of foreign-born parents are U.S. citizens.[35] Given their youth and the relative poverty of their families, the deportation of citizen children's noncitizen parents would have a greater emotional and socioeconomic impact on them than on adults like Herbert and Gaul.

The second argument focuses on punishment proportionality. While the CCA did not compromise Congress's "tough on crime" stance by excluding adults from automatic citizenship, it simultaneously created a loophole by removing a second deterrent and punishment, that of deportation. In passing the CCA, legislators expressed the belief that deportation should not be visited upon persons convicted of minor crimes who have already been punished for the misdeed. However, under the Act, a U.S. citizen parent can rest assured that her legally adopted LPR child will not be deported even if she commits murder because that child will be a citizen.

In contrast, the FRA creates no such loophole, but rather restores the concept of punishment proportionality and fundamental fairness. For example, should the FRA fail, a longtime resident of the United States may be removable upon return from a brief visit abroad if the INS finds out about a minor crime committed many years ago. It doesn't matter whether the LPR is a productive member of society or that his children are U.S. citizens. The tragedy is that unlike my hypothetical new citizen child murderer, the foregoing deportation scenario is what befell Jesus Collado, who was sought to be deported for engaging in what turned out to be a consensual sexual act with his then underage girlfriend many years earlier.[36]

The third reason speaks to both family unity and punishment proportionality. Unlike the CCA, the FRA does not provide automatic relief from deportation for the noncitizen. At best, it provides the Attorney General the opportunity to provide relief from deportation should the individual case so warrant. The noncitizen in such instances is still presumptively deportable, unless exceptional circumstances suggest otherwise. This flexibility allows the decision maker to consider the very issues of family unity and punishment proportionality that made the CCA so appealing. For instance, from a proportionality standpoint, one might contend that Mr. Vasquez's tenuously drug-related conduct described earlier may have been as innocent as the voting conduct subject to the blanket exception created by the CCA.

Finally, the fourth argument addresses the race, gender, and class issue along antiessentialist and antisubordination lines. Although it is true that immigration politics, race, gender, and class are theoretically distinct issues, much has been written about their intersectionality.[37] I do not suggest here that race, gender, and class were definitely at issue, but they may have been in the decision to pass the CCA and yet exempt offspring ages eighteen and older. My desire, therefore, is that when Congress more fully examines the FRA (and other similar immigration legislation) it take into account any underlying biases it may have about race, gender, and class by seeing what role these may have played in the CCA's passage. If the child-adult divide was truly the issue, and not race, gender, and class, then I would hope that when Congress examines the FRA, it considers whether family unity and punishment proportionality are concepts that apply to all races and classes, not just the privileged few. As a thought experiment, it would be useful to imagine a congressional hearing or floor speech in which the stories about the aggravated felons who might benefit from the FRA include a white, upper-middle-class, LPR banker from Ireland convicted of an aggravated DUI[38] or for being a drug coconspirator simply for pointing out a drug dealer at a party (not unlike Mr. Velasquez's situation). Our banker friend has lived in the United States for over thirty years and has three young children, all of whom are U.S. citizens by birth. None of the children has ever visited Ireland. His Irish wife has stayed at home to care for their children all this time, and does not have a paying job herself. I suspect that at least some of the legislators might be able to better relate to that story than to the Herbert or Gaul narratives, if only because they might be able to identify with the Irishman, much as Representatives Delahunt and Schakowsky could share their personal adoption experiences with their colleagues.

## Salvaging the FRA by Keeping the Humanitarian Waiver

Like the CCA, the FRA goes a long way toward promoting family unity, an important immigration policy objective. While I would have preferred the FRA to be passed in its original 2001 form and in its entirety, I would have urged that at the very least Congress adopt a version of the original "humanitarian waiver" provision, which allows the Attorney General (now the Secretary of Homeland Security) or his designate, the immigration judge, to balance "family unity" against the noncitizen's offense.[39] Like the CCA, it is an efficient, insignificant departure from current practice, given that such waivers are common throughout the immigration code, especially where removal would adversely affect either a citizen spouse or child.[40] Second, it captures nicely the themes of "family unity" and "punishment proportionality" without making either one a trump, since it allows the immigration judge to exercise his discretion on a case-by-case basis. Third and finally, unlike the CCA it is not a permanent remedy, in that the waiver does not bestow automatic immunity from deportation through the grant of citizenship. Rather, it simply allows the noncitizen to continue to reside in the United States if the family unification reasons are particularly compelling.

I now return to the beginning. Both LaRaza and NAPALC believe strongly in family unity, and, indeed, our immigration policy embraces it. Proimmigration forces should partner with other like-minded groups to find ways to support bills such as the unvarnished 2001 FRA which ultimately benefit all families. Organizing around a theme of family unity and being able to counteract possible essentialist, oppressive biases inherent in even the most benign of laws such as the CCA should go a long way toward protecting the rights not just of U.S. citizen parents, but of often neglected citizen children as well.

As a U.S. citizen parent of two adopted children from the Philippines, I am thrilled that Ryan and Julia are now U.S. citizens because of the Child Citizenship Act. But I am also a Filipino immigrant who came to the United States as an adult, and I can therefore relate to the beneficiaries of the proposed Family Reunification Act. My hope is that Congress will strive to recognize that family unity should apply to both citizen and immigrant householder families, because in the end U.S. citizens, children as well as adults, benefit from the preservation of this core immigration principle.

From issues of citizenship and relief from deportation in this chapter, I focus next on the constitutional and statutory rights of the 8 to 11 million undocumented immigrants currently residing in America. As I describe in chapter 1, while I have never entered the United States without immigration papers, I was, for a brief time in 1988, without legal documentation. I had fallen "out-of-status," which is the functional equivalent of being an "undocumented" person, because I had no legal right to remain in the United States. Contrary to conventional assumptions, there are a lot of people in the "out-of-status" category of undocumented migrants. Despite the pervasive stereotype of the "illegal alien" slipping across the Mexican border, one-half of all undocumented migration is attributable to those who came with valid documents but fell "out-of-status" and chose to remain in the United States.[41]

And so, as a former "illegal alien," I want to examine the issue of when such persons should be entitled to rights normally afforded U.S. citizens. Unlike green card holders who enjoy the most favored status of "citizens-in-waiting," undocumented immigrants are the pariahs of both U.S. immigration law and the popular imagination. Not only can they be legally deported with fewer administrative and judicial due process protections than other classes of noncitizens, but undocumented immigrants are generally regarded in the public eye as being undeserving of much protection. "They should not be here in the first place," goes the usual justification. Yet most Americans would not completely reject these persons' humanity, either. Thus, while undocumented migrants will not likely be granted the right to vote in a federal election anytime soon, the general public would probably reject torture as a valid means for inducing suspected undocumented migrants into admitting their transgressions. In the next two chapters, I set out to explore the hypothetical "floor" and "ceiling" of the constitutional and statutory rights of undocumented immigrants in the United States.

# 4

# Building the Floor

*Preserving the Fourth Amendment Rights
of Undocumented Migrants*

In this chapter, I contend that the Fourth Amendment right to be free from unreasonable government searches and seizures is a constitutional "floor" that should extend to undocumented immigrants, despite recent pronouncements by some courts suggesting otherwise. The Fourth Amendment is a personal (as opposed to citizenship) right meant to deter unlawful government conduct. Developments in tort premises liability law provide an interesting analogy: just as we should require tortfeasor landowners to compensate persons injured on their property irrespective of their relationship to the plaintiffs, our constitutional law should provide Fourth Amendment protections against the government regardless of the claimant's immigration status.

While the denial of public benefits to lawful permanent residents might define one end of the debate over noncitizens' rights, this chapter chooses to take up the other extreme: the possible denial of domestic Fourth Amendment rights to so-called "illegal aliens," or, less pejoratively, un-documented immigrants. While this issue has been the subject of much debate in the literature,[1] its reexamination is in order in light of a 2003 Utah federal district court's decision entitled *United States v. Esparza-Mendoza*.[2] In *Esparza-Mendoza*, U.S. District Judge Paul Cassell ruled that a previously deported undocumented immigrant was not protected by the Fourth Amendment's prohibition against unreasonable government searches.

The facts of *Esparza-Mendoza* are compelling, although the case starts out rather ordinarily. Around March 1997, Mexican citizen Jorge Es-parza-Mendoza crossed the border into the United States, evading immigration authorities. Two years later, in April 1999, he was convicted in a

Utah state court for felony possession of cocaine. Rather than having him serve his up to five years of prison time, the state handed Esparza-Mendoza over to the INS a month later. The INS deported Esparza-Mendoza to Mexico in May 1999, warning that should he return surreptitiously he would be subject to federal criminal charges. Sometime thereafter, Esparza-Mendoza again entered the United States without documentation. On October 27, 2002, Salt Lake City Sheriff's Officer Tracey Cook apprehended Esparza-Mendoza on federal criminal charges for reentering the United States after having been previously removed.

Had these been the only facts of the case, *Esparza-Mendoza* would appear run-of-the-mill. After all, Esparza-Mendoza had been duly deported based on a state felony conviction and had received notice that he would be charged with a federal crime if he returned. Indeed, Esparza-Mendoza did not dispute any of these facts. Rather, he argued that the government obtained knowledge of his identity unconstitutionally, in violation of his Fourth Amendment rights.

Officer Cook had no reason to suspect that Esparza-Mendoza was an undocumented migrant when she asked to see his identification on October 27, 2002. She encountered Esparza-Mendoza in the course of responding to a call reporting a domestic dispute between Esparza-Mendoza's girlfriend and her sister. When she first arrived at the scene, Officer Cook took statements from the sisters, one of whom claimed that the other threw a brick at Esparza-Mendoza's car. She then asked to speak with Esparza-Mendoza, who stated that the car was actually his sibling's and that he did not want to get involved in the dispute between the sisters.

Here is the Court's description of what happened next:

> Officer Cook stated that she needed to get some identification from him to make sure that everything checked out properly. Esparza-Mendoza responded that he did not want to be involved and did not want to provide his identification. Officer Cook then asked a second time for his identification, stating that she "needed" to see it. It was not put in terms that Esparza-Mendoza had an option to do this, but rather in terms that he was directed to do so. Officer Cook also testified that she had no belief at this time that Esparza-Mendoza had committed any crime.[3]

Officer Cook checked Esparza-Mendoza's name with a dispatch officer, who advised that he was a deported felon and that there was an outstanding warrant for his arrest. After verifying this information with the INS, Officer Cook detained Esparza-Mendoza and the federal government charged him with one count of illegal reentry.

Esparza-Mendoza challenged Officer Cook's conduct as unconstitutional under the Fourth Amendment's prohibition against unreasonable searches and seizures because he was "detained and forced to present his identification without probable cause or even reasonable suspicion."[4] Judge Cassell sided with Esparza-Mendoza on the merits, finding that Officer Cook did not have reasonable suspicion to seek his identification, that she coerced him to present the same, and that his identity was therefore the fruit of an unlawful search in violation of the Fourth Amendment.

The case then took a surprising turn. The Court decided that, despite the Fourth Amendment violation, the government could still introduce the evidence of Esparza-Mendoza's identity because as a "previously removed alien (felon)"—with "felon" in parentheses because Judge Cassell also refers to the category of "previously deported aliens," whether felons or not—Esparza-Mendoza did not belong to the class of persons the amendment was intended to protect.

The rest of the chapter unfolds in three parts. After critiquing Judge Cassell's opinion in *Esparza-Mendoza,* I offer a theoretical alternative to the categorical denial of rights to undocumented migrants or any subset thereof—a more flexible approach to the standing issue based on a parallel to developments in tort premises liability law. I then close with a political critique of *Esparza-Mendoza,* examining the extent to which Judge Cassell's background and politics may have affected his perspective on the facts and law in that case.

## *Critiquing Esparza-Mendoza, Part I—A Legal Analysis*

Judge Cassell provided three reasons for holding that the Fourth Amendment did not protect undocumented migrants previously removed for felony offenses: first, Chief Justice Rehnquist's plurality opinion in *United States v. Verdugo-Urquidez* established that the Fourth Amendment only benefited "the People"—those with sufficient connection to the United States. Second, even if it could not rely on Rehnquist's analysis, the Court's own independent examination of the text, history, structure, and precedents surrounding the Fourth Amendment suggest that "previously removed alien felons" are categorically excluded from "the People" the amendment protects. And third, notwithstanding this categorical denial of Fourth Amendment protection, Judge Cassell opined that the Fifth Amendment's due process clause extends to all "persons," thereby providing a sufficient deterrent against egregious police misconduct. Each of these reasons deserves a closer look.

In *Verdugo-Urquidez*, the Supreme Court rejected a Fourth Amendment challenge brought by a Mexican citizen who was abducted from Mexico and tried in the United States on drug charges; Verdugo-Urquidez attempted to suppress evidence obtained during a search of two of his Mexican residences.[5] Reviewing the text of the Fourth Amendment as well as relevant precedent, the Court held that the Fourth Amendment did not apply to the search of Verdugo-Urquidez's Mexican residences. Despite the strong 6-to-3 agreement on the judgment in the case, three of the justices in the majority penned opinions, the most popular of which, Chief Justice Rehnquist's, could garner no more than four votes on the rationale for when a noncitizen is entitled to Fourth Amendment protection. Nonetheless, Chief Justice Rehnquist's opinion has been cited favorably by some lower courts, including the *Esparza-Mendoza* court.[6]

To determine the class protected by the Fourth Amendment, Rehnquist first distinguished the text of the Fourth Amendment, which purports to protect "the people," from that outlined in the Fifth and Sixth amendments, which aim to protect "persons" and the "accused," respectively, from illegal government conduct.[7] Rehnquist's plurality opinion concluded that "people" was a narrower term of art than either "persons" or "accused" that was selectively used throughout the Constitution to refer to "a class of persons who are part of a national community or who have otherwise developed sufficient connection with this country to be considered part of that community."[8]

Rehnquist drew a distinction here between Verdugo-Urquidez, a Mexican national and resident, and the undocumented immigrant deportees in *INS v. Lopez-Mendoza*, in which the Court implicitly ruled that the Fourth Amendment applied to these noncitizens even though they could not avail themselves of the exclusionary rule in the context of a deportation, as opposed to a criminal, proceeding: "The [undocumented immigrants] in *Lopez-Mendoza* were in the United States voluntarily and presumably had accepted some social obligations; but [Verdugo-Urquidez] has no voluntary connection with this country that might place him among 'the people' of the United States."[9]

Next, reviewing the legislative history of the Fourth Amendment, the plurality decided that the primary purpose of the Fourth Amendment was to deter unreasonable conduct by the U.S. government *domestically,* not extraterritorially. Thus, because Verdugo-Urquidez's residences were in Mexico, the plurality held that the Fourth Amendment did not protect them. Based on this textual and historical analysis, the plurality decided that Mexican national Verdugo-Urquidez had not established sufficient voluntary connections with the United States in order to bar evidence obtained during searches of his Mexican residences.

Despite the fact that Chief Justice Rehnquist never clearly defined what constitutes a "sufficient connection" or "significant voluntary connection" or "substantial connection"[10] to the United States (except to say that Verdugo-Urquidez did not meet the test), the *Esparza-Mendoza* court adopted what Judge Cassell called the "sufficient connection" test, citing Rehnquist's opinion. There are several reasons to be skeptical in applying Rehnquist's test to *Esparza-Mendoza,* not the least of which is that *Verdugo-Urquidez* involved an overseas search while the challenged conduct here happened domestically. As noted above, Rehnquist himself acknowledged that the primary purpose of the amendment was to deter unreasonable domestic, not international, searches. Moreover, even if the "sufficient connections" test was more than dicta, it required an examination of the links between the accused noncitizen and the community—links that were not categorically severed by one's illegal presence. Indeed, the Rehnquist four assumed that some undocumented immigrants might have sufficient connections, citing *Lopez-Mendoza* as a possible example.

Realizing that relying solely on *Verdugo-Urquidez* might not carry the day, Judge Cassell independently studied the text, history, structure, and precedents in order to determine the meaning of "the people" protected under the Fourth Amendment. Relying on many of the same sources as the Chief Justice, Judge Cassell arrived at the same conclusion: that only those with a sufficient connection to the United States need apply.

[I]t appears that the Framers of the Fourth Amendment intended to extend coverage to members of the political community and those closely connected to them—their families, for instance. The question then arises whether aliens . . . have been invited to share the protections extended to the political community. Tourists from overseas and legally resident aliens would appear to be prime candidates for inclusion under a sufficient connection test. But the narrow issue here is not whether these more expansive categories of aliens are covered, but whether a previously deported alien *felon* is covered.[11]

Judge Cassell then applied the "sufficient connection" test in two steps: first, he determined how the framers would have treated criminal noncitizens generally, history revealing that they generally were not viewed as part of the community. Second, he categorically concluded that Esparza-Mendoza, and other previous deportees like him, could not possibly develop sufficient connections:

> For all these reasons, it appears that previously deported alien felons, such as Esparza-Mendoza, are not covered by the Fourth Amendment. In reaching this conclusion, the court has made a categorical determination about previously deported aliens. [A]n individual previously deported alien felon is not free to argue that, in his particular case, he possesses a sufficient connection to this country to receive Fourth Amendment coverage (unless, of course, he could prove that he was in this country lawfully). Any other determination would reward unlawful behavior. It would be perverse to give greater constitutional rights to those aliens who would have most flagrantly flouted the law by unlawfully returning to the United States for the longest periods of time. Therefore, it appears that all previously deported alien felons stand outside "the People" covered by the Fourth Amendment.[12]

Although it will likely be ultimately overturned by the Tenth Circuit, the *Esparza-Mendoza* decision creates a *per se* rule with respect to certain undocumented immigrants' Fourth Amendment rights; that is, under the sufficient connections test, an undocumented immigrant's "illegal" residence in the United States vitiates any legitimate connections the person may have with this country. Judge Cassell's overarching theme is that Esparza-Mendoza was an undocumented immigrant and, therefore, could not have had a legitimate connection to the United States. Interestingly, Esparza-Mendoza's felony record is less of a concern in terms of establishing sufficient connections than his immigration status. Judge Cassell specifically precludes all "previously deported alien felon[s]" from demonstrating their substantial connections unless they can prove lawful presence.

At one level, the court's reasoning is appealing: undocumented immigrants should not be able to claim lengthy, well-established connections with this country when they are not legally entitled to be in the country in the first place. Thus, even though he might have been in this country longer than a tourist on vacation (and who is legally present)[13] in the United States, Esparza-Mendoza's length of stay was automatically nullified because he had not been in this country legally. Aside from encouraging compliance with the law generally, the *Esparza-Mendoza* holding creates a disincentive for noncitizens to immigrate to the United States without the proper documentation. If a right as important as the Fourth Amendment protection against unreasonable searches and seizures can be withheld from persons "illegally" present in the United States, then such persons have a strong interest in pursuing only legal means of entry.

This analysis, however enticing, fails to persuade for two reasons. First, whether one is "legally" or "illegally" in the United States is less an issue of morality than an issue of public policy. Specifically, whether one's status is "legal" or "illegal" upon arrival in the United States without a visa may depend upon one's citizenship. For example, a temporary business visitor from Canada may enter the United States without a valid U.S. visa, while a Mexican national in the same situation may not. Thus, if both the Canadian and Mexican were to enter the United States without visas, the Canadian would be deemed "legal" while the Mexican would not.[14] In addition, the government has, on occasion, granted amnesty to so-called undocumented immigrants by allowing them to apply for citizenship despite their "illegal" status.[15] When it is politically expedient to do so, the government is willing to compromise on the "illegal" versus "legal" "alien" issue.[16]

Second, and more significant, is the court's misguided reliance on the sufficient connections test, whether it emanates from *Verdugo-Urquidez* or from Judge Cassell's own independent analysis. The sufficient connections test to determine Fourth Amendment standing incorrectly shifts the focus of the amendment's purpose from deterring unlawful government conduct (which the Supreme Court in *Verdugo-Urquidez* acknowledges) to allocating rights to individuals based on their relationship with the United States. The sufficient connections test achieves this paradigm shift by highlighting the textual differences between the "people" covered by the Fourth Amendment and the "persons" covered by other constitutional amendments and then creating a relational test that looks at bonds between the noncitizen and the United States as a means of determining whether the Fourth Amendment protects the foreigner. As described earlier, Chief Justice Rehnquist's plurality opinion in *Verdugo-Urquidez* began with a textual exegesis of the Fourth Amendment, concluding that its specific reference to "the people" limited its applicability to a group more closely connected to the United States than the generic "persons" described in the Fifth and Sixth amendments. Accordingly, Rehnquist favored the creation of a "sufficient connections test" to measure the noncitizen's tie to the United States. Although Rehnquist never specifically described the factors the trial court should review to determine whether one's ties are "significant" and "voluntary," or "substantial," the *Esparza-Mendoza* court went even further by specifying a group of individuals—"previously removed alien felons"—who categorically were excluded from the Fourth Amendment's protected class.

Even more objectionable than its indeterminacy is the test's wrongheaded approach toward Fourth Amendment law. Reviewing the landscape of significant Fourth Amendment decisions, it appears that the issues before the Supreme Court often focus on whether a person has a reasonable expectation of privacy or whether a search was reasonably conducted, rather than whether the Fourth Amendment protects the individual in the first instance. In many Supreme Court cases, the person claiming protection may lose on the substantive Fourth Amendment claim not because of who she is, but because she did not have a sufficient privacy interest in the place searched.[17] Thus, *Esparza-Mendoza* and *Verdugo-Urquidez* erode the amendment's objective to deter unreasonable government conduct by creating an obstacle to standing in the guise of the sufficient connections test for a select group of persons.

Because the Fourth Amendment would protect only some individuals under the *Esparza-Mendoza* approach, it would create an incentive for government to be more intrusive in its investigative efforts of, at the very least, previously removed undocumented immigrants, and, at worst, documented nonimmigrants, accused of criminal activity. Suppose, for example, that the leadership of a suspected drug ring is composed of three Europeans—one legal permanent resident, one temporary nonimmigrant holding a valid college student visa, and one undocumented immigrant—and all three have been arrested on the basis of evidence uncovered during an illegal search of their joint business office. Under the *Esparza-Mendoza* analysis, each defendant's ability to raise a Fourth Amendment challenge would vary depending upon her immigration status. Presumably, the legal permanent resident would have no problem asserting her right to be free from an unreasonable search because she would be able to demonstrate her sufficient connections to the United States—her legitimate business interests, her longtime legal residence in the United States, and so forth. The undocumented immigrant might very well be unable to claim any standing because any legitimate connections would be negated by her undocumented status. The remaining defendant, the international student, would be in a middle position. Would her connections be more like those of the permanent resident or those of the undocumented immigrant? While Judge Cassell suggested in dicta that LPRs and tourists might very well have substantial connections, and indeed did not offer his opinion on undocumented immigrants who had *not* been previously deported, the indeterminacy of these persons' protections under the Fourth Amendment is troubling.

The trial court would be able to most effectively weigh the noncitizens' Fourth Amendment claims by adjudicating them on their merits rather than by hiding behind the doctrine of standing, a procedural smoke screen parading as a legitimate constitutional device. As legal expert Lisa Kloppenberg has argued, courts often duck behind procedural rules to avoid ruling on difficult substantive questions involving controversial issues.[18] In my hypothetical drug ring case, because all three of the noncitizens' claims to the business property would involve similar substantive issues, it would behoove the presiding court to take the matters concurrently, ruling on the merits of each argument and achieving consistent outcomes. Proceeding in this way would ensure that law enforcement officers would not be tempted to engage in constitutional violations knowing that their undocumented immigrant targets, and possibly their temporary nonimmigrant targets, would likely have no standing to raise a Fourth Amendment claim.

Judge Cassell would counter with the last of his three arguments—that even if the law categorically prohibited previously removed undocumented migrant felons from receiving Fourth Amendment protection, the Fifth Amendment's Due Process Clause would inhibit the police from engaging in conduct that "shocks the conscience." At least two responses are worth noting: first, the "shocks the conscience" standard is a pretty stringent one. In 2003, the Supreme Court remanded a case to the Ninth Circuit for its determination whether a law enforcement officer who interrogated a severely injured person while he received treatment in the emergency room of a hospital, violated the defendant's Fifth Amendment due process rights to be free from coercive questioning.[19] If that case had to be litigated all the way to the Supreme Court, it appears that the discretion accorded police officers under the Fifth Amendment is exceedingly broad. Second, in the case at hand, Officer Cook violated the Fourth Amendment—a constitutional command—but will receive no sanction for it because the person who claims its protection has no standing to assert it under Judge Cassell's ruling. While Officer Cook will likely learn that what she did was unconstitutional, she would have learned her lesson more effectively had the evidence of Esparza-Mendoza's identity been thrown out.

In sum, application of the *Esparza-Mendoza* sufficient connections test to undocumented immigrants' domestic Fourth Amendment claims could produce several unjust consequences. Although the test would encourage compliance with the immigration laws, it would create that incentive in the midst of a system that burdened some immigrants more than others, depending upon their countries of origin. In addition, creating distinctions in standing among noncitizens dilutes the deterrent effect on law enforcement, effectively leading the government selectively to target vulnerable undocumented immigrants and temporary nonimmigrants for whom compliance with the sufficient connections test might be difficult.

## Critiquing Esparza-Mendoza, Part II—The Tort Law- Immigration Law Parallel and Lessons from Premises Liability Law

In lieu of Judge Cassell's categorical application of the sufficient connections test, I advocate the following: when the Fourth Amendment is at issue in a case, courts should attach less significance to the immigration status of the noncitizen, and should focus instead on *how* the right should apply in the individual case, taking the immigration status of the noncitizen as one factor among many. In reestablishing a floor of Fourth Amendment rights, such a scheme will have two salutary effects: First, it reaffirms the idea that, in applying criminal constitutional rights the personhood of noncitizens should carry more weight than their nonmembership in the U.S. polity; second, it reemphasizes the importance of criminal constitutional rights by correctly focusing on deterring unconstitutional government conduct rather than determining whether rights extend to some individuals but not to others.

To make this case, I will look to domestic tort law and the classifications that govern a landowner's liability in tort for injuries to entrants upon her land. While many states retain the traditional entrant classification system for assessing tort duties in premises liability cases, immigration scholars might look to states such as California and New York that have abolished the tripartite "trespasser," "licensee," and "invitee" classes in favor of a due care standard as models for rethinking U.S. law on the domestic Fourth Amendment rights of undocumented immigrants. States that adhere to the general due care or "reasonableness" standard recognize the equal personhood of all injured entrants regardless of status and limit landowner liability on foreseeability grounds. In such states, an entrant's status might be a factor affecting the foreseeability analysis, but it is not a factor that may foreclose liability. In contrast, traditional entrant classification states presume that the entrant's status limits landowner liability at the outset, thereby privileging the entrant's status over her personhood. Drawing the analogy to immigration and immigrants' rights law, the traditional entrant classification scheme parallels current U.S. immigration and immigrants' rights policy because both are based on classification systems that deny relief to certain persons based on their status. The "reasonableness" standard adopted by other states, however, values the equal personhood of all entrants and provides an arguably more balanced approach to thinking about the citizen-noncitizen dynamic.

You will recall from chapter 1 that since the *Chinese Exclusion Case,* the Supreme Court has affirmed time and again that the Congress has plenary power—virtually unbridled discretion—to formulate immigration policy as it deems fit. Aside from noting the Constitution's mandate that Congress create a uniform rule of naturalization, the Court has located the legislature's power over noncitizens in Congress's implicit foreign relations power. While many commentators have called for the abandonment of the plenary power doctrine, the idea of Congress's unfettered command over immigration policy has remained remarkably resilient.

While the Court has applied the rational basis test to federal alienage classifications outside the strict immigration context,[20] rarely has the Court struck any legislation on rational basis grounds,[21] opting instead to defer to the lawmaking branches of government if "any plausible reason"[22] is proffered for the classification. Because the Supreme Court defers regularly to congressional initiatives in the area of immigration and immigrants' rights, it is not surprising that the Court would also choose to favor the government over the undocumented immigrant when it comes to the Fourth Amendment. To the extent that legal entry into the United States informs the Fourth Amendment standing principle embodied in the sufficient connections test, the Court's deferral to Congress's plenary power over immigration supports and reinforces the membership paradigm implicit in the sufficient connections test. Just as the *Esparza-Mendoza* approach to Fourth Amendment jurisprudence draws a boundary between persons based on whether they are lawfully present within the United States, the plenary power doctrine grants Congress the power to draw a similar line between citizen and noncitizen when allocating certain public goods.

Hence, viewing the problem of undocumented immigrants' Fourth Amendment rights from behind the plenary power prism is an exercise in frustration for those opposed to the sufficient connections test. It is not surprising that *Esparza-Mendoza* was decided as it was when the Supreme Court, aside from sanctioning the ill-defined *Verdugo-Urquidez* sufficient connections test, embraces a view that immigration law is less about immigrants' rights than it is about maintaining congressional power. Put another way, both the sufficient connections test and the plenary power doctrine privilege membership connections to the U.S. community over the inherent rights of an individual, regardless of immigration status. As mentioned earlier, focusing on the membership status of the individual rather than on the individual's rights moves the emphasis of rights analysis away from the person to be protected instead of asking to what extent the person should receive protection under the circumstances.

Just as immigration and immigrants' rights law classifies noncitizens to determine what rights the U.S. government owes them, tort law similarly assigns rights to land entrants against landowners based on an entrant's status. In tort law, there are three general approaches to the question of landowner liability for harms suffered by persons entering the owner's property. Most states[23] follow the common law tradition of examining the status of an entrant to determine landowner liability (Model 1). Thus, if the injured party is an "invitee" (someone who is permissibly on the property for the landowner's benefit), the owner will owe a duty of reasonable care toward the invitee.[24] However, if the injured party is a "licensee" (someone who is permissibly on the property for his or her own benefit)[25] or a "trespasser" (someone who is on the property without permission),[26] the owner will likely have only a lesser duty: for example, the duty not to act willfully or wantonly toward the injured party.[27]

Some states, notably California[28] and New York,[29] have abolished these traditional entrant classifications in favor of a "reasonable person" standard that assumes all entrants are of equal status as persons, and that the foreseeability of harm to the entrant, rather than the entrant's status as invitee, licensee, or trespasser, should determine the landowner's liability (Model 2).

A third group of states has chosen a middle ground by merging the invitee and licensee classifications but retaining the separate trespasser distinction (Model 3). These states see invitees and licensees as those with permission to enter the premises, while trespassers have no permission.[30] Accordingly, this third group of states requires a lesser duty of landowners to injured trespassers, but imposes a "reasonable care" standard vis-à-vis invitees and licensees.[31]

The Model 1 and 3 classification schemes are illustrated in figure 1 below:

FIGURE 1 *Premises Liability under Classification Models 1 and 3*

| Entrant Classification | Entrant's Protection |
|---|---|
| Invitee | Duty of Reasonable Care |
| Licensee | Model 3—Duty of Reasonable Care<br>Model 1—Duty to Avoid Willful/Wanton Acts |
| Trespasser | Duty to Avoid Willful/Wanton Acts |

Shifting our focus for a moment to immigration and immigrants' rights law, if the *Esparza-Mendoza* standard were to gain acceptance and undocumented immigrants were required to first establish sufficient connections to the United States in order to assert Fourth Amendment rights, undocumented immigrants might never meet that initial burden. *Esparza-Mendoza* teaches us that undocumented immigrants may never be able to use their length of stay in the United States as a basis for meeting the sufficient connections test. Indeed, if Judge Cassell's dicta limiting the applicability of the Fourth Amendment to the "people"—that is, to citizens at home and abroad, and to legal permanent residents within the United States—prevails, undocumented immigrants will likely never be able to assert Fourth Amendment protections. Then they will be left only with Fifth Amendment substantive due process protections for truly egregious searches—for example, beating confessions out of defendants—but without any Fourth Amendment relief, which, as discussed earlier, is far from optimal.

*Esparza-Mendoza*, if followed, likely establishes Fourth Amendment protections only for legal permanent residents and nonimmigrants and not for "previously removed alien felons." In addition, *Esparza-Mendoza* is silent on the extent to which undocumented immigrants are protected by the Fourth Amendment, although it suggests that they would not be unless they could establish their lawful immigration status. Accordingly, the matrix of Fourth Amendment rights under the *Esparza-Mendoza* test might appear as set forth in figure 2 below:

FIGURE 2 *The Esparza-Mendoza Test for Fourth Amendment Protection*

| Immigration Classification | Among "The People" per the Fourth Amendment? | Level of Protection from Illegal Searches |
| --- | --- | --- |
| Legal Permanent Resident and Nonimmigrant Visitor | Probably yes | Fourth and Fifth Amendment protections apply |
| Undocumented Immigrant | Unclear, but probably not (unless UI can prove legal status) | Unclear whether Fourth Amendment applies; Fifth Amendment protection applies |
| "Previously Removed Alien Felon" | No | No Fourth Amendment protection; Fifth Amendment protection applies |

Comparing figures 1 and 2, one notices that in both regimes—tort law Models 1 and 3, on the one hand, and the *Esparza-Mendoza* Fourth Amendment regime, on the other—the protective rights granted the different classified groups vary depending on an individual group's significance vis-à-vis the landowner (in tort law) or the United States (in immigration and immigrants' rights law). Specifically, the landowner's level of care falls from that of "reasonable care" to simply avoiding "willful and wanton acts" as the entrant's classification changes from "invitee" to "licensee" to "trespasser." Similarly, under the *Esparza-Mendoza* model, the noncitizen's Fourth Amendment rights diminish and reliance upon the Fifth Amendment's more stringent substantive due process protections increase in accordance with the immigrant's status change from "legal permanent resident" to "previously removed alien felon."

Indeed, the parallels between the two classification systems are quite striking: the landowner in tort law is analogous to the U.S. government in immigration and immigrants' rights law; the invitee, the legal permanent resident; the licensee, the legal nonimmigrant;[32] and the trespasser, the undocumented immigrant. And, as illustrated in figures 1 and 2 above, just as the tort law burdens the trespasser more greatly than the invitee with respect to any claims each may have against the landowner, immigration and immigrants' rights law likewise confers fewer benefits and protections on the undocumented immigrant when compared with the legal permanent resident. (Interestingly, Judge Cassell referred to Esparza-Mendoza as "a trespasser in this country.")

This analogy between the two systems is the "tort law-immigration law parallel," illustrated in figure 3 below:

FIGURE 3 *The Tort Law–Immigration Law Parallel*

| Tort Law: Premises Liability | Immigration and immigrants' rights law |
|---|---|
| Landowner | U.S. Government |
| Invitee | Legal Permanent Resident |
| Licensee | Legal Nonimmigrant |
| Trespasser | Undocumented Immigrant |

The utility of this analogy between tort law and immigration and immigrants' rights law extends beyond the simple parallelism outlined in figures 1 to 3. Immigration scholars might look to the unitary reasonableness standard in premises liability law—in contrast to traditional landowner-entrant classification schemes—to rethink how they might reconstruct the floor of immigrants' Fourth Amendment rights by looking at premises liability law from states that have adopted the Model 2 approach described above, abandoning the traditional classifications in Models 1 and 3.

I will explore that argument in depth by examining the holding in *Rowland v. Christian* abandoning the traditional entrant classification scheme in favor of a "reasonableness" approach to premises liability. In *Rowland v. Christian*, the California Supreme Court was presented with an ideal set of facts that enabled it to depart from the traditional entrant classification scheme in favor of a unitary reasonableness standard. A social guest of Nancy Christian, James Rowland was injured by a defective faucet in Christian's bathroom.[33] Specifically, nerves and tendons in Rowland's right hand were severed. During Rowland's personal injury action against her, Christian moved for summary judgment, despite acknowledging that she had known of the defective faucet and had reported it to her landlord. The trial court granted Christian's motion, holding that because Rowland was a social guest (and therefore a licensee), Christian owed him the duty to refrain from only wanton or willful conduct, which she did. Had the applicable standard been one of "reasonable care," the court would likely have left the determination of liability to the jury, which could have found that Christian owed a duty to inform Rowland of the defective faucet, which she had done.

On appeal, the California Supreme Court saw through the rigidity of the traditional classification system, especially as applied to the facts here, and rejected this approach. While ruling that entrant status is relevant to determining landowner liability, the court dismissed the notion that such a status was outcome-determinative. Instead, the court stated that whether the plaintiff was a "trespasser," "licensee," or "invitee" would be but one factor in assessing whether the landowner defendant acted reasonably under the circumstances. The high court described the traditional system as contrary to California negligence law, which utilizes a standard of ordinary care, and added that the historical bases for favoring the old classifications have become less persuasive over time, as evinced by the growing number of exceptions created to accommodate unusual fact scenarios.[34] For example, courts have imposed the duty of due care toward licensees for "active operations" on the defendant's land, an exception to the general "willful and wanton" rule.[35] Indeed, the inflexible nature of the traditional classification system has prompted the U.S. Supreme Court to describe the classes and their exceptions as a "semantic morass" in *Kermarec v. Compagnie Generale.*[36]

In addition to highlighting the classification system's departure from ordinary negligence law and its growing irrelevance and rigidity in modern society, the *Rowland* court also noted that the traditional classifications drew what appeared to be arbitrary distinctions between persons of equal worth for purposes of limiting landowner responsibility in tort. As the court so eloquently stated, "A man's life or limb does not become less worthy of protection by the law nor a loss less worthy of compensation under the law because he has come upon the land of another without permission [i.e., a trespasser] or with permission but without a business purpose [i.e., a licensee]."[37] Thus, under *Rowland* a plaintiff will be denied recovery because the defendant acted reasonably and not solely because the plaintiff is a trespasser or a licensee, rather than an invitee. Put another way, the *Rowland* court primarily assigns liability based on the plaintiff's and defendant's conduct, which should not vary based on the plaintiff's status.

Following *Rowland,* several jurisdictions have also abandoned the traditional entrant classification;[38] cases from such jurisdictions serve as interesting case studies for seeking new ways to view the question of how to structure immigration policy so as to strike a fair balance between membership and personhood concerns. Specifically, observations gleaned by the *Rowland* court can serve to critique the *Esparza-Mendoza* approach to Fourth Amendment rights.

In *Rowland,* the California court emphasized three principles in justifying its dismantling of the traditional entrant classifications: (1) the traditional scheme was a departure from state negligence law; (2) the historical bases for the entrant classes have had to be modified in order to adapt to modern conditions; and (3) the common law classifications draw arbitrary distinctions between humans whose lives are of equal worth.

These lessons find parallels in the critique of the *Esparza-Mendoza* approach to the Fourth Amendment rights of undocumented immigrants. First, just as the traditional entrant classifications depart from general negligence law, the sufficient connections test departs from traditional Fourth Amendment jurisprudence. In many Fourth Amendment cases, the Supreme Court's focus is on the reasonableness of the government's actions rather than on whether the person challenging the search of her property has the standing to raise the Fourth Amendment claim. That approach is consistent with the amendment's purpose of deterring government conduct. As discussed earlier, focusing on the challenger's standing shifts the focus from government deterrence to individual entitlement to protection. In addition, the deprivation of a noncitizen's constitutional rights based on her immigration status is inconsistent with much Supreme Court alienage jurisprudence. In *Plyler v. Doe,* for example, the Court held that children of undocumented immigrants were protected by the Fourteenth Amendment's Equal Protection Clause.[39] Moreover, the Court has found that the Fifth and First Amendment protections conferred upon citizens apply to noncitizens as well.[40]

Second, just as tort law must adapt to changing conditions, Fourth Amendment law must do the same. The *Esparza-Mendoza* approach derives from a textual analysis of the Fourth Amendment; that is, the Fourth

Amendment limits its protections to the "people" rather than to "persons" generally. Indeed, one might argue that this textual distinction explains why the First, Fifth, and Fourteenth amendments, which do not have such limiting language, apply to noncitizens while the Fourth might not. In addition, supporters of the sufficient connections test might contend that limitations on the conferral of rights is appropriate because, even in the First and Fifth Amendment cases in which noncitizens were granted constitutional protection, these noncitizens were legal permanent residents and therefore had sufficient connections with the United States.

Detractors of the sufficient connections test need not despair. While a historical analysis of the Fourth Amendment's text is a good starting point for determining the provision's scope, it should not be the end point. Indeed, in articulating the purposes of the Fourth Amendment, the Court originally mentioned "preserving judicial integrity" as a primary goal of the exclusionary rule, the primary remedy associated with Fourth Amendment violations. The Court believed that unless tainted evidence was excluded from use at trial, the trial court would be condoning a constitutional violation and would therefore compromise its integrity. However, over time, the goal of government deterrence gained popularity and it is now the primary rationale for the rule.[41]

In assessing whether to apportion Fourth Amendment rights on the basis of citizenship or sufficient connections with the United States, the Court should ask itself whether such right deprivation is consistent with modern trends in immigration policy. An examination of such modern trends will suggest that it is not. Over time, immigration law has begun to level the playing field by tearing down barriers between citizen and noncitizen in certain contexts. In the area of state alienage jurisprudence, for example, the Court held in *Graham v. Richardson* that a state may not discriminate against noncitizens in the distribution of public benefits absent compliance with "strict scrutiny." Even within the federal alienage cases, the Court has held Congress to a rational basis standard for legislation that discriminates between noncitizen groups in Medicare disbursements.[42] Indeed, these cases involving greater scrutiny of government action involved only the distribution of public economic benefits, not the conferral of a constitutional right. If, despite the resilience of "plenary power," the Court is willing to closely scrutinize government action with respect to the conferral of public benefits, it should be willing to subject government searches and seizures to even closer examination regardless of whether the target of such action is a citizen. Surely, one's interest in personal liberty outweighs any economic interest in government support.

Third, and perhaps most importantly, the *Esparza-Mendoza* sufficient connections test draws arbitrary distinctions between humans much in the same way that the traditional tort entrant classes do. If the modern goal of the Fourth Amendment is to deter the government from unreasonably invading individual privacy, then it should not matter whose privacy is being invaded—the citizen's or the noncitizen's. Just as the injured tort plaintiff should not be arbitrarily denied recovery depending on her land entrant status, so too the constitutional grievance suffered by the criminal defendant is just as serious whether that defendant is a citizen or a noncitizen.

Thus, just as the *Rowland* court incorporated the traditional entrant classifications into its due care approach, courts should likewise bypass the standing requirement imposed upon noncitizens by the sufficient connections test in favor of adjudicating the merits of the Fourth Amendment claim. This unitary approach to Fourth Amendment rights avoids the problem of the slippery slope; rather than trying to discern whether a defendant has standing under the sufficient connections test *ex ante*, trial courts will address each search and seizure on its merits, balancing the defendant's right to privacy against the government's need to secure evidence to assist in the proper prosecution of a case.

Aside from the evenhanded nature of a unitary approach, granting Fourth Amendment protections to all noncitizens is also prudent foreign relations public policy. As Justice Brennan suggested in his *Verdugo-Urquidez* dissent, subjecting a noncitizen defendant to U.S. criminal sanctions creates an obligation upon the courts to accord such defendants the corresponding protections of U.S. criminal procedural law.[43] This "mutuality"[44] of obligation engenders trust among the world's nations and signals the commitment of the United States to due process for foreigners subject to its law. In addition, affording noncitizen defendants the protection of American constitutional law is consistent with the Universal Declaration of Human Rights, which provides for similar protections against unlawful searches and whose provisions the Supreme Court itself has invoked on at least one occasion.[45]

Finally, having a presumption of standing to assert Fourth Amendment claims breaks down existing race-based stereotypes of the undocumented immigrant as the "other": for instance, the unfortunate but pervasive image of the dark-skinned "illegal alien" from Mexico[46] who crosses the border with his pregnant wife to live off welfare and to avail himself of the birthright citizenship of his daughter once she arrives in this world. Acknowledging that the Fourth Amendment deters all government over-reaching regardless of the citizenship of the accused helps to bridge the gap between the presumptively white or black American and the presumptively brown or yellow "alien."[47] Put another way, presuming Fourth Amendment standing for all persons regardless of citizenship is but another step toward recognizing the personhood of citizens and noncitizens alike. To the extent that race and alienage stereotypes intersect, breaking down the citizen-noncitizen barrier likewise dismantles the majority-minority racial divide. For example, subjecting law enforcement officers to a single Fourth Amendment standard regardless of the target's citizenship ensures that officers inclined to harass minority citizens with "foreign" appearances or "foreign-sounding names"[48] are fully deterred.

Some may contend that the tort law-immigration law parallel may be most useful as a hypothetical construct and intellectual exercise, but that the goals of private tort law are substantially different from public law, in this case, constitutional law and immigration policy. Specifically, tort law is premised on the notion of compensating injured plaintiffs reasonably, while public constitutional law is about the preservation of individual rights. However, at one level both types of law seek to deter undesirable conduct. In tort law, one of negligence law's chief objectives is to achieve the optimal level of accidents in society by assigning liability to deter unreasonable conduct. Similarly, the Supreme Court has recognized that both the exclusionary rule and the threat of *Bivens*[49] suits in the Fourth Amendment context aim to deter unreasonable government conduct. Moreover, in both the *Rowland* approach to tort liability and Fourth Amendment jurisprudence generally, the courts rely on a rule of reasonableness—due care in *Rowland*, a reasonable search in Fourth Amendment precedent—to strike the proper balance between the parties' legitimate interests.

Even assuming the validity of the tort law-immigration law parallel, others may argue that applying a *Rowland*-like "reasonableness" approach to Fourth Amendment claims by doing away with the standing requirement would open the floodgates to nonmeritorious defenses. There are two counterarguments to this: first, presumably defense counsel will likely not raise spurious Fourth Amendment claims if she believes she cannot win on the merits; and second, in the event of an unlikely increase in frivolous claims, the price of protecting constitutional rights might be worth sacrificing some judicial resources to make sure justice is served.

Some may submit that the unitary approach to Fourth Amendment law is soft on crime and on undocumented immigration. If the rule of law is meant to encourage law abidance, creating a presumption of standing for all undocumented immigrants in one sense rewards illicit activity. Why should immigrants who enter the country illegally and then stand charged with a crime benefit from these actions by being able to challenge searches that would not have taken place but for their illegal activity and illegal presence in the United States? This argument fails for two other reasons. First, all criminal defendants are entitled to constitutional criminal procedural protections, such as a right to a fair and impartial jury trial; yet society generally does not view such safeguards as protecting criminals only. Rather, these rights are believed to be minimal rights that ensure that all who stand accused may be given more protection than the empty phrase "presumption of innocence" seems to provide. Second, as mentioned earlier, a noncitizen's status as "legal" or "illegal" is based on many factors that favor noncitizens from certain countries over others. It is hard to be persuaded that someone is an "illegal alien" when she might not have been adjudged "illegal" had she arrived from Canada.

A final argument that one might raise against a unitary approach in the Fourth Amendment context is that even within tort law most jurisdictions have retained the traditional entrant classification system or, at the very least, have retained the "trespasser" distinction, the analogue to the "undocumented immigrant" under the tort law-immigration law parallel.[50] This suggests that most courts would be unreceptive to an argument for a unitary Fourth Amendment approach utilizing the tort law-immigration law parallel because most states have chosen not to follow the *Rowland* approach advocated here. While this may be a practical hurdle, it is not an insurmountable one. The challenge will be to persuade courts of the merit of this approach.

Specifically, by emphasizing that the conferral of Fourth Amendment standing upon all noncitizens serves the multiple goals of effective government deterrence, equal treatment for all defendants regardless of citizenship, the establishment of a practical rule of reasonableness, and the dismantling of negative stereotypes of the undocumented immigrant, a persuasive case can be made. A unitary Fourth Amendment standard furthers antiessentialism by dismantling stereotypes of, in this case, undocumented migrants. The sufficient connections test, on the other hand, exacerbates prejudicial action by assuming without evidence that undocumented migrants cannot develop such ties. Antisubordination is likewise enhanced by raising the standing prospects of those at the bottom of the immigration food chain to equal those at the top.

## Critiquing *Esparza-Mendoza*, Part III— The Politics of Judge Cassell

Scrutinizing individual justices' opinions provides clues as to how they might rule on future cases: Justices William Brennan and Thurgood Marshall were strong supporters of individual rights and a "living Constitution"; Justices Antonin Scalia and Clarence Thomas believe just as strongly in states' rights and more narrow, historical analyses of the document. As a general rule, liberal judges tend to be less wary of government intervention, especially for the benefit of society's less fortunate; conservative jurists value smaller government accountable to the electorate and not the courts, but will support legislation designed to maintain law and order.

A review of *Esparza-Mendoza* and its author's conservative background[51] suggests that similar conclusions may be drawn here. U.S. District Judge Paul Cassell was appointed to the federal bench by George W. Bush, and, from the conservative perspective, for good reason. Prior to his appointment, Paul Cassell held the same occupation I do now—he was a law professor at the University of Utah. This is where the similarities between Cassell and myself pretty much end. A native of Idaho, Cassell was President of the *Stanford Law Review,* and a law clerk to then U.S. Court of Appeals Judge Scalia and Supreme Court Chief Justice Warren Burger. Cassell further cultivated his conservative credentials by joining then President Ronald Reagan's Justice Department as a federal prosecutor. He even met his wife Patricia at a conservative Federalist Society luncheon, boasting that he is the first person to ever use the organization as "a dating service."[52]

Prior to his judicial appointment, Paul Cassell was well known for his belief that the law unduly favored criminal defendants, and had focused his professional and academic work in three core areas: defending the death penalty, promoting a constitutional amendment to protect victims' rights, and attacking the Supreme Court's 1966 decision in *Miranda v. Arizona,* which mandates that criminal suspects be read their rights. In Cassell's view, current laws are too soft on crime and criminal defendants, without sufficiently vitiating the rights of their victims. While many in the legal academy have challenged both Cassell's specific claims as well as his conservative crusade, the Bush administration saw it fit to elevate the former law professor to the status of federal trial judge.

Reviewing his background, it is perhaps unsurprising that Judge Cassell opted for a categorical denial of Esparza-Mendoza's rights. From Cassell's perspective, Esparza-Mendoza is a criminal who should not be afforded any constitutional rights against a police officer who, acting in good faith, conducted a technically illegal search. Just as he views *Miranda*'s command that police officers remind suspects of their "right to remain silent," Judge Cassell believes it unnecessary to place too many trivial obstacles in the way of upstanding officers like Tracey Cook who committed a minor error. Put another way, the cost of throwing away the evidence of Esparza-Mendoza's crime far outweighs the benefit of teaching Officer Cook to be more prudent.

I believe that Judge Cassell has the analysis backward. Being in the country "illegally" is a technical violation; the government abusing its investigatory powers in violation of the Fourth Amendment (which Judge Cassell acknowledged) is not. A commitment to antiessentialism and antisubordination helps support this position. By categorically denying to a class of noncitizens certain fundamental rights, Judge Cassell's *Esparza-Mendoza* ruling perpetuates the stereotype of the "illegal alien"—the brown "wetback" sneaking across the border. As discussed earlier, not all undocumented persons are Mexican, nor are all illegal border crossers, especially when American immigration policy often determines whether one needs immigration documentation based on one's national origin. My *Rowland* proposal—treating noncitizens the same as U.S. citizens for Fourth Amendment purposes—furthers antiessentialist notions and levels the playing field for persons without the proper documents who are consigned to the lowest rungs of the immigration inferno.

Just as this chapter advocates a "floor" of rights, the next one focuses on a possible "ceiling" on undocumented migrants' rights by asking to what extent such individuals should have access—under either constitutional or statutory law—to governmental aid for postsecondary education, something many U.S. citizens take for granted.

# 5

# Hitting the Ceiling
## The Right to a College Education

While one could certainly argue that the Constitution guarantees undocumented immigrants both Fourth Amendment protection and governmental aid, or that it conveys neither, I start from the premise that the Bill of Rights are generally regarded as "negative" rather than "positive" in nature—they protect people from unreasonable government intrusion into their lives, but they do not obligate the government to provide positive goods like food, clothing, and shelter to its citizenry.[1] Thus, the Fourth Amendment (along with its constitutional brethren) might serve as a "floor" of rights—that which the government cannot take away. In contrast, government benefits such as welfare or tuition assistance, might form a "ceiling"—rights reserved to citizens or citizens-to-be only.

In the following chapter, I test the limits of this hypothetical ceiling by examining a growing problem in America today—the increasing number of undocumented persons who are college-eligible but cannot qualify for government financial aid because of their immigration status. In this post-9/11 era of impoverished state budgets, federal concerns about national security, and increasing public ambivalence about immigration, can financial aid for postsecondary education be a viable constitutional or statutory right that can be claimed by undocumented immigrants?

## The Problem: Producing Highly Educated Farmworkers

Carmen Medina is the Executive Director of the Adams County Delinquency Prevention Program, a state-sponsored initiative designed to attend to the needs of school-age children in south-central Pennsylvania. While perhaps best known as the site of the Battle of Gettysburg, Adams County is also an agricultural powerhouse, producing more apples and peaches than virtually any other area of the United States. Because of its agrarian economy, Adams County is also home to a large number of Mexican farmworkers, many of whom came to this country without proper work or immigration papers, their young children in tow, in search of a better life. It is with these farmworkers' children that Medina's office is most concerned. Aside from providing these children with social, cultural, and educational support, Medina's office also strongly encourages them to work hard at school so that they may maximize their opportunities after high school.

Yet Medina has grown increasingly uncomfortable dispensing such advice. By her estimate, 97 percent of these children are undocumented like their parents and therefore are effectively barred from pursuing postsecondary education because of their undocumented status, their poverty, or both. Indeed, undocumented status and poverty are mutually reinforcing obstacles to advancement. While colleges and universities are not barred from admitting them, undocumented immigrants cannot effectively compete for postgraduation jobs for which they have been trained because employers can be sanctioned for knowingly hiring such persons. In addition, undocumented immigrant students are largely ineligible for federal and state financial aid, ensuring their continued occupancy of the lower rungs of the socioeconomic ladder. Thus these two factors—undocumented status and poverty—work in tandem to preclude many undocumented children, like most of those in Adams County, from pursuing a college degree, leading Medina to comment sarcastically that all her program is doing is to help create a class of well-educated farmworkers.

Not surprisingly, the problem Medina describes is not unique to Pennsylvania but is one which many states with increasing immigrant populations have confronted, and are just beginning to address: should longtime undocumented immigrants have the same opportunity as lawful permanent residents and U.S. citizens to attend state colleges and universities? There are two typical justifications for denying them such opportunities. First, treating undocumented immigrants as in-state residents discriminates against U.S. citizen nonresidents of the state. Second, and more broadly, undocumented immigration should be discouraged as a policy matter, and therefore allowing undocumented immigrant children equal opportunities as legal residents condones and perhaps encourages "illegal" immigration. This chapter responds to these two concerns by surveying state and federal solutions to this issue.

## Existing Federal and State Legislation

For most of U.S. history, immigration law has been a federal mandate. At the same time, public education has been primarily a state and local governmental affair. Despite this general division, the federal government has often used its immigration power to influence state policies affecting immigrants. Whether it is exercised under the purview of constitutional preemption or differential Equal Protection analysis, Congress's plenary power over immigration, and the immigration service's administrative mandate to enforce the same, afford the federal government broad power to affect immigrant policy in areas traditionally left to the states. Thus, Congress has passed legislation involving immigrants' welfare entitlements[2] and criminal law obligations,[3] two fields often viewed as primarily local in scope. Yet those who favor such incursions justify them as a necessary means to control immigration. After all, immigrants seek to become citizens of the United States, not California or New Jersey. Thus, even if such federal legislation does not directly affect foreign ingress and egress, its impact on state and local legislation is considerable.

### 1. Bars to State Largesse: A Critique of IIRAIRA Section 505

On the issue of public education, current federal law states that

> [a noncitizen] who is not lawfully present in the United States shall not be eligible on the basis of residence within a State . . . for any postsecondary education benefit unless a citizen or national of the United States is eligible for such a benefit (in no less an amount, duration, and scope) without regard to whether the citizen or national is such a resident.[4]

This provision was enacted in 1996 as section 505 of the infamous Illegal Immigration Reform and Immigrant Responsibility Act of 1996 (IIRAIRA), which has been vilified by commentators for its establishment of certain anti-immigrant rights provisions, such as expedited removal and curtailment of judicial review of most deportation orders. Aside from fulfilling IIRAIRA's general objective of deterring undocumented immigration, this postsecondary education law protects U.S. citizens from discrimination by a state that might be inclined to grant in-state tuition benefits to some but not others. Put another way, Congress wanted to ensure that undocumented immigrants would not be made better off than U.S.

citizens by some states. This chapter will examine the validity of both these goals: first, to protect U.S. citizens over undocumented immigrants, and second, to deter undocumented immigration generally.

As to the first objective, closer scrutiny of the law suggests that there is no rational basis for necessarily favoring nonstate resident U.S. citizens over in-state resident undocumented persons given the myriad exceptions to residency requirements that already appear in state law. Many residency requirements use as their determining factors two criteria: (1) whether an individual *intends* to reside in-state and (2) the *duration* of the person's stay in-state. I will refer to these as the "intent" and "duration" requirements of traditional residency laws.

In an excellent, pre-IIRAIRA study, legal scholar Michael Olivas demonstrated the inconsistent and incoherent assumptions underlying most state residency laws, effectively arguing that many state institutions grant in-state status to nonresidents who have satisfied neither the intent nor duration requirements.[5] I have a personal example to share on this point that questions the essentialist assumptions of the current federal law. When our family moved from California to Pennsylvania, my wife received in-state tuition for her master's program at the University of Maryland because she was simultaneously offered a job as a graduate research assistant. She had no intention of living in Maryland after graduate school, since I had accepted a permanent teaching position in Pennsylvania. As Olivas explains, "Graduate students rarely are paid well and certainly provide important instructional or research services to institutions. Paying their tuition seems a modest benefit and one well worth preserving, but using the residency requirement to deem the students 'residents' is a curious bookkeeping maneuver, one that undermines the residency determination system."[6]

Returning to the example of the Adams County farmworker children, why should they, who likely meet both intent and duration requirements under the traditional residency test, not be entitled to in-state college tuition when my wife, who had fulfilled neither criterion, was eligible? The answer cannot be that my wife worked as a research assistant, thereby conferring upon the university (or more accurately, the professor for whom she worked) some benefit. Indeed, some Adams County high school graduates have long contributed to the economy of Pennsylvania (and to the people of the United States) through their many years of work in the local apple and peach orchards. Thus, current federal law allows my wife, a U.S. citizen but nonresident of Maryland, to be favored under state law over the Adams County farmworker kids, simply because of her federal citizenship and in spite of her Maryland nonresidency. In contrast, Pennsylvania may not benefit the Adams County children—longtime past, present, and likely future, residents of the Commonwealth, simply because they are not members of the national community—despite their long-standing contributions to the state.

In response, one might argue that undocumented immigrants should not be favored over U.S. citizens because the latter pay taxes and the former do not. Hence, only the latter should be able to benefit from a subsidized public education. The underlying assumption is that undocumented immigrants create a net economic loss to the United States and its states by drawing more upon public funds than they contribute to society. The best evidence on this point is equivocal.[7] Moreover, within the realm of higher education itself, it appears that a negligible percentage of undocumented immigrants avail themselves of these particular benefits—for example, by the state's own estimates, far less than 1 percent of undocumented persons in California are enrolled in its public community colleges.[8] This is a particularly telling statistic because California is one of the largest havens for undocumented immigration,[9] moderating the view that more undocumented persons lead to greater strains on the public fisc.

If favoring certain out-of-state U.S. citizens or residents over undocumented immigrants defies traditional residency measures of intention and duration, then what else can be used to justify IIRAIRA's prohibition on unilateral in-state benefits to undocumented persons? A second justification underlies the essence of IIRAIRA: discouraging states from granting unilateral benefits to undocumented immigrants provides a disincentive to enter without inspection. Even assuming that this is true as an empirical matter, this deterrent would not apply to the majority of the Adams County farmworker teens. Many of these college-age children entered the United States at a young age, often not understanding what they were doing when their parents brought them into the United States. Their blameworthiness at the time of their entry is therefore speculative as they were unsuspecting accomplices to U.S. immigration violations. More importantly, this measure would do nothing to specifically deter them from continuing in their undocumented status. These individuals probably view themselves as American rather than foreign, thereby making it unlikely that their ineligibility for postsecondary school assistance would compel them to either voluntarily depart the United States or submit themselves to deportation proceedings.

Finally, it is unclear that the law has served as a general deterrent to those seeking to enter the country without documentation. Again, a brief anecdote on this point. One of my former Immigration Law students served on the Border Patrol in Arizona for three years before entering law school. He shared with his classmates that he saw many pregnant Mexican women try to enter the country without documentation so they could give birth to their children stateside, thereby conferring U.S. citizenship upon them. One would be hard-pressed to conclude that these individuals would have ceased attempting the dangerous trek across the border had they been aware of IIRAIRA's limits on postsecondary education benefits.

In sum, IIRAIRA section 505 does not appear to be based on sound policy. While the law aims to protect out-of-state U.S. citizens, the states themselves often provide exceptions to the usual intention and duration requirements of residency laws that redound to the benefit of such citizens, while leaving the most deserving longtime residents, undocumented workers, without relief. Further, it likely does not serve as an effective deterrent to undocumented entry either generally or specifically. Hence, the law perpetuates the hierarchical status quo: nonresident U.S. citizens are sometimes allowed in-state status, while undocumented persons, who would qualify for residency under the traditional measures of intent and duration but for their immigration status, are not. Put differently, IIRAIRA Section 505 violates the equality principles of antiessentialism and antisubordination by allowing states to favor U.S. citizens over undocumented nonresidents despite the fact that in many instances the latter might be more productive, and hence more worthy, recipients of state largesse.

## 2. State Initiatives to Grant Undocumented Immigrants Postsecondary Tuition Benefits despite IIRAIRA Section 505

While close to twenty state legislatures have tuition benefit bills currently before them, fewer than ten states have enacted laws providing in-state tuition to long-term college-bound undocumented residents in an effort to comply with IIRAIRA section 505.[10] Interestingly, all but Texas passed their laws after 9/11. All have circumvented IIRAIRA's restrictions by expanding their residency requirements to afford in-state tuition to both U.S. citizens and noncitizens. Although some of their specifics vary, these laws allow for in-state tuition at certain public colleges and universities if a person can prove the following: attendance at a private or public high school within the state for at least two or three years and graduation from high school or the equivalent thereof.[11] In addition, the laws require undocumented students to provide affidavits that they will seek to pursue lawful immigration status as soon as they are able.[12] These modest gains have not come easily. In California, for example, it took more than two years for the legislation to finally gain approval, with Governor Gray Davis having vetoed the first bill which he believed violated IIRAIRA section 505.[13] On the flip side, a handful have taken steps in the opposite direction, seeking ways to specifically restrict undocumented students' access to college.[14]

Thus, there is both good news and bad news for immigrants' rights advocates when looking at current state law. The good news is that, despite IIRAIRA section 505, several states have chosen to provide undocumented immigrants in-state tuition benefits by revising their residency requirements and many more are considering doing the same. This is particularly encouraging because in six of the states bills were signed into law after the terrorist attacks of September 11, 2001, thus undermining conventional wisdom that no proimmigrant legislation was likely to follow such a catastrophe.[15]

The bad news is that only seven states have decided to pass such legislation close to eight years after IIRAIRA section 505 took effect, three have acted to *restrict* undocumented student access, and it is unclear how many more proimmigrant laws will pass in this isolationist, post–September 11 political climate in which states are suffering financial crises. More importantly, IIRAIRA section 505 looms like a specter over this entire issue, making any promise of widespread, national relief through federal legislation seem illusory.

Even if the gains in Texas and its sister states bear fruit elsewhere, these initiatives are necessarily limited in scope in two important ways. First, despite their eligibility for state support, undocumented students in these states still do not qualify for federal financial aid. Second, without a guarantee that an undocumented person can achieve lawful immigration status following graduation from college, such a person will always live under the double threat of being ineligible to lawfully hold a job and possible removal from the United States. And since immigration regulation is a federal power, state legislatures cannot tie academic achievement or state residency to immigration status. The power to change one's immigration status rests solely on Congress's shoulders.

## The Solution: The Proposed Student Adjustment Act of 2003

To the extent that the ideal solution to this problem is a federal one, I advocate passage of the proposed Student Adjustment Act of 2003, which had its initial incarnation in 2001 and was reintroduced on April 9, 2003.[16] I believe that a federal law such as the Student Adjustment Act would be a practical and fair solution to the problem of access to higher education, as it is wholly consistent with much of current immigration policy. The rest of this discussion unfolds in three parts. First, I examine and critique the proposed Act. Second, I place the Act in a larger conceptual framework of immigration law and policy. And third, I explain why such a proposal should be politically palatable to policymakers and the public alike.

### 1. The Student Adjustment Act of 2003: A Critique

Originally proposed in the House of Representatives in May 2001 and reintroduced in April 2003, the Student Adjustment Act (SAA) addresses the two primary concerns identified in the opening narrative as bars to undocumented immigrants' enrollment in public colleges and universities—undocumented status and poverty—in three specific ways. First, the SAA repeals IIRAIRA section 505, thereby returning to the states the unfettered power to determine residency requirements for in-state tuition benefits at public schools. Second, it permits undocumented students to adjust their immigration status to lawful permanent residence, provided they comply with certain age, character, educational, and residency requirements. And third, it allows adjusting immigrants the opportunity to apply for federal financial aid. In sum, the SAA allows undocumented immigrants the same opportunities for postsecondary education and postcollege work as the law currently provides lawful permanent residents.

At a press conference, original sponsor Congressman Chris Cannon (R-Utah) argued that the bill not only benefited undocumented immigrant students, but also society as a whole. Cannon noted that "[e]ach year, ten thousand undocumented students who have lived in the U.S. for at least five years graduate from U.S. high schools."[17] Most had no choice in the decision to immigrate without inspection, that choice having been made for them by their parents, and yet they are consigned, like Medina's Pennsylvania farmworker children, to limited futures because of their immigration status and concomitant poverty. The SAA corrects this injustice wrought upon those whose "illegal" presence was involuntary.

More importantly, the SAA works to benefit society by providing a substantial number of children the opportunity to reach their full potential through postsecondary education. Cannon stated that among the undocumented high school graduates are "valedictorians, straight-A students, creative talents, and idealistic youngsters committed to bettering their communities."[18] Society loses out on these students' contributions by not allowing them the opportunity to flourish. The SAA helps ensure this possibility.

The U.S. Supreme Court's decision in *Plyler v. Doe*[19] supports some of Cannon's rhetoric, specifically the unfairness visited upon the undocumented children as well as the importance of education in helping persons reach their full potential. In *Plyler,* the Court struck down a Texas law that denied free public primary and secondary education to undocumented immigrant children. Like Cannon, Justice Brennan took great pains to differentiate the children's culpability from that of their parents:

> The children who are plaintiffs in these cases are special members of this underclass. Persuasive arguments support the view that a State may withhold its beneficence from those whose very presence within the United States is the product of their own unlawful conduct. These arguments do not apply with the same force to classifications imposing disabilities on the minor *children* of such illegal entrants. At the least, those who elect to enter our territory by stealth and in violation of our law should be prepared to bear the consequences, including, but not limited to, deportation. But the children of those illegal entrants are not comparably situated. Their "parents have the ability to conform their conduct to societal norms," and presumably the ability to remove themselves from the State's jurisdiction; but the children who are plaintiffs in these cases "can affect neither their parents' conduct nor their own status."[20]

Just as Justice Brennan chided Texas for visiting hardships upon minor children who were not responsible for their undocumented status, Cannon similarly questioned the wisdom of depriving undocumented students of the effective ability to attend college.

Aside from addressing this issue of fairness to innocent undocumented students, Brennan, like Cannon, also stressed the importance of education in helping children realize their full potential as productive members of society. Citing the Fourteenth Amendment's Equal Protection Clause, Justice Brennan extolled the leveling power of education as a means of bridging the gap between haves and have-nots:

> [D]enial of education to some isolated group of children poses an affront to one of the goals of the Equal Protection Clause: the abolition of governmental barriers presenting unreasonable obstacles to advancement on the basis of individual merit. Paradoxically, by depriving the children of any disfavored group of an education, we foreclose the means by which that group might raise the level of esteem in which it is held by the majority. But more directly, "education prepares individuals to be self-reliant and self-sufficient participants in society."[21]

Some might argue that this nod to *Plyler* is inappropriate because the Court did not intend to grant broad rights to undocumented children; it merely aimed to prevent states from denying a free, basic education to its residents. In contrast, the SAA provides so much more by making all longtime, college-bound, undocumented immigrants eligible both for federal funding and immigration adjustment, and includes the possibility of additional state subsidy. The argument concludes that *Plyler* was intended to establish a constitutional floor, not a ceiling.

However, this reference to *Plyler* was not to suggest that its promises mirrored those of the SAA, only that both appear to espouse principles of fairness and equality. Both *Plyler* and the SAA pursue the common goals of enhancing fairness to blameless undocumented students and equality among persons. Put differently, providing an education to undocumented immigrants furthers equality norms without compromising notions of fairness, given the nonculpability of most college-bound, undocumented persons for their immigration status.

The many objections to proposals such as the SAA boil down to two principal types: a moral objection and an economic argument. The moral objection stems from the belief that any law allowing undocumented immigrants the opportunity to adjust status will encourage illegal immigration. The lobbying group Federation for American Immigration Reform (FAIR) frames the argument this way: "[S]ome proponents of allowing [tuition benefits] couple their advocacy with the proposal that the illegal aliens be given legal resident status. This is a form of amnesty and is objectionable for all of the reasons that any amnesty for illegal aliens is objectionable—most importantly, that it encourages others to follow in their footsteps and sneak into the country."[22]

The idea here is that the law prohibiting undocumented immigration is not a serious one because people can easily adjust their status over time. FAIR cites the example of so-called "parachute kids"[23] taking advantage of *Plyler*'s guarantee of free public education for all schoolchildren regardless of immigration status. There are at least two responses to this argument. First, as an empirical matter, most undocumented children who will likely avail themselves of this law are students who arrived here as youths along with their parents, as Cannon, Justice Brennan, and Medina have observed. Thus it is difficult to make the moral claim that the sins of the parents should be visited upon the innocent children, who had no control over their immigration status. Arguably, even the "parachute kids" may not be morally culpable parties if they acted solely at the behest of their parents. Second, children who knew that they were engaged in an "illegal entry" still might be ineligible for adjustment under the SAA for want of "good moral character."

The economic argument relates to the moral one. If the SAA passes, it will create an added incentive to enter without inspection, the incentives of higher education benefits and the prospect of employment aside. As mentioned earlier, there has not been much evidence that most undocumented immigration is due to a desire to pursue free or subsidized public education. However, assuming for a moment that this is true, the age and residency requirements (as well as the "good moral character" provisions) will preclude many would-be undocumented immigrants from realizing the benefits of the SAA.

But perhaps the most interesting assumption that underlies the opposition to schemes such as the SAA is the treatment of work as separate from education, and that while one might be a fair means for achieving membership, the other might not. In the next section I challenge that notion, suggesting that the pursuit of higher education should be considered "work," thereby supporting the idea of amnesty within the SAA.

### 2. "Education as Work": A Theoretical Justification for the Student Adjustment Act

The FAIR website proffers the following argument against tuition benefit proposals: "The apologists for illegal aliens claim that their benefit to the U.S. economy is that they will do work that Americans will not do. However, their argument for [tuition benefits] is that these illegal aliens should not be forced by lack of education to do unskilled work. Thus, the advocates are arguing out of both sides of their mouths."[24]

FAIR's contention has some surface appeal. If immigrants' rights proponents insist that undocumented immigration should be tolerated because it fills a need for unskilled labor, then providing such immigrants education benefits will deplete the labor source. However, FAIR conflates two groups of undocumented persons in its statement: those who have chosen to enter the country to work and those who did not choose to immigrate. As mentioned earlier, the typical migration pattern involves the movement of a family in which the parents make the calculated choice to enter the United States with the underlying goals of working and eventually providing their children a better life. The children, as noted by Justice Brennan and Rep. Cannon, have no say in their immigration and may provide labor as part of their perceived family duties.

Critics might respond that regardless of their intent, many undocumented immigrant children and young adults provide unskilled labor that will be diminished if tuition benefits facilitate their college attendance. But as an empirical matter, the percentage of eligible college-bound undocumented workers is quite small, thereby not depleting the labor pool as greatly as some might suspect. Medina attests that at most two to three undocumented Mexican students a year from her antidelinquency program would be able to attend college should financial aid be forthcoming.[25] In California, the number of undocumented students in public community colleges totals "far less than one percent."[26] Furthermore, even with such depletion there will likely be more adults who will replace the few college-bound children of the prior migration wave through both lawful and undocumented entry into the United States.

More importantly, underlying FAIR's argument is the assumption that education is not work. By asserting that tuition benefits deplete the unskilled labor pool by providing undocumented immigrants postsecondary education, FAIR implies that pursuing further education does not qualify as work. This is perhaps more clearly stated in the following argument: "The fact is that illegal aliens may not hold a job in the United States. Therefore, tax dollars expended on the higher education of these illegal aliens in order to prepare them for professional jobs is wasted."[27] The image here is that state and federal taxpayers would be subsidizing undocumented immigrant education instead of undocumented immigrants earning their keep through low-end labor. Yet pursuing one's education, especially one's postsecondary education, is work. In contrast to most jobs, the monetary benefit of this work is deferred rather than immediately realized.[28]

To FAIR's credit, it acknowledges that higher education serves as preparation for professional jobs, and in that sense, recognizes that one must work (by studying) to become a professional. Few would quibble with the notion that pursuing one's doctorate or law or medical degree is work. Indeed, many law and medical students have the opportunity to practice their profession prior to graduation in live clinic settings. Surely, such "practical skills" education is work.[29] However, FAIR's conclusion—that subsidizing such education is a waste because undocumented persons cannot engage in postcollege work—fails to appreciate the potential of translating the "education as work" metaphor into a viable conduit to legalization.

By and large, immigrants to this country are lawfully permitted entry in any of the following four ways: family sponsorship, an employment relationship, success in the diversity lottery, or refugee status.[30] Thus, one of the four primary modes of entry is by virtue of one's work—the theory being that one might be a valuable economic contributor to American society, especially when the U.S. market is in need of particular work that the domestic labor supply cannot provide.

But an arguably untapped source of potential future labor would be those undocumented postsecondary school students who are precluded from pursuing a college education because of their immigration status or limited finances. If Congress would formally acknowledge that education is work, and that superior high school performance leading to college admission is a sign of employment potential, it would avail the country of a future labor source already educated within and familiar with the U.S. school system. Just as an employment-based immigrant visa may be viewed as a fair exchange for the anticipated contributions of the immigrating employee, the SAA's adjustment of status provision implicitly acknowledges the work undocumented high school students have done to gain acceptance into a U.S. college or university.

Furthermore, there is support for this "education as work" metaphor in other areas of the law. In the area of family and disability law, courts have sometimes blurred the distinctions between work and education for purposes of determining a parent's eligibility to pay child support or a claimant's eligibility for Social Security Act benefits. Hence, courts will consider the impact on future income that a parent's decision to attend graduate school might have on his ability to pay child support.[31] Similarly, in computing social security benefits awards, courts have consistently upheld agency determinations that reduce awards due to the fact that the claimant was employed or was in school.[32] In the eyes of the law, sometimes postsecondary education *is* work.

On principle, critics might object that, regardless of the economic benefits that might accrue to the United States, no undocumented person should be able to receive amnesty regardless of her productivity or potential, that is, if you entered illegally, you should not benefit from that illegal act. However, at the time of their adjustment under a bill such as the SAA, undocumented students would have already contributed to the U.S. economy through their labor both within and sometimes outside school. In contrast, foreign-based recipients of employment-based immigrant visas provide little, if any, direct contribution to the United States prior to their immigration. In a sense, tuition benefits and the opportunity to adjust status are but fair compensation for the labor already expended by and benefits received from undocumented immigrants. Viewed from this perspective, the idea of adjusting status based on the "education as work" metaphor seems more in line with current immigration policy.

Finally, allowing undocumented immigrants to attend college free and clear of immigration or financial aid hurdles unshackles them from the fetters of low-end farm labor. In other words, the SAA would help solve Medina's problem of the "highly educated farmworker" by permitting undocumented high school graduates to re-create their identities, giving them the opportunity to enter professional, high-skilled work under the same terms as other U.S. residents.

## 3. The Student Adjustment Act Is Politically Palatable

Even after accepting the notion that education is work, the greatest obstacle to the passage of a tuition benefits-adjustment of status proposal such as the SAA might be its political unpopularity after September 11, 2001. Neither Congress nor the American public appears ready to support an amnesty proposal legalizing "illegal aliens" in this climate of heightened concern over homeland safety. If the public is already skeptical about a temporary guest worker program like the one proposed by President Bush in 2004, how likely is it that a permanent amnesty plan like the SAA will succeed?

Post–September 11 sentiment has largely focused on two aspects of national security: ensuring that those who enter the United States are not terrorists and ridding our polity of terrorists already in our midst. The SAA does nothing to affect national policy on the first point, since it addresses only those noncitizens already in the United States. And as for internal security, the SAA specifically denies adjustment of status to those individuals who might pose a security risk.[33] Further, even if a person qualifies for adjustment, the bill does not automatically grant citizenship; it simply legalizes the individual's immigration status. Thus, if later in her life the now lawfully admitted college student turns out to be a security risk, the government will have better information on that student. Keeping tabs on a documented individual is certainly much easier than monitoring those without immigration papers.

It is encouraging that almost all the states that have enacted an in-state residency amendment did so after September 11. Such promulgation is a testament to these state governments' realization that terrorism and alienage are, more often than not, mutually exclusive, and that acknowledging the value of higher education, especially for the least fortunate, knows no bounds of citizenship.

From undocumented immigrants, I turn in chapter 6 to the question of foreign partners in a binational same-gender relationship. Although these two groups appear to share little in common, like undocumented immigrants, foreign same-gender partners may face deportation even if they enjoy state benefits pursuant to a marriage with a U.S. citizen. Thus, a foreign gay man who lives in a loving, stable relationship, who enjoys the same rights of survivorship, the custody of children, and other state-recognized benefits that married heterosexual spouses do, may nonetheless risk expulsion because our current immigration laws do not confer spousal status on the noncitizen partner. It is this often overlooked link between gay rights and immigration status that will be a key American civil rights issue in the near future.

# 6

# A Peek into the Future?

*Same-Gender Partners
and Immigration Law*

Would the federal government's decision to selectively deport the foreign same-gender partners of U.S. citizens based solely on their sexual orientation violate the Constitution? This controversial question captures three major themes highlighted in the last three chapters on nonterrorist "others." Chapter 3 on mixed-immigration status families examined the theme of family unity held to be an important bulwark of immigration law; binational same-gender partners also seek to use the immigration laws to keep their families together. Chapter 4 focused on possible limitations on the Fourth Amendment rights of undocumented persons—usually those who enter the United States surreptitiously—to be free from unreasonable governmental searches; here, I analyze the constitutional rights of "overstays," noncitizens whose entry documents have expired, thereby rendering them undocumented. And finally, chapter 5 questioned whether the denial of governmental financial aid to undocumented college-bound residents violated federal constitutional or statutory law; similarly, I question the wisdom of a policy that forbids gay and lesbian citizens from legally petitioning their same-gender foreign partners, a benefit enjoyed by heterosexual binational couples.

By revisiting these three themes of family unity, undocumented migrants' constitutional rights, and federal benefits, I hope to provide the reader with yet another view of important issues that affect the noncitizen community, while adding the dimension of sexual orientation to test our Constitution's commitments to its citizens and their foreign partners.

## A Thought Experiment: The Selective Deportation of Foreign Same-Gender Partner Overstays

Consider the following American love story set in the not-too-distant future. Mexican national Maria Camacho is a foreign student at the University of Massachusetts. In her junior year, Maria falls in love with classmate Susan Sanders, a U.S. citizen. Their relationship grows and the couple decides to celebrate their love by marrying under Massachusetts law after graduation.[1] Realizing that Maria's foreign student visa is about to expire, Susan applies with the U.S. Citizenship and Immigration Services (USCIS) to adjust Maria's status from nonimmigrant to immigrant on the basis of their Massachusetts marriage. The USCIS demurs, noting that current federal law and relevant case precedent do not confer immigration benefits upon noncitizen same-gender partners. Despite the rebuff, Maria decides to thwart the federal law and sets up to live permanently in Massachusetts with Susan. She therefore lets her visa expire, reasoning that at least Massachusetts recognizes that theirs is a valid marriage and does not believe that the Bureau of Immigration and Customs Enforcement (ICE) would seek to deport her. However, as more and more same-gender mixed immigration-status couples begin to flock to Massachusetts, marry, and then thwart the immigration law, the ICE is left with no choice but to begin deporting Maria and others like her.

The skeptical reader might question the Camacho-Sanders hypothetical on two grounds: first, same-gender marriages themselves are rather rare since Massachusetts is the first state to mandate them and indeed, did so in early 2004.[2] Less rare, however, are civil unions, domestic partnerships, and similar state-sanctioned relationships between gay and lesbian partners. Take Vermont's civil unions, for instance: How likely is it that there would be many *binational* same-gender unions? "More than you think," the following facts suggest:

- In 2000, Vermont celebrated the civil unions of over three thousand individuals that year, 78 percent of whom were from other states, Washington, D.C., or other countries, including Canada, England, Venezuela, Mexico, Philippines, Australia, Netherlands, Germany, India, and Guatemala.[3]
- Opportunities for U.S. citizens and noncitizens to establish long-term monogamous relationships have been enhanced not just by advances in technology and transportation, but by the continuing attractiveness

of American educational institutions to foreign students. Of the various categories of nonimmigrants, student visa holders constituted the second largest group behind temporary tourist and business visitors during fiscal year 2001.[4]

- A 2003 study by the Pew Research Center has found that opposition to gay marriage is decreasing.[5] Similarly, a 2003 Gallup poll reports that 72 percent of Americans eighteen to twenty-nine years old favor same-gender marriages,[6] which suggests that more states will likely follow Massachusetts and Vermont by enacting marriage or civil union laws[7] in the years to come.

These facts imply that not only is there a greater probability of same-gender binational relationships developing today than in the past, but greater acceptance by the American public and the availability of formal civil union status in Vermont may also increase the number of formal, government-sanctioned relationships among binational same-gender partners.

This raises a second question for skeptics: if America is growing ever more tolerant of same-gender relationships, why would the foreign partners of gay and lesbian U.S. nationals be deported? If a growing number of U.S. residents accept gay and lesbian unions as acceptable lifestyle choices, would not the number of deportations of foreign same-gender partners actually decrease over time rather than increase? The answer would depend on whether the current ban against homosexual U.S. citizens from petitioning their foreign partners to immigrate as their "spouses" is ever lifted. In *Adams v. Howerton*,[8] the Ninth Circuit upheld the constitutionality of interpreting Immigration and Nationality Act (INA) section 201(b), which permits immigration based on certain familial relationships, to limit the conferral of "immediate relative" status to those noncitizen "spouses" involved in a heterosexual, but not homosexual, marriage. While the statute placed no such explicit limitation on the term "spouse," the court ruled that the INS's implementation decision to limit immigration benefits to heterosexual couples was constitutionally rational. Despite the plaintiffs' attempts to have the relevant provisions more strictly scrutinized, the court cited Congress's well-established plenary power over the field, which mandated a much more perfunctory review of the contested legislation. Nonetheless, the Ninth Circuit noted that there might be limits to Congress's plenary power over immigration:

The scope of this very limited judicial review has not been further defined; the Supreme Court has not determined what limitations, if any, the Constitution imposes upon Congress. Faced with numerous challenges to laws governing the exclusion of aliens and the expulsion of resident and non-resident aliens, the Court has consistently reaffirmed the power of Congress to legislate in this area.[9]

Perhaps more important than this sterile recitation of the law from *Adams* is recognizing the practical effect the decision has had on its protagonists. Today, Australian national Anthony Sullivan lives as a fugitive from the law somewhere in the United States together with his U.S. citizen partner, Richard Adams. After years of futilely trying to get the federal government to recognize their valid state marriage license, Sullivan now manages to live beneath the immigration authorities' radar screen, although he blames his "outlaw" status for the couple's current financial difficulties: "We would probably own our own home. We both love to travel. We would have been able to travel. I would have been a professional of some kind."[10]

The *Adams* plenary power-backed decision is further supported by the 1996 passage of the Defense of Marriage Act (DOMA), which limits the definition of "marriage" to heterosexual unions for federal purposes and permits individual states not to recognize same-gender unions from other jurisdictions, domestic or international.[11] Applied to our hypothetical, this means that Maria and Susan could neither get other states to recognize their Massachusetts marriage, and more importantly for our purposes, nor could Susan avail herself of current immigration law to petition her spouse, Maria, to remain in the United States legally.

This hypothetical thus illustrates a bind for binational same-gender partners wrought, in part, by the U.S. federal system: despite Massachusetts's recognition of their relationship, which would lead to their enjoyment of the same *state* government benefits given to its heterosexual married couples, Maria and Susan would be barred under *federal* law from living together anywhere within the United States as a legally united couple and indeed, unless Maria could find some other way to maintain a lawful immigration status (say, through employment or asylum), Maria would have to leave the country. (Unlike in the *Adams* case, my research revealed no deportation cases against foreign same-gender partners, although it is quite plausible that most have, like Sullivan, been able to evade detection or that they have found other legitimate ways of remaining in the country. As Pradeep Singla, who worked for the Lesbian and Gay Immigration Rights Task Force shared with me when I began this research, "[O]ne of the most frequently asked questions [we receive] pertains to entering into a civil union in Vermont and seeking recognition of this relationship by INS for immigration benefits.")[12]

Since *Adams,* the plenary power doctrine, and DOMA combine to create a formidable barrier to any *judicial* recognition of binational same-gender marriage, gay rights groups have sought to lobby Congress for ways around *Adams,* including the Permanent Partners Immigration Act of 2003, which seeks to create immigration benefits for same-gender partners while leaving the INA definition of "spouse" intact.[13] Support for the bill recently reached as high as a quarter[14] of those in the House of Representatives, presenting, once again, both good news and bad news. The good news is that this support is unprecedented; never before have so many congresspersons been so supportive of a gay rights bill. The bad news is twofold: a quarter is nowhere close to a majority and the bill itself is rather limited in scope, for it does nothing to dismantle DOMA. In addition, columnist Andrew Sullivan suggests that there are increasing signs of a growing backlash against gay rights in general.[15] President Bush has openly declared his opposition to same-gender marriages and the Vatican has likewise denounced such unions as "deviant."[16] Some in Congress support a constitutional amendment that would limit all marriages to heterosexual couples only.[17]

Apart from this societal tug-of-war between gay rights activists and opponents, the recent appearance of Massachusetts as a haven for same-gender couples—including binational ones—and the likelihood that we will see more states recognizing same-gender marriages in the future, prompts consideration of a different constitutional law question than that addressed in *Adams*: would it be constitutional for the Bureau of Immigration and Customs Enforcement (ICE) to choose to deport the foreign same-gender partner overstay of a U.S. citizen married in Massachusetts solely because of her sexual orientation? While *Adams* focused on the constitutionality of denying immigration benefits to same-gender partners, this inquiry does not challenge any congressional action; it asks only whether the ICE has the power under the Constitution to selectively deport someone based solely on her sexual orientation.

While the foregoing story may strike some readers as a most improbable scenario, the narrative appears more credible when viewed from the lens of the U.S. Supreme Court's 1999 decision in *Reno v. American-Arab*

*Anti-Discrimination Committee (AADC),*[18] mentioned briefly in chapter 1, and described in greater detail here. In *AADC,* in a scenario not unlike the one described above, the INS singled out for deportation six nonimmigrants and two permanent residents because of their membership in the Popular Front for the Liberation of Palestine (PFLP), believed by the government to be an international terrorist organization. Though accused of no crimes, the "LA 8"[19] were deemed guilty of terrorism by association.

On appeal to the Supreme Court, the deportees alleged that they had been selectively targeted by the INS in violation of their First Amendment right to join the PFLP. The Court chose to address their constitutional claim only *in dicta,* ruling instead on statutory grounds. Nonetheless, Justice Scalia's majority opinion used strikingly broad language in addressing the constitutional issue: "As a general matter—and assuredly in the context of claims such as those put forward in the present case—an alien unlawfully in this country has no constitutional right to assert selective enforcement as a defense against his deportation."[20] After supporting this statement, he went on to qualify: "To resolve the present controversy, we need not rule out the possibility of a rare case in which the alleged basis of discrimination is so outrageous that the foregoing considerations can be overcome."[21]

The difference between deporting noncitizen overstays who are terrorist affiliates, on the one hand, and those who are same-gender partners, on the other, might strike some as so glaring that the analogy is unconvincing. However, the line between the noncriminal terrorist affiliate and the noncriminal same-gender partner might not be particularly obvious to some. Both types of overstays might be viewed as being engaged in intimate relationships with undesirables—terrorists in one instance, gays or lesbians in another—and their "illegal" immigration status provides the government with a good reason to deport them. Indeed, former INS Commissioner Doris Meissner's November 2000 memorandum on prosecutorial discretion recounts that the agency prosecutes immigration violations to further several goals, including "protecting public safety,[22] promoting the integrity of the legal immigration system, and deterring violations of the immigration law."[23] Just as the deportation of overstaying terrorist affiliates might arguably promote all three goals, in some people's minds the removal of same-gender partner overstays would be similarly effective. Analogously, DOMA was probably enacted in part because of the perceived threat that there would be a great increase in the number of jurisdictions that might recognize same-gender marriages.

While it is true that Commissioner Meissner's memorandum explicitly leaves the exercise of prosecutorial discretion in the hands of high-level INS (now ICE) officials, should there be a sizable number of cases that emerge in future years not only out of Massachusetts but also from other states that seek to pass similar legislation, there might be an impetus to begin deporting same-gender partner overstays, especially if one holds the view that morally such persons are not much different from the "LA 8" and that, regardless, the continued violation of the immigration laws should be stopped through their removal. Unfortunately, there is precedent for government officials taking hard-line stances on immigration violations even in the face of enforcement discretion. In an infamous episode from 2002, Colorado Congressman Tom Tancredo called for the deportation of Jesus Apodaca, an undocumented high school honors student who agreed to be interviewed by a local newspaper for a story on the unavailability of government financial aid for undocumented persons.[24] (Ironically, Tancredo relented somewhat when it was revealed that the firm he had hired to help remodel his house had employed two undocumented workers: "I have never, to my knowledge, hired anybody illegally," the Congressman protested.)[25]

Finally, if, as Andrew Sullivan has suggested, a conservative backlash against gays and lesbians is imminent, what better way to constitutionally implement such an antigay policy than to utilize the immigration laws—laws that have been subject to minimal judicial scrutiny—to selectively deport foreign same-gender partners of U.S. citizens? (Think about the message it sends: "If we, the federal government, can't prevent rogue states like Massachusetts from granting marriage rights to gay and lesbian citizens, we can surely limit the number of such unions by deporting foreign same-gender partners under existing immigration laws!") At one level, such a strategy would be no different from Attorney General Ashcroft's antiterrorism plan detailed in chapter 2: if we can't prove that a person is a terrorist or a criminal, we can at least remove him from the United States because of his technical immigration violation.

While the day of homosexual removals *en masse* is not upon us, the specific government targeting of homosexuals since 1986 highlighted in recent Supreme Court decisions—to prevent them from enacting protective state legislation,[26] to exclude them from private leadership positions in organizations,[27] and to criminalize their private, consensual sexual activity[28]—suggests that the selective immigration prosecution of homosexuals might not be so far-fetched. Indeed, as I noted in chapter 1,

Supreme Court opinions on the immigration exclusion of certain select groups, specifically on racial and ideological grounds, is a well-established source for affirming congressional plenary power over the field. Thus the specific targeting of same-gender partner overstays captures antigay and anti-immigrant sentiment that has long been a part of Supreme Court history, both ancient and recent.

Thinking back to the Camacho-Sanders hypothetical, does the mass deportation of overstaying same-gender partners constitute an outrageous "rara avis" under *AADC* or does it constitute a permissible enforcement of immigration law, not unlike the removal of terrorist sympathizers such as the "LA 8"? Part of the answer to this question might depend on how the Court views not only immigrants in general, but *homosexual* immigrants specifically. To this end a review of the Court's most recent pronouncement on gay rights, *Lawrence v. Texas,*[29] and on immigrants' rights, *Demore v. Kim,*[30] might be useful.

In *Lawrence v. Texas,* the Supreme Court voted 6-to-3 to overturn its nearly twenty-year-old decision in the infamous *Bowers v. Hardwick* case, ruling that Texas could not criminalize private sexual activity between two consenting persons of the same gender. How the case came to be prosecuted is disturbing. After receiving a false report about a weapons disturbance, Harris County police in Houston, Texas, dispatched officers to an apartment where they found John Lawrence and Tyron Garner having sex. While the informant was charged with filing a false report Lawrence and Garner were also prosecuted under the Texas Penal Code for engaging in "deviate sexual intercourse," which included anal sex between persons of the same gender.

Writing for a majority of five (Justice O'Connor wrote a separate opinion), Justice Kennedy held that the petitioners here—"two adults who, with full and mutual consent from each other, engag[ing] in sexual practices common to a homosexual lifestyle"[31]—enjoy a "right to liberty under the Due Process Clause [which] gives them the full right to engage in their conduct without intervention of the government."[32] Specifically, the Court stated that it had erred in *Hardwick* by concluding that laws against homosexual conduct had "ancient roots"; more accurately, societies banned sodomy engaged in by both hetero- and homosexual couples. Moreover, the Court noted that, despite the presence of these laws on the books, they were not enforced among consenting adults acting privately within their homes. While predatory acts of older men against male and female children, for example, were prosecuted, consensual sex between adults was not. Relying on a string of privacy cases from *Griswold v. Connecticut* (recognizing a privacy right to obtain contraception) to *Planned Parenthood v. Casey* (upholding a woman's right to an abortion), Kennedy concluded that Texas had no legitimate reason for "circumscribing personal choice"[33] in matters of consensual, private sex among adults.

*Lawrence v. Texas* is a most welcome opinion for gay rights' activists. Not only did the Court overrule *Hardwick,* but it also established a baseline of privacy for all individuals, regardless of their sexual orientation. But *Lawrence* was not the only Due Process case the Court decided in 2003. Indeed, in *Demore v. Kim,* the Court rejected a challenge to the Due Process Clause in an immigration case that might shed light on the selective deportation issue.

In *Demore v. Kim,*[34] the Court split 5-to-4, holding that the mandatory detention of lawful permanent residents pending their deportation did not violate the Due Process Clause. Korean citizen Hyung Joon Kim immigrated to the United States as a child, obtaining lawful permanent residence status by age eight. As an adult, Kim was convicted of two theft crimes in California, after which the INS sought to deport him. Without first determining whether he was a flight risk or a danger to others or himself, Kim was detained for over five weeks before being charged as deportable. Kim argued that because he was a lawful permanent resident, the Due Process Clause required that the government grant him a hearing at which an individualized determination is made before he may be detained.

Writing for the majority, Chief Justice Rehnquist opined that the mandatory detention provisions of the Immigration and Nationality Act did not violate Due Process because Congress's plenary power over immigration matters allowed it to reasonably conclude that such detention was necessary to ensure that persons like Kim would be properly processed and deported.

*Lawrence* and *Kim* are the Supreme Court's latest statements on the controversial issues of gay and immigrant rights, respectively. Indeed, five of the six[35] justices who signed on to the *AADC* majority opinion—Rehnquist, Scalia, Thomas, Kennedy, and O'Connor—were the same five who sided with the government in *Kim.* Taking *AADC* and *Kim* together, one might think that Ms. Camacho and Ms. Sanders in the opening hypothetical would receive little support from these five justices; yet, *Lawrence* states that private, consensual sexual conduct is beyond government regulation, irrespective of one's sexual orientation, which implies an opening for the Camacho-Sanders couple to argue that selective prosecution would be similarly outrageous under *AADC*.

As mentioned earlier, conventional wisdom might suggest that Ms. Camacho and Ms. Sanders should seek relief from Congress by having it amend the immigration code to allow for same-gender sponsorship. To the extent that immigration and naturalization are the province of the federal government, any relief for same-gender partners must be sought in the halls of Congress, not in the courts, so the argument goes. This is a powerful argument, and indeed, one that I have made several times in this book in advocating that Congress pass the Family Reunification Act (chapter 3) and the Student Adjustment Act (chapter 5). It is an especially useful argument in the same-gender binational partner context because this deportation scenario is fictional. Having the law changed to allow immigration benefits for same-gender partners would render the foregoing hypothetical moot.

This chapter, however, will take a different path. Even though there have been no reported cases of selective deportations based on sexual orientation, *AADC*, *Lawrence*, and *Kim* make exploration of the Camacho-Sander hypothetical worthwhile. By examining the possibility that such selective deportations might occur in this context, the hope is that advocates of putative deportees would have a litigation resource; it would be better still if the ICE never adopted such a policy at all.

Thus, the next section explores the contours of the majority's statement in *AADC* and takes seriously the opening story to suggest that Ms. Camacho has a strong constitutional argument not to be selectively deported because of her homosexual status. A review of its noncitizen and gay rights jurisprudence reveals that, despite its deference to the political branches under most circumstances, the Court will not hesitate to strike down legislative or executive action in cases of extreme discriminatory treatment. Whether the vehicle for such judicial intervention is called "equal protection" or "due process," the result is that even on a conservative court such as the present one, there will likely be five votes in favor of the individual rights claimant, despite her being a lesbian noncitizen.

Hence, the "outrageous" test articulated by Scalia in *AADC* is but another version of a "minimal protection" test. Under this scheme, the Court will strike down legislative or executive action only if two things are present: (1) it views the plaintiff as having been unfairly deprived of a right open to all, and who asks only for "equal," as opposed to "special," treatment; and (2) it can identify no legitimate governmental interest to preserve majority sentiment, expressed either through legislative policy, executive action, or a core constitutional value. Although there are doctrinal arguments to suggest otherwise, on balance a majority of the Court should find that the selective deportation based on sexual orientation offends common notions of decency and justice, thereby rendering such an act "outrageous."

This chapter concludes with a brief revisit to *Adams,* placing the same-gender immigration benefits debate within a broader international context and arguing that sooner or later the U.S. government will have to address the larger issue of same-gender partnerships and their inferior status vis-à-vis traditional, heterosexual marriages.

## *What Constitutes "Outrageous"?*
## *A Review of Recent Cases on Gay and Immigrants' Rights*

I have shared the hypothetical about mass deportations of foreign same-gender partner overstays with many people, both lawyers and non-lawyers, to test its relevance and to examine gut reactions to the story. Most believe that the ICE would never engage in such an act because they would have no particular incentive to do so, despite the overstays' continued unlawful presence. Underlying this argument, I suspect, is a belief that such a scenario would be ludicrous—that it would be un-American to deport homosexual overstays just because we could, especially if they were part of a legal same-gender union under state law. However, when asked to indulge my paranoia and consider the hypothetical at face value, the same people assume that most U.S. residents would affirm the ICE's decision, even if the deportees were selectively targeted because of their homosexuality, on two related grounds: first, that the federal government has virtually unlimited power over immigration matters, and second, that the real issue is the noncitizen's "illegal" status, and not her sexual orientation. Ms. Camacho's sexual orientation should not excuse her violation of a valid law.

From this admittedly most unscientific of surveys, I detect a disconnect. On the one hand, many believe that the selective deportation of foreign same-gender partner overstays would be highly unlikely, and yet there is also consensus that the federal government would have the power to carry out such a directive.

It is this disconnect that I plan to explore in the context of the following statement from *AADC*: "To resolve this present controversy, we need not rule out the possibility of a rare case in which the alleged basis of discrimination is so outrageous that the foregoing considerations can be overcome."[36] If, in a sense, the opening narrative is "outrageous" because it offends our idea of how America treats visitors within its boundaries, why is it no less "outrageous" should the government actually carry out this scenario? Put differently, if the thought of deporting same-gender partner overstays *en masse* offends our sensibilities, why would the Supreme Court approve such a project?

### 1. *Reno v. AADC*: What Is "Outrageous" Conduct?

In *Reno v. AADC,* the Supreme Court stated that, generally, noncitizens could not assert a First Amendment selective prosecution claim to challenge their otherwise valid deportation order. In a case more popularly known as the "LA 8 case," the INS sought to deport eight noncitizens (two of whom were permanent residents) because of their affiliation with the Popular Front for the Liberation of Palestine (PFLP), which the government described as a terrorist organization.

In the convoluted lower court litigation, the government contended that while the First Amendment would protect the rights of U.S. citizens to affiliate with groups such as the PFLP, the same protection does not extend to noncitizens. As then-FBI Director William Webster admitted, "If these individuals had been United States citizens, there would not have been a basis for their arrest."[37] Several variations of the government's argument were presented in the federal district and appeals courts, but they were soundly rejected each time. The lower courts agreed with the noncitizens that the First Amendment required that they not be selectively targeted for deportation solely because of their political affiliations.

The Justice Department pursued an appeal to the Supreme Court, which resolved the First Amendment issues in its opinion, although it initially declined to do so because the parties left them unbriefed. Although the case was resolved on statutory grounds, the Court nonetheless opined on the selective prosecution argument, siding with the government and noting that the First Amendment typically did not prevent the INS from choosing whom to deport among noncitizens illegally present: "[A]n alien unlawfully in this country has no constitutional right to assert selective enforcement as a defense against his deportation."[38] Writing for the majority, Scalia reasoned that allowing such claims would unnecessarily hamper the operations of the executive branch as it seeks merely to enforce the immigration rules set by Congress:

> Even when deportation is sought because of some act the alien has committed, in principle the alien is not being punished for that act (criminal charges may be available for that separate purpose) but is merely being held to the terms under which he was admitted. And in all cases, deportation is necessary in order to bring to an end an ongoing violation of United States law. The contention that a violation must be allowed to continue because it has been improperly selected is not powerfully appealing.[39]

Without specifying a concrete example, the Court did note, however, that there may be rare cases in which the alleged basis of discrimination is so outrageous that the balance tips in the noncitizen's favor: "To resolve the present controversy, we need not rule out the possibility of the rare case in which the alleged basis of discrimination is so outrageous that the foregoing considerations can be overcome."[40]

Scalia noted that selective enforcement claims are generally disfavored in the criminal context and should be even further discouraged in deportation proceedings for at least three reasons. First, allowing the full adjudication of all selective deportation claims will lead to delays, which permit the deportee to continue to remain in the United States in violation of the law. Second, greater scrutiny of INS (now ICE) action will chill law enforcement by leading to the disclosure of sensitive foreign-policy objectives. And third, unlike in criminal prosecutions, deportations seek only to hold the noncitizens to the terms of their admission; deportation is not punishment, and hence constitutional safeguards may properly be relaxed in this context.

Although the Court's members voted 8-to-1 in favor of upholding the INS's deportation decision on statutory grounds (even if for different reasons), the justices split on the proper constitutional analysis. Five of the justices—Rehnquist, Thomas, O'Connor, Kennedy, and, in a separate opinion, Stevens—subscribed to Scalia's notion that, absent outrageous government conduct, noncitizens were barred from raising selective enforcement as a constitutional defense to deportation. Two others—Ginsburg and Souter—set forth separate opinions which expressed a greater willingness to consider selective deportation claims. Breyer was the only one not to express his view on the constitutional availability of selective deportation claims. To summarize, the justices were split 6-to-2 in favor of the general bar, with one abstention. Despite the fact that Scalia's analysis has not been developed further in subsequent cases and is arguably dictum, a solid majority of the Court accept Scalia's test, even though two—Ginsburg and Souter—might prefer stronger judicial review of selective deportation claims. It is worth exploring, therefore, how our same-gender partner overstay might fare under such a test.

For someone who usually takes care to only address issues squarely before the Court, Justice Scalia's selective deportation section not only was unnecessary to the resolution of the case, but was also an issue the parties did not brief. That he would go out of his way to rule on this issue suggests that the types of claims he might consider "outrageous" might be limited, indeed. Justice Stevens's opinion supports the idea of a limited exception, further distinguishing between punishment in the criminal justice context and the less adverse consequences of deportation. Stevens asserted that while Congress could not punish innocent persons because of their membership in a terrorist organization, he had "no doubt that the Attorney General may give priority to the removal of deportable aliens who are members of such an organization," per Scalia's analysis.[41] If the other four justices in the majority agree with Scalia and Stevens, our hypothetical same-gender partner overstay appears to have a tough road ahead, given what looks like a rather narrow window of relief.

While she focused mostly on the statute's construction, Justice Ginsburg devoted part of her concurrence to address Scalia's selective enforcement analysis. While initially concluding that this issue was not before the Court, Ginsburg stated that she was "not persuaded that selective enforcement of deportation laws should be exempt"[42] from judicial scrutiny, citing the Court's review of selective prosecution cases in the criminal law context. While Scalia drew a distinction between criminal proceedings and civil deportation hearings (which he argued counseled against judicial intervention in selective deportation claims), Ginsburg stressed the hardships wrought by deportation, including separating families. This suggests that Justice Ginsburg is more likely than the majority to recognize a broad selective deportation claim beyond creating special exemptions for "rare cases."

Justice Souter's dissenting opinion also expressed displeasure with the Court's discussion of the unbriefed selective deportation claim, quickly dismissing it as dictum. While he, too, believed that the differences between criminal and immigration law do not obviate the need for a selective deportation defense, Souter disclaimed siding with the noncitizen on this issue: "I do not assume that the Government would lose the argument."[43] Like Ginsburg, Souter would probably be more receptive to a selective deportation claim than Scalia and his colleagues in the majority.

Leading commentary on the *AADC* case has construed the majority's rejection of selective deportation claims as being rooted in a desire to limit remedies available to acknowledged deportees. Legal scholars Gerald Neuman, David Cole, and David Martin all agree that the best analysis of Scalia's opinion is one which gives credence to the Court's fear that if deportees were successful in establishing a selective enforcement claim, they might be entitled to permanent injunctive relief from removal, an arguably unjust result when the noncitizen concedes deportability.[44] A fairer response, Neuman argues, would be to remand the case "for an exercise of enforcement discretion untainted by the [constitutionally] impermissible motive."[45] Such reconsideration would properly balance the constitutional interests of the noncitizen against the government's desire to halt an admitted immigration violation. But even under this analysis, the ICE retains much unfettered power to proceed against deportable noncitizens as it wishes, constrained only by the yet-to-be-defined standard of "outrageous" conduct. This indeterminacy should give us pause as it parallels a debate raised earlier in chapter 4 about the proper scope of the Fourth Amendment: is the "outrageous" conduct test more like the less protective "due process" limits on unreasonable searches of undocumented persons articulated by Judge Cassell, or is it more like the regular Fourth Amendment jurisprudence that applies to police action?

Furthermore, although the *AADC* plaintiffs and the lower courts based their selective deportation claim on the First Amendment, the Supreme Court's constitutional analysis was broader in scope. Justice Scalia's reasoning in *AADC* did not even mention the noncitizens' speech or associational rights as being bases of a valid constitutional claim, focusing instead on the more ambiguous term "outrageous" governmental action. As David Cole has noted, "[T]he decision is about selective enforcement claims in particular, and not about the First Amendment rights of aliens more generally."[46]

Scalia's selective deportation analysis, agreed to by five other justices, appears to defer broadly to the government to enforce immigration laws as it sees fit, constrained only by a vague standard of "outrageous" conduct. At best, we know that the selection of admittedly deportable noncitizens based on their suspected terrorist affiliations is not outrageous. But we know little beyond that.

This chapter attempts to give content to Scalia's test by contending that "outrageous" selective enforcement is one in which the government intends to oppress an individual or group based on a disadvantaged status, rather than an objective desire to enforce the immigration laws. Put another way, the "outrageous" test is but another version of a "minimal protection" test akin to equal protection or due process "rational basis" scrutiny. Under this scheme, as noted earlier, the Court will strike down legislative or executive action only if: (1) it views the plaintiff as having been unfairly deprived of a right open to all, and who asks only for "equal," as opposed to "special," treatment; and (2) it can identify no legitimate governmental interest to preserve majority sentiment, expressed either through legislative policy, executive action, or a core constitutional value.

This analysis is based on a review of the Court's more recent writings in the area of gay and immigrants' rights—both constitutional and subconstitutional—concluding that while the Court is sometimes willing to protect the constitutional rights of homosexuals and noncitizens, it is generally reluctant to do so absent particularly discriminatory governmental conduct and the absence of a legitimate, countervailing interest. The "outrageous" test outlined in *AADC* is but a variant of the constitutional and subconstitutional analyses employed in the cases described below.

## 2. The Court's Recent Opinions on Gay Rights

Effectively comprehending the Court's gay rights jurisprudence requires us to compare two sets of cases—*Bowers v. Hardwick, Romer v. Evans,* and *Lawrence v. Texas,* on the one hand—and *Hurley v. Irish-American Gay, Lesbian, and Bisexual Group of Boston* and *Boy Scouts of America v. Dale,* on the other. In each we see the Court struggling with conceptions of substantive due process, equal protection, and First Amendment rights that might provide us with bases for measuring the scope of the rare "outrageous" selective prosecution case hypothesized by Justice Scalia.

## A. *Hardwick, Evans,* AND *Lawrence*:
## SUBSTANTIVE DUE PROCESS AND
## EQUAL PROTECTION AS APPLIED TO GAY RIGHTS

Michael Hardwick's appearance before the Supreme Court was the result of a concerted effort to find a test case to challenge the legality of state sodomy laws. Hardwick was arrested for engaging in sex with another man in the privacy of his apartment after being discovered there by a Georgia police officer who had been invited in by a friend. The officer was there to serve a warrant on Hardwick for public drinking, an offense for which Hardwick had already paid a fine, unbeknownst to the officer. Although originally arrested and temporarily jailed under the state's sodomy law, Hardwick's charges were quickly dropped, but not before an ACLU attorney had persuaded Hardwick to file suit challenging the Georgia law.[47]

As the case wound its way up to the Supreme Court, one of the leading issues was whether the Court would be willing to extend its conception of constitutional protection of private conduct against charges of immorality by a substantial number of the populace. During the late 1960s and early 1970s, the Court protected a wide range of private activity under the rubric of Fourteenth Amendment "substantive due process," including the choice to use contraception in *Griswold v. Connecticut* and the right to an abortion in *Roe v. Wade.* Thus, one key question was whether the Court would protect from governmental sanction the right to consensual sexual activity conducted in the privacy of one's home.

In a 5-to-4 decision, the Court answered in the negative. *Bowers v. Hardwick*[48] stands for the proposition that the Due Process Clause of the Fourteenth Amendment does not provide homosexuals a constitutional right to engage in sodomy, thus affirming a state's right to criminalize such conduct. Joined in the majority by Justices Burger, Powell, Rehnquist, and O'Connor, Justice White noted that homosexual sodomy was not a substantive liberty right "deeply rooted in this Nation's history and tradition." On the contrary, laws prohibiting such acts "have ancient roots." Further, White confirmed the majority's reluctance to expand the concept of substantive due process to recognize new rights "without express constitutional authority," invoking the historical wrangling over unenumerated socioeconomic rights during the 1930s. Finally, the Court rejected Hardwick's claim that prevailing public sentiment about the immorality of homosexuality was irrational, leaving intact the sodomy laws of then some twenty-five states.

The four dissenters questioned the Court's narrow characterization of the issue before it, broadly depicting the right at stake as "the right to be let alone." From that premise, both Justice Blackmun's and Stevens's opinions focused, albeit in slightly different ways, on the legacy of privacy carved out by the Court's precedents in the realm of personal choice that they believe protected the "right to engage in nonreproductive, sexual conduct," even if it offends others.[49]

The deeply divided Court was not aided by revelations that Justice Powell had originally sided with the dissenters in conference, but later switched his vote to side with the majority in upholding the Georgia sodomy law. He attempted to soften the decision's blow by writing a concurrence raising the possibility of an Eighth Amendment objection, had Hardwick's sodomy prosecution gone forward.[50]

When questioned four years later about his decision in *Hardwick,* Powell reflected that "he probably made a mistake in that one," noting that his subsequent reading of the opinions in the case suggested to him that the dissenters had the better argument.[51] As Powell's biographer, John Jeffries, explains, "As startling as his change of heart may have seemed, it was really no more than his continuing unease at choosing between sodomy as a crime and sodomy as a fundamental right. He had never come to rest on that question."[52] Powell would have preferred to split the difference, not recognizing a homosexual's right to engage in sodomy, but not allowing for the criminal persecution of gays. Indeed, Justice Powell feared the slippery slope. Again, from Jeffries:

> After all, if homosexuals had a constitutional right to engage in sex, would they not also have the right to object to any form of regulation or restriction disadvantaging them for having done so? Would gays then have a constitutional right to serve in the military or in the intelligence agencies? Would they have a right to teach in public school or work in day care centers? Would there be a constitutional requirement that the law allow homosexual adoption or same-[gender] marriage?[53]

It was a further fall along the slippery slope that likely gave rise to the litigation in *Romer v. Evans,* the Court's next major foray into the arena of gay rights. On the heels of successful local initiatives to provide protection from sexual orientation discrimination in such cities as Denver and Boulder, the citizens of Colorado decided to amend their constitution to prohibit any state or local governmental body from taking steps to protect gays and lesbians.[54] Pro–"Amendment 2" advocates described the law as a way to ensure that gays and lesbians did not receive special privileges from the government, arguing that civil rights statutes should be reserved for the truly deserving, like racial minorities. Some of the supporting rhetoric likened gay rights legislation to special protections for white males:

> Example: Young-Caucasian-males-without-disabilities aren't a protected class. Claims of discrimination are not accepted on the basis of being a Caucasian-male-without-disabilities. But does this mean that someone belonging to this group has no legal recourse? Of course not. Just ask a Caucasian male, Allen Bakke. If he hadn't had legal recourse, there wouldn't be a famous Supreme Court reverse-discrimination case named after him. For Bakke to get that recourse, however, we didn't have to make Caucasian-males a specially protected class, or declare them, as a group, immune from discrimination. That would have destroyed the whole meaning of civil rights. And so will protected status for homosexuals. []
> Once more for the record: anti-discrimination laws were written to protect specially protected classes—groups who've proven they need help.[55]

In response, oppositionists had difficulty diffusing the force of the "special rights sound bite" unleashed by the law's supporters. As one anti–Amendment 2 activist remarked, "[T]here is no good phrase or slogan to counter 'special rights.' It takes fifteen minutes of real discussion to undo the damage that phrase does."[56]

> Amendment 2 passed by a narrow margin: 53.4 percent voted for it, while 46.6 percent voted against it. Ironically, polls conducted by the Denver Post before and after the vote suggest that most Coloradans did not believe in discriminating against homosexuals in the areas of employment and housing, for example, which Amendment 2 would have allowed.[57]

Just as Justice Powell's *Hardwick* concurrence struggled over how to protect homosexuals from criminal prosecution without conferring upon them new constitutional entitlements, the Colorado voters faced a similar dilemma: would approval of Amendment 2 promote gay rights beyond providing them with the protection from prosecution voters believe they should receive? It is in this factual context that this next debate over gay rights came before the Supreme Court.

In *Evans*, six justices struck down Colorado's Amendment 2 on the grounds that it violated the Equal Protection Clause of the Fourteenth Amendment. Specifically, Justices O'Connor, Stevens, Souter, Ginsburg, and Breyer joined Justice Kennedy's opinion declaring that even though homosexuals are not a constitutionally protected class, the Amendment's avowed purposes fail to pass even the deferential rational basis standard:

> Amendment 2 fails, indeed defies, even [the rational basis test]. First, the amendment has the peculiar property of imposing a broad and undifferentiated disability on a single named group, an exceptional and, as we shall explain, invalid form of legislation. Second, its sheer breadth is so discontinuous with the reasons offered for it that the amendment seems inexplicable by anything but animus toward the class it affects; it lacks a rational relationship to legitimate state interests.[58]

More specifically, the Court thought Amendment 2's unprecedented blanket denial of access to legal protection imposed upon homosexuals thwarted the very purpose of equal protection jurisprudence, and that the avowed rationales for the provision bore no rational relationship to a legitimate state purpose other than to discriminate against homosexuals *qua* homosexuals.

Joined by Chief Justice Rehnquist and Justice Thomas in dissent, Justice Scalia viewed the battle over Amendment 2 as pure politics with which the Court should not have involved itself. In his view, "the constitutional amendment before us here is not the manifestation of a 'bare . . . desire to harm' homosexuals, but is rather a modest attempt by seemingly tolerant Coloradans to preserve traditional sexual mores against the efforts of a politically powerful minority to revise those mores through use of the laws."[59]

More pointedly, Scalia chastised the majority for not even mentioning *Bowers v. Hardwick*, which he characterized as "the case most relevant to the issue before us today." He put the issue squarely: "If it is constitutionally permissible for a State to make homosexual conduct criminal, surely it is constitutionally permissible for a State to enact laws merely disfavoring homosexual conduct."[60]

One can distinguish *Hardwick* and *Evans* on doctrine and on fact: doctrinally, *Hardwick* is a due process case, while *Evans* sounds in equal protection. Factually, the Georgia sodomy law in *Hardwick* was to be applied only to homosexual conduct, while Amendment 2 in *Evans* was to be extended to status. Yet the *Evans* majority's failure to point out these differences and the apparent incongruity of results which Justice Scalia suggests made for an uneasy peace. Worse still, the availability of both *Hardwick* and *Evans* as valid Supreme Court precedent made prognostication on future gay rights rulings difficult. But perhaps this is what the Supreme Court intended. As legal scholar William Eskridge explains:

> Judges are no longer constrained by *Hardwick* in equal protection cases and can follow *Evans*'s lead if they choose to do so. But judges desiring to reject challenges to antigay policies can follow *Hardwick* and limit *Evans* to its unusual facts. This lack of authoritative guidance is probably what the Supreme Court expected after *Evans*: state courts and lower federal courts would struggle with issues of sexual orientation discrimination on a case-by-case basis, less constrained by Supreme Court precedent because of the *Hardwick* versus *Evans* choice now available.[61]

The Court finally resolved this incongruity in 2003 with its decision in *Lawrence v. Texas* in which five of the justices, led by Kennedy, squarely overturned *Hardwick*. Following up on his forceful opinion in *Evans*, Justice Kennedy took his cue from the *Hardwick* dissenters, stating, as Justice Powell had belatedly realized, that they had the stronger argument and that the majority in *Hardwick* had "fail[ed] to appreciate the extent of the liberty at stake":

> To say that the issue in [*Hardwick*] was simply the right to engage in certain sexual conduct demeans the claim the individual put forward, just as it would demean a married couple were it to be said marriage is simply about the right to have sexual intercourse. The laws involved in [*Hardwick*] and here are, to be sure, statutes that purport to do no more than prohibit a particular sexual act. Their penalties and purposes, though, have more far-reaching consequences, touching upon the most private human conduct, sexual behavior, and in the most private of places, the home. The statutes do seek to control a personal relationship

that, whether or not entitled to formal recognition in the law, is within the liberty of persons to choose without being punished as criminals.[62]

For Justice Kennedy and the majority in *Lawrence,* the scope of the Due Process Clause was broad enough to protect the liberty of gays and lesbians to engage in consensual sexual conduct in the privacy of their own homes, free from the disapprobation of a different-minded majority.

Writing separately, Justice O'Connor concurred to provide the sixth vote, but she based her decision on the Equal Protection Clause, and not the "liberty" right enshrined in the Due Process Clause:

> [T]he [s]tate cannot single out one identifiable class of citizens for punishment that does not apply to everyone else, with moral disapproval as the only asserted state interest for the law. The Texas sodomy statute subjects homosexuals to a "lifelong penalty and stigma. A legislative classification that threatens the creation of an underclass . . . cannot be reconciled with" the Equal Protection Clause.[63]

While Kennedy expressed concern that reliance on equal protection might tempt Texas and other states to reenact legislation that penalized both hetero- and homosexual sex acts, O'Connor appeared untroubled by this prospect, citing Justice Jackson in *Railway Express Agency, Inc. v. New York*: "The framers of the Constitution knew, and we should not forget today, that there is no more effective practical guaranty against arbitrary and unreasonable government than to require that the principles of law which officials would impose upon a minority be imposed generally."[64]

Justice Scalia's dissent was joined by Chief Justice Rehnquist and Justice Thomas. He took both Kennedy and O'Connor to task for what he believed was their elevation of the petitioners' rights claims to "fundamental" status, which subjected the Texas law to more substantial scrutiny than was warranted by the traditional "rational basis" test. Scalia asserted that the Texas legislature's disapproval of homosexual conduct reflected its citizenry's legitimate belief in its immorality. As such, Scalia believed that *Hardwick* was correctly decided because it refused to draw distinctions between antihomosexual laws and others regulating sexual conduct, such as state laws against "bigamy, same-sex marriage, adult incest, prostitution, masturbation, adultery, fornication, bestiality, and obscenity. . . . The impossibility of distinguishing homosexuality from other traditional 'morals' offenses is precisely why [*Hardwick*] rejected the rational-basis challenge."[65]

Now that *Hardwick* has been overturned by *Lawrence*, due process claims by gays and lesbians become another litigation option aside from the favorable equal protection ruling in *Evans*. In the context of our hypothetical selective deportation of same-gender partner overstays, however, *Lawrence* and *Evans* by themselves provide more limited guidance because they review state, rather than federal, restrictions on gay rights. An ICE decision to deport will be viewed with considerably more deference than a state statute, even for constitutional purposes, because of the plenary power and *Chevron* doctrines, which confer virtually limitless discretion upon Congress and administrative agencies, respectively. Before we explore an answer to the opening hypothetical, however, it might be useful to first examine the justices' views in *Lawrence* and *Evans* for some hint as to how they might vote.

Since it is Justice Scalia's *AADC* opinion on what might constitute an "outrageous" selective deportation that ultimately concerns us, let us start with him. Scalia's dissents in *Lawrence* and *Evans* suggest that he might be reluctant to afford any "special rights" to deportable same-gender partners in light of a long-standing deference to legislative fiat in the area of immigration. Just as Scalia was willing to defer to Colorado's democratic process which led to Amendment 2's passage and to Texas's decision to criminalize same-gender sexual practices, he might likewise be willing to leave foreign policy matters to the better judgment of the federal political branches, especially in the case of a nonsuspect class such as gays and lesbians. Then again, Scalia must have had something in mind when he set forth his "outrageous" theory; the open question is whether the selective deportation of a nonsuspect class by a federal government otherwise properly exercising its immigration power is sufficiently "outrageous."

Like Scalia, Kennedy did not participate in *Hardwick,* although he penned the majority opinions opposite Scalia's dissents in both *Evans* and *Lawrence*. Kennedy's words reveal a justice who is willing to protect a nonsuspect class even under the normally deferential "rational basis" test. Would he be willing to protect the same class of individuals when the federal government exercises its well-established power over immigration by conducting a selective, but otherwise legitimate, removal of a same-gender partner overstay? This is difficult to answer at this juncture, but a review of several other cases in the gay rights and immigration rights areas suggest perhaps an affirmative answer, which will be more fully developed below.

Like Scalia and Kennedy, four others on the current Court were not sitting when *Hardwick* was issued: Justices Thomas, Breyer, Ginsburg, and Souter did not participate in the 1986 decision. However, unlike Scalia and Kennedy, these four did not issue opinions in *Evans* and *Lawrence* either, with the exception of Thomas's two-paragraph originalist paean. At best, we can take note of their alliances—Thomas sided with Scalia in both the *Lawrence* and *Evans* dissents; Breyer, Ginsburg, and Souter joined Kennedy in the majority opinions in both cases. Although not an uncommon alignment, this configuration does not tell us how each of these individuals would rule on the constitutionality of our selective deportation narrative. But it does provide us a small piece to what is admittedly a complex puzzle.

That leaves us with the three justices who participated in *Hardwick, Evans,* and *Lawrence*: Rehnquist, Stevens, and O'Connor. During the seventeen years between *Hardwick* and *Lawrence,* the Court saw the ascendancy of Justice Rehnquist to the Chief's position. Rehnquist authored opinions in none of the three cases, but voted with the majority in *Hardwick* and the dissent in *Evans* and *Lawrence,* suggesting his reluctance to grant much constitutional protection to homosexuals.

Justice Stevens provides us with more guidance and some useful language. His opinion in *Hardwick* and his decision to join Justice Kennedy's majority opinion in *Lawrence* (indeed, Kennedy quoted Stevens's *Hardwick* dissent with approval) suggest his willingness to extend the same substantive due process rights to homosexuals engaged in private, consensual sex acts already enjoyed by heterosexuals. More importantly, his discussion of the selective application of a neutral sodomy law in *Hardwick* against homosexuals provides an insight into how he might view the selective deportation of same-gender partner overstays:

> A policy of selective application must be supported by a neutral and legitimate interest—something more substantial than a habitual dislike for, or ignorance about, the disfavored group. Neither the State nor the Court has identified any such interest in this case. The Court has posited as a justification for the Georgia statute "the presumed belief of a majority of the electorate in Georgia that homosexual sodomy is immoral and unacceptable." [] But the Georgia electorate has expressed no such be-

lief—instead, its representatives enacted a law that presumably reflects the belief that all sodomy is immoral and unacceptable. Unless the Court is prepared to conclude that such a law is constitutional, it may not rely on the work product of the Georgia Legislature to support its holding. For the Georgia statute does not single out homosexuals as a separate class meriting special disfavored treatment.

Nor, indeed, does the Georgia prosecutor even believe that all homosexuals who violate this statute should be punished. This conclusion is evident from the fact that the respondent in this very case has formally acknowledged in his complaint and in court that he has engaged, and intends to continue to engage, in the prohibited conduct, yet the State has elected not to process criminal charges against him.[66]

Stevens's language implies a strong reluctance to condemn the selective enforcement of criminal laws against homosexuals, especially where the laws themselves are generally not enforced against known offenders. As applied to the context of the same-gender partner overstay, Stevens might very well disapprove of the same selective discrimination even within the context of a civil deportation proceeding. Moreover, his decision to join the *Lawrence* and *Evans* majorities, albeit *sans* opinion, strengthens the assumption that he would be sympathetic to a same-gender partner's selective prosecution claim. The one wrinkle in this analysis, however, is that Stevens clearly distinguished between *civil* immigration and *criminal* law enforcement in *AADC,* believing that government had more power to selectively enforce deportation orders. Thus, Stevens's sympathy toward our same-gender protagonist might depend on whether he believes her rights to be treated equally to heterosexuals trump the government's right to enforce its immigration laws, albeit in a manner that prefers heterosexual marriages to gay and lesbian ones.

Unlike the anti-gay-rights Rehnquist or pro-gay-rights Stevens, Justice O'Connor switched positions from an anti-gay-rights ruling in *Hardwick* to a pro-gay-rights stance in both *Evans* and *Lawrence,* utilizing Equal Protection as her mode of analysis. More specifically, in the only opinion she penned among the three cases—her *Lawrence* concurrence—she stated that she would not vote to overturn *Hardwick* on substantive due process grounds, but instead believed that the Texas law violated the rights of gays and lesbians to be treated equally, an issue different from that raised in *Hardwick:*

In [*Hardwick*], we held that a state law criminalizing sodomy as applied to homosexual couples did not violate substantive due process. We rejected the argument that no rational basis existed to justify the law, pointing to the government's interest in promoting morality. The only question in front of the Court in [*Hardwick*] was whether the substantive component of the Due Process Clause protected a right to engage in homosexual sodomy. [*Hardwick*] did not hold that moral disapproval of a group is a rational basis under the Equal Protection Clause to criminalize homosexual sodomy when heterosexual sodomy is not punished.

This case raises a different issue than [*Hardwick*]: whether, under the Equal Protection Clause, moral disapproval is a legitimate state interest to justify by itself a statute that bans homosexual sodomy, but not heterosexual sodomy. It is not. Moral disapproval of this group, like a bare desire to harm the group, is an interest that is insufficient to satisfy rational basis review under the Equal Protection Clause.[67]

Even though she did not issue an opinion in *Hardwick,* a report of O'-Connor's views during the justices' conference support her position in *Lawrence,* suggesting that she may have regarded Mr. Hardwick's claim narrowly: "The right of privacy's source is the Fourteenth Amendment's guarantee of personal liberty. But this right is not absolute and does not extend to private, consensual homosexuality. The state's legislative power to enact this [antisodomy] law is not unconstitutional as exercised."[68] Like Justice Kennedy in *Evans,* Justice O'Connor is willing to give "bite" to the usually toothless rational basis test when the government appears to be singling out a class of people—even a nonsuspect class such as gays and lesbians—for no apparent reason than that it disapproves of their way of life. And like Kennedy's and Stevens's view on the subject, O'-Connor's opinion on the selective deportation of same-gender partners is difficult to discern. Which part of the phrase "selective deportation" would capture O'Connor's fancy—"selective," therefore implying that the government is "outrageously" singling out gays and lesbians—or "deportation," suggesting that civil deportation proceedings are not as pernicious as criminal matters, and so more deference to the ICE is warranted?

In sum, this brief review of the Court's Fourteenth Amendment gay rights jurisprudence provides us with the following very tentative array with respect to how the individual justices might rule on whether the selective deportation of a same-gender partner was "outrageous," under

Justice Scalia's *AADC* opinion: Justices Scalia, Rehnquist and Thomas would likely be unsympathetic; Justices Kennedy, Stevens, Breyer, Souter, and Ginsburg would likely be sympathetic. Justice O'Connor is the only person whose gay rights position changed between *Hardwick* and *Evans/Lawrence,* and is therefore the most difficult to predict.

But irrespective of the particular votes of this particular Court's members, on the broader issue of rights' claims by a minority group that is not a suspect class, six of the justices—Kennedy, O'Connor, Stevens, Breyer, Souter, and Ginsburg—have demonstrated their willingness to protect such claims even under the most deferential "rational basis" test if they believe that the only reason for the government's action is an unwillingness to treat the group with the same rights as others of a different sexual orientation. Scalia, Rehnquist, and Thomas, on the other hand, do not view the Court's role as the proper arbiter of a dispute over gay rights; instead, they believe that aggrieved groups seek redress from the political branches of government: the legislatures who enact the law and executive officers who enforce it.

## B. *Hurley* AND *Dale*:
### FIRST AMENDMENT LIMITS ON GAY RIGHTS

Aside from its Fourteenth Amendment substantive due process and equal protection decisions in *Hardwick/Lawrence* and *Evans,* respectively, the Court has twice examined the First Amendment rights of groups who wish not to express prohomosexual beliefs.

In *Hurley v. Irish-American Gay, Lesbian and Bisexual Group of Boston,* a unanimous Supreme Court overturned a Massachusetts court's decision to enforce the state's antidiscrimination law by requiring parade organizers to allow a gay, lesbian, and bisexual organization to participate. Since 1947, the South Boston Allied War Veterans Council has applied for, and has been granted, the right to stage Boston's annual St. Patrick's Day parade, an event that had previously been organized by the city. In 1993, the Council denied GLIB, an organization of gay, lesbian, and bisexual descendants of Irish immigrants, permission to march in the parade as an organization, although it did not discriminate against individual members from participation.[69]

In a single, unanimous opinion by Justice Souter, the Court held that the Council's decision to exclude GLIB was constitutionally protected from government coercion under the First Amendment. After finding that the parade constituted a protected expressive activity, the Court reasoned that the Council's action to exclude GLIB because of its disagreement with the latter's message was constitutionally permissible. "[W]hatever the reason, it boils down to the choice of a speaker not to propound a particular point of view, and that choice is presumed to lie beyond the government's power to control."[70] The Court also emphasized the difference between government regulating acts versus speech: "While the law is free to promote all sorts of conduct in place of harmful behavior, it is not free to interfere with speech for no better reason than promoting an approved message or discouraging a disfavored one, however enlightened either purpose may strike the government."[71]

As in *Hurley,* the *Dale* court was asked to review a state court's decision to enforce its antidiscrimination law in favor of a homosexual against a private organization. However, unlike the unanimity with which the Court decided *Hurley,* a closely divided Court produced the 5-to-4 split in *Dale* for which Chief Justice Rehnquist's majority opinion appeared next to dissents by Justices Stevens and Souter, the author of *Hurley.*

In *Boy Scouts of America v. Dale,* Justices Scalia, Thomas, Kennedy, and O'Connor joined the Chief Justice's opinion holding that the Boy Scouts could not be required by New Jersey's antidiscrimination law to readmit James Dale as an assistant scoutmaster. Dale, a longtime scout and adult member, was expelled from the Boy Scouts when they found out he was gay and a gay rights activist. The New Jersey Supreme Court ruled that the state public accommodations antidiscrimination law mandated that the Boy Scouts reinstate Dale, and that the *Hurley* case was inapposite since Dale's participation in the Boy Scouts would not compel them to express any message to which they demurred.[72]

Chief Justice Rehnquist and four others disagreed with the New Jersey court. Indeed, the majority found *Hurley* controlling:

> Here, we have found that the Boy Scouts believes that homosexual conduct is inconsistent with the values it seeks to instill in its youth members; it will not "promote homosexual conduct as a legitimate form of behavior." [] As the presence of GLIB in Boston's St. Patrick's Day parade would have interfered with the parade organizers' choice not to propound a particular point of view, the presence of Dale as an assistant scoutmaster would just as surely interfere with the Boy Scout's choice not to propound a point of view contrary to its beliefs.[73]

The Court then balanced this burden on the Boy Scouts' First Amendment rights against New Jersey's desire to protect homosexuals from discrimination, concluding that enforcement of the statute would materially interfere with the group's constitutional rights. Rehnquist noted that the state's interests did not permit such a "severe intrusion," a result which was apparently anticipated by the *Hurley* opinion.

Justices Stevens and Souter, *Hurley*'s author, each filed a dissenting opinion. Ginsburg and Breyer joined each of the opinions; Souter joined Stevens's opinion, but Stevens did not join Souter's.

Justice Stevens's six-part dissenting opinion focused largely on distinguishing *Hurley* in two key respects: first, Stevens engaged in a lengthy review of the record in this case, concluding that the Boy Scouts' allegations that its deep-seated belief that homosexuality is not "morally straight" is supported not by the underlying facts but only by bald statements in their briefs. And second, while he conceded that the Boy Scouts have a right not to have Dale advocate homosexuality in his role as assistant scoutmaster, Stevens disagreed with the majority's conclusion that Dale's very presence in a scoutmaster's uniform sends a message the Boy Scouts do not want to express:

> Dale's inclusion in the Boy Scouts is nothing like the case in *Hurley*. His participation sends no cognizable message to the Scouts or to the world. Unlike GLIB, Dale did not carry a banner or a sign; he did not distribute any fact sheet; and he expressed no intent to send any message. If there is any kind of message being sent, then, it is by the mere act of joining the Boy Scouts. Such an act does not constitute an instance of symbolic speech under the First Amendment.[74]

Thus, Stevens concluded that the only viable justification for the majority's opinion is that "homosexuals are simply so different from the rest of society that their presence alone—unlike any other individual's—should be singled out for special First Amendment treatment."[75]

Justice Souter's dissent began with an affirmation of the first five parts of Stevens's piece, but then disavowed allegiance to the sixth part, which focused on society's growing acceptance of homosexuals. Joined by Breyer and Ginsburg, Souter asserted that there is no constitutional significance to Stevens's observations: "The fact that we are cognizant of this laudable decline in stereotypical thinking on homosexuality should not, however, be taken to control the resolution of this case."[76] Thus Souter limited the grounds for his opposition to the fact that the Boy Scouts have not made "sexual orientation the subject of any unequivocal advocacy," a point Stevens highlighted in his dissent to distinguish the case from *Hurley.*

Following *Hurley,* a gay rights activist might be encouraged that *Dale* was not a unanimous opinion. However, examining the Court's language regarding the relevance of antigay stereotypes in First Amendment jurisprudence, it is clear that, save for Justice Stevens, the Court's members believe that public pro- or antihomosexual rhetoric plays no role in the Court's constitutional analysis of a free expression claim. This is evident not just in the passage from Souter's opinion quoted above, but in Chief Justice Rehnquist's admonition that greater societal tolerance of homosexuality "is scarcely an argument for denying First Amendment protection to those who refuse to accept these views." To the extent that the seven other justices—all but Stevens—signed on to either Rehnquist's or Souter's statements suggest that there is little sympathy on the Court for considering popular trends in ruling on a First Amendment challenge, even if they are supported by democratically enacted antidiscrimination legislation. Indeed, as Rehnquist opines, "[T]he fact that an idea may be embraced and advocated by increasing numbers of people is all the more reason to protect the First Amendment rights of those who wish to voice a different view."[77]

Yet, while he might agree with Rehnquist about the irrelevance of antigay sentiment in analyzing a First Amendment claim, Souter appears to welcome the idea that negative stereotypes are fading from view. Specifically, he applauds the "laudable decline" in such thinking. To the extent that Justices Breyer and Ginsburg also signed on to the Souter opinion, it is not unfair to suggest that they might likewise agree with his assessment. Justice Stevens clearly supports this belief, as demonstrated by Part VI of his opinion. Finally, given Kennedy's and O'Connor's pro-gay-rights stance in *Evans* and *Lawrence,* it is possible that these two swing voters would likewise applaud the decline of invidious sexual orientation stereotyping, especially given their apparent distaste for negative gender stereotypes, as will be explored below.

Thus, despite the fact that two (*Hurley* and *Dale*) of the four viable (i.e., *Lawrence* overruled *Hardwick*) gay rights precedents reviewed here might be described as anti–gay rights, there might be sufficient sentiment on the Court for protecting homosexuals more than is to be expected. Specifically, *Lawrence* and *Evans* teach us that a majority of the Court—

Justices Stevens, Souter, Breyer, Ginsburg, O'Connor, and Kennedy—may be unwilling to tolerate much stereotypical, animus-based discrimination against homosexuals outside the confines of a First Amendment debate. From the Court's perspective, if the core constitutional value to be protected in the First Amendment realm is that each individual should be free to express her ideas, no matter how repugnant, then discriminatory principles deserve as much protection as egalitarian ones. Outside the realm of free speech, however, the Court is less willing to tolerate discriminatory acts, even against nonsuspect classes like gays and lesbians.

Further, the Court has stated that issues of discrimination are properly raised within the context of the Fourteenth Amendment, as opposed to being grounded elsewhere in the constitution. In *Whren v. United States,* for example, the Court rejected the plaintiffs' assertions that they were constitutionally protected from racially motivated traffic stops by the Fourth Amendment's provisions for reasonable searches and seizures. Instead, the Court stated that any selective prosecution claims should be brought as alleged violations of the Fourteenth Amendment's Equal Protection Clause.[78] Interestingly, the Court in *Hurley* specifically noted that GLIB did not raise an equal protection claim and that the case was to turn instead on the Boy Scouts' First Amendment expressive association argument. While it might have had difficulty persuading the Court that sufficient state action was involved to keep the claim alive, one wonders whether GLIB might have been better off pursuing the equal protection argument, knowing now that 1996's *Evans,* another equal protection decision, followed on the heels of the 1995 *Hurley* decision.

Our hypothetical same-gender partner overstay might glean the following lesson from the preceding analysis of the Supreme Court's gay rights cases. It appears that she would be best off emphasizing discrimination claims outside the realm of First Amendment free expression (as in *Hurley* and *Dale*). Instead, a due process or equal protection analysis that emphasizes the deprivation of liberty based on extreme, animus-driven conduct by the government grounded solely on sexual orientation would be a better theme (as in *Lawrence* and *Evans*). Put another way, the justices appear reluctant to either create new rights or violate third parties' constitutional rights. Nonetheless, a majority of the Court will uphold the cause of persons unduly discriminated against because of their status rather than conduct.

This pattern of minimal judicial intervention is also reflected in the Court's recent immigration and nationality cases: *Miller v. Albright,*

*Nguyen v. INS, Demore v. Kim,* and a consolidated case—*Zadvydas v. Davis/Ashcroft v. Ma.* When it believes that the government is unfairly discriminating against a group or individual based on noncitizen status, the Court steps in to protect; if the government has a strong countervailing federal interest in maintaining the discriminatory practice, however, the Court will not interfere.

### 3. The Court's Recent Opinions on Immigrants' Rights

#### A. THE PARALLEL TO *Hardwick/Lawrence-Evans*: *Miller-Nguyen*

Just as the characterization of the claims in *Hardwick/Lawrence* (substantive due process) and *Evans* (equal protection) played such a crucial role in these cases' outcomes, so too did characterization matter in *Miller v. Albright.*[79] However, the analysis in *Miller* depended less on the constitutional claim that was asserted (equal protection) than who was asserting the right (citizen versus noncitizen). In the end, the Court's failure to reach consensus on the equal protection claim here prompted it to grant certiorari in *Nguyen v. INS*[80] on the same issue.

In *Miller v. Albright,* the Supreme Court issued a 6-to-3 decision where no opinion mustered more than three votes (indeed, the two dissenting opinions were the threesomes). Lorelyn Penero Miller, the daughter of a Filipina mother and American father who had never married, challenged a provision in the Immigration and Nationality Act requiring U.S. citizen fathers, but not mothers, to assert their paternity within eighteen years of the child's birth. Miller's primary argument was that this was a form of unconstitutional gender discrimination built into the immigration code, especially given the enhanced scientific methods of proving paternity today that made the INA provision appear to endorse the outmoded stereotype of the uncaring father. The Court upheld the statute with three pairs of justices issuing different opinions to support the holding.

Justice Stevens, writing for himself and Chief Justice Rehnquist, thought that a rational basis test (just as in *Evans*) applied to this equal protection challenge on the theory that immigration policy is subject to the plenary power of Congress. But even if a heightened form of scrutiny applied, Stevens believed that Congress's concern over fostering a good relationship between father and child while the child is a minor, among other reasons, satisfied this more stringent test.

Justice Scalia, joined by Justice Thomas, asserted that the Court had no power to provide the relief Miller requested. To the extent that Miller sought citizenship as her remedy, Scalia asserted that only Congress could confer this upon her, even if the Court was to agree with her equal protection claim.

Justice O'Connor, joined by Justice Kennedy, seemed to suggest that the viability of the gender-based equal protection claim was governed by who brought the suit. Because Miller was a noncitizen, the challenged statute, as applied to her, would be upheld under the most deferential "rational basis" standard of review. O'Connor therefore concluded that Stevens's analysis of the statute was correct. However, in an interesting piece of dicta, O'Connor noted that had Miller's father, who had been erroneously dismissed from the case, remained in the suit, the heightened scrutiny befitting a gender-based claim would have applied, and O'Connor would have voted to strike down these provisions.

The O'Connor opinion is particularly intriguing because its gender discrimination analysis tracks that of the dissenters in *Miller,* all three of whom voted to strike down the legislation. Over the course of two opinions, Justices Ginsburg, Breyer, and Souter agreed with the heightened scrutiny standard mentioned in the O'Connor dicta. Unlike O'Connor, however, none of the three justices found standing to be a relevant issue, paving the way for Miller to assert her father's gender-based claim as a third party.

The *Miller* decision is therefore as frustrating as it is encouraging for individual constitutional rights claims. On the positive side, a solid five-person majority on the Court asserted that gender-based stereotypes could not survive an equal protection challenge even within the realm of immigration and nationality law. On the other hand, the thrust of O'-Connor's dicta spoke only to the rights of citizens in conferring citizenship upon their noncitizen children born out of wedlock, rather than directly affirming the rights of the noncitizen herself. Indeed, even the Breyer dissent noted that a deferential standard of review applies "in [cases] involving aliens."

*Nguyen v. INS* resolved the issue which *Miller* left open: could the gender-based distinction governing the conferral of citizenship to an out-of-wedlock foreign child survive heightened scrutiny under the Court's equal protection jurisprudence? In a sharply divided 5-to-4 vote, Justice Kennedy, joined by Scalia, Thomas, Rehnquist, and Stevens, held that it did. Justice O'Connor, joined by Souter, Ginsburg, and Breyer, filed a dissent.

Interestingly, both the majority and dissent agreed on the proper standard to be applied here, that of heightened or intermediate scrutiny as befits gender-discrimination claims. As such, the government was charged with asserting an important governmental objective that was substantially related to the challenged gender-based classification. It was in the application of the test that the two sides differed. The majority found that the dual interests in assuring that: (1) "a biological parent-child relationship exists" and (2) "the child and the citizen parent have some demonstrated opportunity or potential to develop . . . a relationship that . . . consists of the real, everyday ties that provide a connection between child and citizen parent and, in turn, the United States" were substantially related to the gender-based classification, while the dissent rejected these ideas as the province of speculation and stereotype.

Despite Kennedy's authorship, Justice Stevens's influence was in evidence throughout the majority opinion. Aside from anchoring his analysis on two governmental objectives first identified by Stevens in *Miller,* Justice Kennedy specifically mentioned Stevens as having argued that the gender neutrality advocated by the dissent masks the real biological difference between mother (who is always present at the child's birth) and father (who may not be). Following Stevens's reasoning, Kennedy concluded that "the differential treatment is inherent in a sensible statutory scheme, given the unique relationship of the mother to the event of birth."

It is curious that Kennedy, who had joined O'Connor in *Miller,* and not Stevens, adopted much of Stevens's reasoning in *Nguyen.* This is particularly noteworthy given O'Connor's (and thus implicitly, Kennedy's) specific disavowal of Stevens's assertion in *Miller* that the statute would survive heightened scrutiny. Having been described as one with a "streak of independence"[81]—a phrase most closely associated with Stevens's jurisprudence[82]—Kennedy's decision to break ranks from his usual conservative allies was noted earlier in *Evans* and *Lawrence.*

This time, however, he abandoned the liberal wing perhaps because of his concern about granting automatic citizenship to a large number of children born of U.S. servicemen and their foreign partners. Although never explicitly stated, Kennedy's caution surfaced during his discussion about the biological differences between verifying maternity versus paternity. After stating that, unlike biological mothers, fathers may not be physically present at a child's birth, Kennedy invoked the image of the millions of American soldiers stationed abroad, noting that the vast majority are male. The implication is that Congress did not want to grant automatic citizenship to binational "G.I. babies," and that therefore the Court should be reluctant to thwart legislative intent by opening the floodgates to a stream of new citizens. While "invasion" arguments are as old as the *Chinese Exclusion Case* described in chapter 1, they are seldom tested empirically. Even assuming that automatic citizenship was conferred upon the hypothetical millions of children sired by U.S. servicemen and birthed by noncitizen women, it is likely that only a fraction of these children raised in a foreign country would opt for American citizenship, often given class, cultural, and distance barriers.

Further, Kennedy might have believed that the hardship imposed upon fathers is reasonable, unlike what he viewed as the virulent campaign waged against homosexuals in *Evans*.[83] Kennedy noted that the challenged code section provides three ways by which a parent may confer citizenship upon a child: by legitimation, court paternity order, or written acknowledgment of paternity. In addition, a child may seek citizenship separate and apart from his relationship to his biological father based on the child's own ties to the United States. In contrast, Colorado's Amendment 2 would have rendered homosexuals powerless to effect any antigay change in that state's law.

In her dissent, Justice O'Connor took the opposite view from Kennedy. She focused on the Court's departure from their recent gender-based equal protection jurisprudence, giving only lip service to the idea of heightened scrutiny. First, O'Connor questioned whether the majority's proffered interest in providing fathers the potential to have a relationship with their out-of-wedlock offspring was based on pure postlitigation argument rather than on congressional intent. But even assuming the validity of this purported goal, O'Connor argued that a gender-neutral statute requiring the physical presence or awareness of the child's birth would have satisfied this interest. Second, because of the ease of determining paternity through modern methods such as DNA testing, O'-Connor contended that protecting the statute's gender-based classification perpetuated an impermissible stereotype of the differences between mothers and fathers. Thus, O'Connor concluded that the majority's application of heightened scrutiny was incorrect, hoping that time will reveal *Nguyen* to be an aberration in the Court's equal protection jurisprudence.

Even though he penned no opinion in *Nguyen,* Justice Stevens's vote was not a surprise, given his endorsement of the challenged provision in *Miller.* Like Kennedy, Stevens probably viewed this statute as simply equalizing the parenting responsibilities placed upon mothers and fathers with respect to their illegitimate offspring. Moreover, given Stevens's prior rejection of the Court's tripartite equal protection analysis,[84] perhaps Stevens felt no qualms about upholding the challenged provision under either the "intermediate scrutiny" or "rational basis" tests. Indeed, if Stevens's ultimate concern was protecting the rights of the disadvantaged, then one can reconcile his votes in *Evans* and *Lawrence* on the one hand, and *Nguyen* on the other, by distinguishing the hardships visited by restricted voting rights and criminal sanctions based on one's sexual orientation with the less onerous burden on a father to actually take responsibility for his offspring by declaring his paternity for citizenship purposes before the child's eighteenth birthday.

Yet this analysis is not completely satisfying. Behind the citizen fathers in *Miller* and *Nguyen* were noncitizen children who were denied citizenship by virtue of the Court's rulings. Indeed, in earlier cases involving both documented and undocumented immigrants, Stevens has shown compassion for a class he has described as "already subject to disadvantages not shared by the remainder of the community," invoking the language of "discrete and insular" minority status reminiscent of the *Carolene Products*[85] case. But perhaps the question of hardship is one of degree for Stevens (and likely for Kennedy as well): notwithstanding the arguably blameless status of the noncitizen children in *Nguyen* and *Miller,* Stevens would likely distinguish the inability of homosexuals to thwart Colorado's Amendment 2 or Texas's criminal sanctions for private sexual activity from the relatively less burdensome task of seeking a declaration of paternity from one's father within an eighteen-year period under the federal law.

Of course, even this characterization fails to capture the reality that for many noncitizen children the labyrinthine Immigration and Nationality Act enforced by an overburdened federal agency may make even this apparently wide-open window of opportunity seem particularly narrow. As Stevens acknowledged previously, noncitizens "are not entitled to vote and . . . are often handicapped by a lack of familiarity with our language and customs." Add to this the difficulty Ms. Penero Miller faced in trying to have her U.S.-based father acknowledge her existence while she resided in the Philippines, and the burdens faced by the *Evans-Lawrence* and *Miller-Nguyen* plaintiffs appear not so different.

We are thus left to speculate as to how *Nguyen* might influence our analysis of a same-gender partner's selective deportation claim, in light of the *Hardwick-Lawrence* and *Evans* line of gay rights cases. One thing is clear: even though *Evans* and *Lawrence* permit an avenue of equal protection and due process argument that barred a *state's* action against homosexuals, the landscape changes when the *federal* government's interests over immigration are at stake. Justices whose views on gay rights are as diverse as Rehnquist and Stevens agree that when it comes to immigration decisions Congress has virtually unlimited power to regulate admissions and exclusions, as evidenced by their joint opinion in *Miller.* Moreover, the entire Court agreed to apply a heightened scrutiny test to the federal statute in *Nguyen* that appeared to be a shadow of the robust rational basis review applied to the state antihomosexual laws struck down in *Evans* and *Lawrence.* As Justice O'Connor noted in her *Nguyen* dissent:

> No one should mistake the majority's analysis for a careful application of this Court's equal protection jurisprudence concerning sex-based classifications. Today's decision instead represents a deviation from a line of cases in which we have vigilantly applied heightened scrutiny to such classifications to determine whether a constitutional violation has occurred. I trust that the depth and vitality of these precedents will ensure that today's error remains an aberration.[86]

The constitutional immigration law cases we have examined thus far—*Miller, Nguyen,* and *AADC*—appear to grant much power to the government in the areas of immigration and nationality law, leaving only an undefined egregious selective enforcement claim as possible constitutional armor for deportable noncitizens. When viewed in light of the gay rights cases explored earlier—*Lawrence, Evans, Hurley,* and *Dale*—the case of our foreign same-gender partner overstay might appear to be a loser: of the seven cases examined so far, the individual rights claimant— either the homosexual or the noncitizen—has lost five of the seven times, prevailing only in *Evans* and *Lawrence,* both of which are gay rights, and not immigration, cases.

Yet the "outrageous" language from *AADC* coupled with the holdings in *Lawrence* and *Evans* might provide sufficient ammunition for our hypothetical deportee when viewed in the light of three cases—in reality, one pair of related cases and one constitutional due process case—recently decided by the Supreme Court. Each of the previous seven cases reviewed emphasizes two important factors that the Court weighs in deciding whether to uphold the individual rights claim: whether the plaintiff asks for equal rather than special treatment in response to the government's discriminatory conduct and whether there is a legitimate countervailing federal or constitutional interest to justify the prejudice. The following analysis will demonstrate how egregious, unjustifiable governmental conduct raises serious constitutional questions, even within the political, often nonjusticiable realm of immigration law.

## B. THE COURT'S JUNE 2001 SUBCONSTITUTIONAL DECISION ON INDEFINITE DETENTION — *Zadvydas*

Thus far we have examined the direct application of constitutional norms to immigration and nationality cases by reviewing the Court's decisions in *Miller, Nguyen,* and *AADC.* In each of these three cases, we have noted how the Court has deferred to congressional and INS power over immigration matters, even when it has claimed to be exercising a heightened review of their actions, as in *Nguyen.* Given the ineffectiveness of directly applying constitutional norms in immigration cases, legal scholar Hiroshi Motomura has identified a second way by which the Court has historically protected noncitizens' rights through phantom subconstitutional norms to circumvent the question of the political branches' plenary power over immigration.[87] Motomura argues that because the plenary power doctrine has by and large insulated anti-immigrant legislation from review, federal courts have often chosen to protect immigrants by interpreting immigration statutes in their favor.

Relatedly, the Court's June 2001 subconstitutional decision on indefinite detention within deportation might shed some light on the availability of five votes in favor of our hypothetical same-gender partner overstay. The issue in *Zadvydas* was not constitutional in nature—indeed, the Court took great pains to describe its holding as statutory—yet, the Constitution informed how the five-person majority found in favor of the immigrants. Specifically, the Court held that the statutory provision had to be read to avoid a serious constitutional question, which is a well-known canon of statutory construction.[88]

The issue before the Court involved whether the federal government had the power to indefinitely detain a noncitizen who could not be deported because no country was willing to receive her. In the consolidated cases *Zadvydas v. Davis* and *Ashcroft v. Ma* (collectively *"Zadvydas"*) the Court held that the statutory provision governing the INS's power to detain pending deportation must be construed to avoid a Fifth Amendment substantive due process violation, thereby requiring that a reasonable limitation be placed on the government's power though no such language appears in the statute's text. Both Kestutis Zadvydas and Kim Ho Ma had been adjudged deportable after having committed certain criminal offenses; after they had been detained pursuant to statute, however, they could not effectively be deported because their respective receiving countries would not grant them entry. Indeed, for Ma, the prospect of ever returning to Cambodia had been made even less likely because Cambodia had no repatriation agreement with the United States at the time.[89]

Justice Breyer, joined by O'Connor, Stevens, Souter, and Ginsburg, noted that "the Due Process Clause applies to all 'persons' within the United States, including aliens, whether their presence here is lawful, unlawful, temporary, or permanent." In the past, indefinite civil detention has been reserved for particularly dangerous individuals whose mental incapacity, for example, rendered them a continuing threat to society. In contrast, Breyer noted that deportees do not generally impose such a threat, nor is their detention to be construed a punishment, unlike in the criminal law context.

Next, Breyer distinguished the deportees' condition from that of a person first entering the United States. In response to the government's assertion that its plenary power over immigration supported its action here, the Court held that, unlike the indefinite detention on Ellis Island of a former U.S. resident in *Shaughnessy v. U.S. ex rel Mezei*[90] (discussed in chapter 1), the indefinite detention of one who has already entered the United States was subject to closer constitutional examination than the detention and exclusion of a returning noncitizen who has technically not entered the country. Breyer concluded by reading a presumptive 180–day limit on detention into the statute; should the government be unable to prove that the noncitizen would foreseeably be deported, she must be granted supervised release. To do otherwise would be to deny her a substantive right under the Due Process Clause to be free from arbitrary indefinite detention without any realistic chance of being deported.

Both Justices Scalia and Kennedy filed dissenting opinions, with Thomas joining Scalia, and Rehnquist joining Kennedy. Scalia asserted that a deportee had no constitutional right to be paroled into the United States when she enjoyed no right to be here in the first place:

> A criminal alien under final order of removal who allegedly will not be accepted by any other country in the reasonably foreseeable future claims a constitutional right of supervised release into the United States. This claim can be repackaged as freedom from "physical restraint" or freedom from "indefinite detention," but it is at bottom a claimed right of release into this country by an individual who concededly has no legal right to be here. There is no such constitutional right.[91]

He then distinguished precedents involving the torture or commitment to hard labor of a deportee, arguing that such cases have nothing to do with the claimed right to supervised parole, which was the issue here. Under no circumstances, Scalia concluded, could the federal courts require the INS to release an individual who had been fairly adjudged deportable according to established administrative processes. *Mezei,* the case involving the possible indefinite detention on Ellis Island, controlled Scalia's analysis here and marked his departure from the majority's view.

Kennedy's opinion took less strict a stance than Scalia's by not ruling out the possibility of judicial intervention in some instances. Kennedy disagreed with the majority's construction of the statute at issue, especially its creation of a specific time period after which supervised release must be provided should deportation no longer be forthcoming. Describing this new rule as having been "invented by the Court," Kennedy then moved on to uphold the statute's constitutionality, stating that a person who has substantive objections to a detention order may challenge them in a habeas proceeding where the facts can be fully litigated:

> The Government has conceded that habeas jurisdiction is available under 28 U. S. C. §2241 to review an alien's challenge to detention following entry of a final order of deportation, although it does not detail what the nature of the habeas review would be. As a result, we need not decide today whether, and to what extent, a habeas court could review the Attorney General's determination that a detained alien continues to be dangerous or a flight risk. Given the undeniable deprivation of liberty caused by the detention, there might be substantial questions concerning the severity necessary for there to be a community risk; the adequacy of judicial review in specific cases where it is alleged there is no justification

for concluding an alien is dangerous or a flight risk; and other issues. These matters are not presented to us here.[92]

Unlike the majority, Kennedy preferred a lower court's case-by-case analysis of a specific detention rather than a blanket subconstitutional rule outlawing indefinite detention, which Congress did not intend. Put differently, Kennedy saw the possible constitutional issue as one involving procedural due process, which he believed was satisfied by the current safeguards even if they led to possible indefinite detention, rather than the broader substantive due process violation that the majority hoped to avoid through a narrower reading of the INS's power under the statute.

## C. THE COURT'S 2003 CONSTITUTIONAL LAW DECISION IN *Demore v. Kim*

In April 2003, the Court had the opportunity to apply its holding in *Zadvydas* in yet another 5-to-4 decision in *Demore v. Kim.* As mentioned earlier, while *Zadvydas* was a statutory interpretation case, constitutional law claims prominently undergirded both the majority's and the dissent's analysis. In *Demore v. Kim,* a majority of the Court chose to address the constitutional due process issue head on, rather than rely on statutory analysis.

In *Kim,*[93] Chief Justice Rehnquist was joined on the merits by Scalia, Thomas, Kennedy, and O'Connor in holding that Congress could require that a lawful permanent resident be detained pending deportation without violating the Due Process Clause of the Fifth Amendment. Korean citizen Hyung Joon Kim, a lawful permanent resident since the age of eight, was sought to be deported by the INS following his commission of two theft crimes in California. He was immediately detained pursuant to the mandatory detention provisions of the Immigration and Nationality Act. After spending three months in detention while awaiting his deportation hearing, Kim filed for habeas relief, arguing that because he was a lawful permanent resident, the Due Process Clause of the Fifth Amendment entitled him to be free from detention while he awaited his hearing, absent a showing by the government that he was either a flight risk or a public danger. The district court reviewing his habeas petition agreed, citing *Zadvydas,* and opined that as a lawful permanent resident, Kim had a due process liberty right to be free from mandatory detention unless the government could otherwise justify his incarceration. The Ninth Circuit affirmed.

The Supreme Court reversed, 5-to-4. Writing for the majority, Chief Justice Rehnquist began his constitutional analysis by citing the federal alienage benefits case of *Mathews v. Diaz,* which signaled that the Court would rely on the "plenary power" doctrine to subject Congress's action to minimal scrutiny. As we have discussed throughout this book, citation of the plenary power doctrine is virtually determinative of the outcome; the result was no different here. Rehnquist rejected Kim's substantive claim because he believed *Zadvydas* was distinguishable in two respects: first, *Zadvydas* involved noncitizens who could not reasonably expect to be deported to their home countries, whereas the mandatory detention statute in *Kim* involved only those who were being detained pending their eventual deportation. Thus the purposes of the mandatory detention were different in the two cases: in *Kim,* mandatory detention was Congress's way of ensuring that noncitizens would be physically present throughout the proceedings prior to their eventual removal; in contrast, in *Zadvydas,* mandatorily detaining deportees who could not be removed served no reasonable goal consistent with due process. Second, the detention in *Zadvydas* was potentially indefinite because of the government's inability to effect deportation; in *Kim,* detention would last only until the noncitizen was adjudged deportable and could be removed, which in most cases was completed within two months.

Justice Souter, joined by Ginsburg and Stevens, read *Zadvydas* more broadly, arguing that because Kim was a lawful permanent resident, the Constitution granted him more protection than other noncitizens such that he was presumed to be free from detention for immigration law enforcement purposes unless the government could prove that he was a flight risk or a public danger. Drawing from the Court's precedents in criminal procedure, Souter argued for a more stringent review of the mandatory detention statute: "[T]he Fifth Amendment permits detention only where 'heightened, substantive due process scrutiny' finds a 'sufficiently compelling' governmental need." Thus Souter noted that Kim had already served his time for the California offenses, had not been adjudged deportable by any immigration court, and had not been found to be a flight risk or a public danger. Even though he was charged with a deportable offense, the government had the burden to prove that he was in fact deportable based on the crimes he had committed, and it had not done so. Unless it could prove that Kim would otherwise abscond or endanger others, the government had no right to detain him while he waited for his day in immigration court, Souter concluded.

Justices O'Connor, Kennedy, and Breyer wrote separately to draw distinctions from the Rehnquist and Souter positions. O'Connor (joined by Scalia and Thomas) would have dismissed the case for lack of jurisdiction; she believed that Congress had precluded the courts from reviewing Kim's habeas petition. While he joined Rehnquist's opinion in full, Kennedy wrote to reiterate his position from *Zadvydas*, that Kim might be entitled to a hearing should there be proof that the government was detaining him for a reason other than to effect his deportation. Breyer also fell back on his *Zadvydas* opinion. Instead of siding with Souter to rule on the constitutionality of the mandatory detention provision, Breyer opted instead to import limiting rules from criminal procedure that would provide Kim sufficient protection to avoid a constitutional problem.

Let us examine O'Connor's and Kennedy's voting patterns in the immigrants' rights cases we have discussed. In *Miller* and *Kim*, they agree on the merits, while they disagree in *Nguyen* and *Zadvydas*. And as applied to our selective deportation issue, the question for these two justices inevitably becomes one of degree: To what extent is the government's conduct so "outrageous" that constitutional equality norms found in the Equal Protection and Due Process clauses require the Court to check such action? Put another way, how do we balance the fact that foreign same-gender partners of U.S. citizens are "double-minorities" (i.e., alienage and sexual orientation) on the one hand, against the government's legitimate need to enforce its immigration law as part of its sovereign power, on the other?

The other seven justices appear to be clearer on this issue, with perhaps the exception of Justice Stevens, who, as discussed earlier, sometimes defers to the federal legislative and executive enforcement bodies when it comes to immigration and citizenship matters. Justices Scalia, Thomas, and Rehnquist generally favor the government over individual rights claimants, whether gays and lesbians or immigrants. Justices Breyer, Souter, and Ginsburg fall on the opposite end, siding more often with the disfavored class against the government.

Thinking back to the two equality norms of antiessentialism and antisubordination, Scalia, Rehnquist, and Thomas see their role as justices as largely divorced from the political policymaking that might help give shape and substance to one's interpretation of antiessentialism and antisubordination. Put differently, these justices believe that the legislature is the appropriate branch for discussions of whether and how individuals might be grouped and characterized (antiessentialism) and helped or hindered (antisubordination). As Justice Thomas noted in his *Lawrence* dissent siding with upholding the Texas ban against homosexual sodomy:

> If I were a member of the Texas Legislature, I would vote to repeal it. Punishing someone for expressing his sexual preference through non-commercial consensual conduct with another adult does not appear to be a worthy way to expend valuable law enforcement resources.
>
> Notwithstanding this, I recognize that as a member of this Court I am not empowered to help petitioners and others similarly situated. My duty, rather, is to "decide cases 'agreeably to the Constitution and laws of the United States.'" And, just like Justice Stewart, I "can find [neither in the Bill of Rights nor any other part of the Constitution a] general right of privacy," or as the Court terms it today, the "liberty of the person both in its spatial and more transcendent dimensions."[94]

Breyer, Ginsburg, and Souter, on the other hand, see their roles as justices as affirming antiessentialist and antisubordination principles through their interpretation of the Due Process and Equal Protection clauses of the Constitution. Unlike the others, it appears they are not as troubled by broader interpretations of the Constitution's text or precedent, if such interpretations are consistent with modern antiessentialist and antisubordination principles. In *Miller,* for example, Justice Breyer took the majority to task for adhering to stereotypical and discriminatory views in holding that biological differences between men and women could constitutionally be codified in U.S. citizenship law:

> Since the founding of our Nation, American statutory law, reflecting a long-established legal tradition, has provided for the transmission of American citizenship from parent to child—even when the child is born abroad. Today's case focuses upon statutes that make those children, when born out of wedlock, "citizens of the United States at birth." The statutes, as applied where only one parent is American, require the American parent—whether father or mother—to prove the child is his or hers and to meet a residency requirement. The statutes go on to require (1) that the American parent promise to provide financial support for the child until the child is 18, and (2) that the American parent (or a

court) legitimate or formally acknowledge the child before the child turns 18—*if and only if the American parent is the father,* but not if the parent is the mother.

What sense does it make to apply these latter two conditions only to fathers and not to mothers in today's world—where paternity can readily be proved and where women and men both are likely to earn a living in the workplace?[95]

In between these two positions lie Justices Kennedy and O'Connor, and to a lesser extent Justice Stevens. While all three appear to feel strongly about the rights of gays and lesbians, they just as forcefully embrace the idea that immigration law and policy are the province of the legislative and executive branches, not the courts. To the extent that these justices embrace the principles of antiessentialism and antisubordination (as Stevens did in *Hardwick,* and Kennedy and O'Connor did in *Evans* and *Lawrence,* respectively) in the context of our selective deportation hypothetical, they will need to be convinced that the government is unfairly singling out a vulnerable group. Otherwise, they would likely defer to the need to enforce our immigration laws, irrespective of whether they personally agree with these laws or not (à la Thomas in *Lawrence*). Legal scholar Cass Sunstein has coined the phrase "judicial minimalism," arguing that cautious, precise adjudication on the facts presented is the hallmark of wise judicial decision making, and often holding up Justice O'Connor's opinions as exemplars of this approach.[96] While we certainly want our judges to be careful, we also want them to be wise. Opinions such as *Brown v. Board of Education* (and perhaps over time, *Lawrence v. Texas*) are commonly believed to be landmark decisions because they reflect the Supreme Court's ability to defend subordinated groups in the face of majoritarian prejudice, irrespective of whether they pass muster under a particular constitutional theory.

These particular justices' views aside, the next section explores what a Court's opinion might look like should it choose to favor our hypothetical plaintiff, on the one hand, or rule in favor of the government, on the other. It concludes that, on balance, the selective deportation of same-gender partner overstays should constitute an "outrageous" case under the *AADC* test.

## Why the Selective Deportation of Same-Gender Partner Overstays Should Constitute the "Rara Avis"

The "outrageous" test articulated by Scalia in *AADC* appears to be another version of the "minimal protection" test that has led to the protection of individual rights in both the gay rights and immigrants' rights cases. In *Evans*, the Court applied what appeared to be a heightened scrutiny test masquerading as rational basis to prevent particularly invidious sexual discrimination under the Equal Protection Clause; it did the same with the Due Process Clause in *Lawrence*. In *Zadvydas*, substantive due process was invoked as a limit on the statutory interpretation of immigration laws that might otherwise excessively curtail noncitizens' rights.

However, the cases in which the Court chose to protect the homosexual or the noncitizen stand in contrast to the majority of the cases reviewed in which the Court deferred to majoritarian sentiment against gays and noncitizens because it believed these groups sought special rights rather than minimum equal treatment. In *Hardwick*, the Court narrowly characterized the case as a claim for a special right to engage in homosexual sodomy rather than as a broader right of privacy to deny protection under the disfavored substantive due process doctrine. Similarly, the *Miller-Nguyen*, *Kim*, and *AADC* courts chose not to interfere in the executive and legislative branches' decisions over immigration matters, even though in *Nguyen* the Court purported to apply heightened scrutiny to the challenged legislation. Finally, in *Hurley* and *Dale* the Court refused to give credence to the dictates of a single state's law over the national, constitutional rights owing to private groups who choose to discriminate against homosexuals.

Thus, the Court will strike down legislative or executive action only if a majority believes two elements have been fulfilled: (1) the plaintiff has been unfairly deprived of a right open to all and asks only for "equal," as opposed to "special," treatment; and (2) there is no legitimate governmental interest in protecting the will of the majority of the people opposed to providing equal treatment, either through legislative policy, executive action, or the expression of a core constitutional value.

### 1. Equal, but Not Special, Rights

To make her case, the same-gender partner overstay will, like the plaintiffs in *Evans* and *Lawrence*, need to convince the Court that her selective deportation is particularly egregious—indeed, "outrageous"—and not the product of some rational distinction between homosexuals and other deportees. Though not a constitutional law decision, *Zadvydas* might provide her with analogous facts, urging the Court to broaden its protection of nonimmigrants currently in the United States so that they are treated like all other deportees whose sexual orientation conforms to societal norms.

The decision to deport same-gender partner overstays simply because they are homosexual has the same sweeping, irrational quality to it that Amendment 2 had in *Evans* and the Texas antigay sodomy statute had in *Lawrence*. While admittedly more narrow in its scope because a deportation order affects the noncitizen homosexuals' immigration status only, for the noncitizen the barrier erected by that decision is arguably as insurmountable as the virtual dilution of voting power created by the Coloradans or the criminalization of private sexual activity under the Texas code. Indeed, because the ICE's policy would be of national scope, it would have a far more widespread impact on gays and lesbians than a single state's discriminatory act. Thus, a class action claim would be the best vehicle for a frontal assault on such a policy.

To prove that theirs is an "equal rights" (and not "special rights") claim, our hypothetical class action plaintiffs should: (1) present specific evidence of homophobic conduct by the ICE; (2) show that they are productive members of society; (3) emphasize that they seek no change in existing law, but only that their deportability be considered separate and apart from their sexual orientation; and (4) draw analogies to the Court's decision in *Zadvydas*, arguing that extreme unfairness may not be visited upon even non-U.S. citizens.

To bolster the analogy, persuasive evidence will first need to be gathered to demonstrate the animus required by *Evans*. A written formal or informal policy of deporting same-gender partners supported by documentary evidence of invidious discrimination would provide the best case. A good example would be the INS letter that *Adams v. Howerton* plaintiffs Richard Adams and Tony Sullivan received regarding their request that Mr. Sullivan, an Australian, be classified as Mr. Adams's spouse:

Upon consideration, it is ordered that your visa petition filed on April 28, 1975 for classification of Anthony Corbett Sullivan as the spouse of a United States citizen be denied for the following reasons: You have failed to establish that a bona fide marital relationship can exist between two faggots.[97]

Second, evidence that the ICE generally does not deport productive out-of-status noncitizens would likewise suggest animus. In March 2000, the *New York Times* reported that the INS (now ICE) doesn't even bother deporting undocumented immigrants any more, only those who they discover later have criminal records.[98] Because of the then-booming U.S. economy and these undocumented immigrants' willingness to do work no U.S. workers would perform, the INS had decided to concentrate its deportation efforts elsewhere, targeting mostly those with criminal records. If our hypothetical overstays demonstrated their contributions to the general welfare through employment, the payment of taxes, caring for children, volunteer work, or a host of other productive activities, then the immigration authority's policy of selectively choosing them becomes even more suspect, especially in light of current prosecutorial discretion guidelines.

A third point, and one crucial to the deportees' claim, would be to assert that they are not looking to have the law changed to promote homosexuality. As discussed above, the thrust of their argument is that they be treated as any heterosexual overstay, without consideration of their homosexual relationships. They would do well to avoid the *Hardwick* trap by not claiming a special right to which gays should be entitled. Relying instead on the *Evans* and *Lawrence* analysis along with strong evidence of animus and a vow not to change existing law, our fictional deportees could provide the Court with a firm doctrinal basis for finding the selective deportation constitutionally "outrageous" under *AADC*.

Fourth and finally, analogies should be made to the deprivation of rights discussed in *Zadvydas*. Read broadly, *Zadvydas* stands for the proposition that there exists a minimum level of protection afforded noncitizens regardless of Congress's plenary power over immigration and the ICE's *Chevron* power to enforce the law. Just as the government may not indefinitely detain certain noncitizens, neither may it rely on sexual orientation as a basis for prioritizing deportability.

In response, the government might characterize the selective deportation argument as a claim for special treatment by a nonsuspect class, relying on *Nguyen* and *Hardwick* by drawing distinctions between homosexuals and heterosexuals. It might also argue that *Evans, Lawrence,* and *Zadvydas* be read narrowly to apply to only extreme deprivations of liberty and due process, just as it did in distinguishing *Zadvydas* from *Kim*. As will be shown below, such arguments fail to persuade because they offend our common sense of justice and fair play.

First, the government might look to *Nguyen* for guidance, not so much doctrinally as thematically. In *Nguyen,* the Court applied an intermediate scrutiny test in a most deferential way, finding that the actual differences between men and women supported Congress's gender-based citizenship statute. Thus, the Court concluded that the statute's distinctions were not rooted in invidious stereotype. Similarly, the ICE may argue that its decision to deport same-gender partner overstays may be based on rational bases and not homophobic animus or stereotype. To the extent that Congress's decision to pass the Defense of Marriage Act stemmed from a desire to preserve the traditional institution of heterosexual marriage and not to condemn homosexuality, the ICE would contend that its decision to deport same-gender partner overstays simply enforces that national policy. Like the father in *Nguyen,* the hypothetical overstay is not entitled to special treatment, but is rather subject to differential treatment based on her different sexual orientation, which provides her no unique protection under the law as even the *Evans* majority acknowledged.

While the above arguments from *Nguyen* appear doctrinally sound, they fail to pass the "common sense" test (and certainly violate our equality themes of antiessentialism and antisubordination). *Nguyen* did not involve the specific targeting of a disadvantaged group because of its status; rather, the Court acknowledged the reality that males in the armed services should be held responsible for their foreign-born, out-of-wedlock offspring, a responsibility that is borne solely by the noncitizen mother. Gays and lesbians deported *en masse* because of their same-gender relationships suffer a much greater disability than U.S. citizen fathers, both within immigration law and in society generally. Put another way, homosexuals of both genders fit the description of a "discrete and insular minority" more closely than heterosexual males in the armed services, and therefore deserve more protection. In antisubordination terms, fathers are a privileged class, while gays and lesbians are not.

Even if the Court found the themes in *Nguyen* inapposite, the ICE might contend that the deprivation of immigration benefits does not confer upon the same-gender partner overstay as broad-based a disability as Amendment 2 envisioned. Just as the noncitizen in *Nguyen* had available several different ways of establishing citizenship despite having a U.S. citizen father, the same-gender partner overstay need not rely on her U.S.

citizen partner to remain in the United States. Indeed, both employment and diversity visas are avenues open to all prospective immigrants, same-gender partners included.

However, as argued earlier, mass selective deportation based on sexual orientation has the potential to affect a greater number of homosexuals than Colorado's Amendment 2, which would have applied only to state residents. In addition, the availability of other avenues for remaining in the United States does not legitimize a homophobic deportation policy. An analogy to interracial marriages might clarify this point. Because a black noncitizen can immigrate to the United States by obtaining either an employment or diversity visa does not justify denying him the opportunity to obtain a family-based visa because he chooses to marry a white U.S. citizen. In our hypothetical, the same-gender deportee does not even go that far. She does not ask that the immigration code be changed to allow for same-gender immigration benefits; she wants only to be treated as any heterosexual overstay.

Finally, the ICE might argue that analogies to *Lawrence* and *Zadvydas* are unconvincing, describing criminalization of private sexual activity and indefinite detention, respectively, as more extreme abuses of governmental power than the decision to deport an admittedly removable noncitizen, albeit one who was selectively chosen. *Kim,* the government would argue, is the more persuasive precedent. The decision to temporarily detain someone to effect her deportation is like the decision to deport someone, even if the basis for that deportation does not apply to all noncitizens. To put this more concretely, Ms. Camacho knew when she applied for her student visa that hers was a temporary status and that she could not remain in the United States as an immigrant despite her marriage to Ms. Sanders. Yet she decided to overstay anyway. Just as the *Kim* court upheld the logical decision to detain deportees pending their removal, the government would argue that, similarly, the Court should uphold the civil, not criminal, deportation of foreign same-gender partners for failing to comply with the terms of their conditional entry.

While *Lawrence* and *Zadvydas* focus on arguably more extreme deprivations of due process, there is no principled reason to limit either case to its specific facts. That Lawrence, Garner, Zadvydas, and Ma suffered significant hardships does not mean that same-gender partner overstays selectively chosen for mass deportation would not. Selectively choosing someone to be deported because that person is gay offends our sensibilities much in the same way that criminalizing homosexual sodomy and indefinite detention do. All three governmental acts are abuses of power that the Court should not tolerate.

On balance, despite the government's best efforts to ground its defense of a sexual orientation–based selective deportation policy in doctrine and traditional values, our hypothetical same-gender partner overstay's claim sounds not in special rights but in equal rights when viewed from the vantage point of basic fairness. Common sense suggests that the selective targeting of homosexuals for deportation based on their status alone imposes upon an already vilified class of persons a sweeping disability, not unlike discrimination based on race or gender.

## 2. No Countervailing Federal or Constitutional Interest in Selective Deportation of Same-Gender Partner Overstays

Even if it accepts the view that our same-gender partner overstay seeks only equal and not special treatment, the Court will still inquire whether there is a legitimate countervailing governmental interest to preserve majoritarian antigay and anti-immigrant outcomes through legislative fiat, executive action, or constitutional imperative. Despite the fact that the majority of the cases reviewed here suggest that the Court usually defers to antigay and anti-immigrant legislative or executive action, the following discussion demonstrates that there is no legitimate reason for the Court to support the selective deportation of foreign same-gender partner overstays.

*Evans, Zadvydas,* and *Lawrence* all suggest that, while it is often reluctant to do so, the Court will intervene to elevate the rights of gays and noncitizens if there is no good countervailing reason to do otherwise. In *Evans,* the Court concluded that the very essence of equal protection was the requirement that all have access to the political process, something denied homosexuals for no other reason than their sexual orientation. In *Zadvydas,* indefinite detention was adjudged too punitive a consequence that would deprive due process rights to even those individuals adjudged deportable. And in *Lawrence,* the Court overruled *Hardwick* to conclude that due process "liberty" protects gays and lesbians against criminal sanctions for engaging in purely private, consensual sexual activity. Analogously, the Court might find that the government has no rational reason to deport same-gender overstays based solely on their sexual orientation and that they should be considered for deportation or deferral like any other group.

But despite this line of precedent, the Court may submit to the expertise of federal executive and legislature decision makers or may seek to preserve a constitutional core value. Regardless of the motive behind the Court's action, the result would nonetheless sustain discrimination against gays and lesbians. Thus, the *Miller-Nguyen, Kim,* and *AADC* courts chose not to interfere in the executive and legislative branches' decisions over immigration matters, even though in *Nguyen* the Court purported to apply heightened scrutiny to the challenged legislation. Where the Court appears to trust the relative expertise of the political branches on immigration and nationality issues, it chooses to give credence to the proffered reasons for the government's action. In *AADC,* for instance, the Court was unwilling to intervene despite the assertion of a First Amendment right on the part of the deportable noncitizens for fear of diminishing the political branches' power to combat international terrorism. Similarly, in *Kim,* the Court distinguished its holding in *Zadvydas,* upholding Congress's blanket decision to detain all deportees prior to their hearings. And in *Nguyen,* the Court was reluctant to strike down a gender distinction that could effectively lead to the conferral of automatic citizenship on numbers greater than those contemplated by Congress. Finally, in *Hurley* and *Dale* the Court refused to give credence to the dictates of a single state's law over the federal constitutional rights owing to private groups who choose to discriminate against homosexuals.

Yet, unlike in *Nguyen, Kim, AADC,* or *Hurley-Dale,* there is no valid reason to defer to Congress and the ICE should they decide to single out same-gender partner overstays for deportation. Unlike in *Nguyen, Kim,* or *AADC,* there is no threat of unduly interfering with the legislature or executive's power over immigration since the remedy sought by the deportee is that the decision to deport her first be examined without regard to her sexual orientation. Should the ICE still decide she should be deported, it may pursue her removal. Furthermore, unlike fears of the automatic conferral of citizenship in *Nguyen,* the flight risk or public danger posed by criminal deportees in *Kim,* or the promotion of terrorism in *AADC,* asking the ICE to reconsider its deportation decision free of sexual orientation bias carries no similar negative consequence for immigration policy. Lastly, unlike in *Hurley* or *Dale,* there is no private party with a vested interest in preventing the same-gender partner overstay from asserting a right to equal treatment. While Congress has passed the Defense of Marriage Act to limit the federal rights of same-gender couples, our protagonist does not seek to be accorded federal marriage benefits in a way analogous to Dale wanting to be part of the Boy Scouts. The same-gender partner overstay seeks only to be treated like any other overstay, and the government has no apparently good reason to do otherwise.

## Epilogue: The United States Lags Behind on Gay Rights Issues in Immigration Law

U.S. citizen Richard Adams and Australian national Tony Sullivan were married by a Boulder city clerk in Colorado in 1975, hoping to be able to reside permanently in the United States just as any heterosexual binational couple could.[99] Because the Ninth Circuit construed the INA term "spouse" to refer to those involved in heterosexual marriages only and denied Sullivan's claims of hardship should he be deported,[100] however, Sullivan has been forced to live in the United States as a fugitive from the ICE just so that he can be with Adams.

The deported foreigner is not the only person adversely affected; the U.S. citizen partner is likewise harmed. For instance, one U.S. citizen in another binational relationship expressed sadness about being effectively "forced to leave his own country because of his own government's discriminatory laws."[101] This couple has since moved to Canada where gays and lesbians are more protected under the law.

Aside from Canada, fifteen other nations also provide immigration benefits to same-gender partners.[102] Indeed, one of the fifteen recently took the next step in moving toward parity for homosexual relationships. As of April 1, 2001, all same-gender marriages performed in the Netherlands have the same force and effect as traditional heterosexual marriages.[103] As of this writing, developments in Belgium and Canada suggest that these nations are not far behind.

Two commentators predict that soon enough, an American citizen will marry a Dutch citizen in a same-gender ceremony in the Netherlands and then seek recognition of that union in the United States.[104] While this scenario implicates more than the conferral of immigration benefits, it does present a problem that will likely require governmental attention at some point in the not-too-distant future. In an effort to resolve this complex issue, many others have argued for the extension of immigration benefits to same-gender couples[105] or the national legalization of gay marriages.[106]

This chapter has a much less ambitious agenda: it seeks only to explore the possibility that the selective deportation of a same-gender partner who has overstayed her visa constitutes an outrageous case under the *AADC* test. Its modest goal is to discourage the ICE from ever pursuing such a strategy, knowing that there are probably many who believe that same-gender partner overstays, even if married in Massachusetts, are not the ideal candidates for "suspect class" status (and therefore, unlike racial minorities, do not enjoy substantial constitutional protection). That notwithstanding, common sense, equality principles, and sound doctrine suggest that, despite the many antigay and anti-immigrant decisions handed down since 1986, the Court will not hesitate to halt egregious government conduct when the plaintiff is being deprived of equal rights and there is no legitimate countervailing reason to justify the discrimination. In the hypothetical mass deportation of same-gender partner overstays, this chapter applies such an approach while breathing life into the as-yet-undefined "outrageous" exception test created by the *AADC* Court.

# 7

## The Equal Noncitizen
### *Alternatives in Theory and Practice*

The previous chapters surveyed the myriad ways in which the American legal system fails to fulfill the Constitution's promise of equality regarding its treatment of noncitizens. Throughout the book I have attempted to provide concrete solutions to the problems posed, some theoretical, some practical, always measuring their viability against the twin yardsticks of antiessentialism and antisubordination. Chapter 1 explored the persistence of the plenary power doctrine as a constitutional limit on immigrants' rights, noting the racial and ideological contexts underlying the cases, as well as highlighting the way the doctrine and its biases have affected my navigation of American immigration and citizenship law as a Filipino native. In chapter 2, I focused on the role immigration policy and racial profiling have played in the government's post-9/11 war against terrorism. Chapters 3 through 6 examined the case of certain nonterrorist "others"—foreign-born adoptees, undocumented migrants, and same-gender partner overstays—and questioned whether our laws and policies provided them sufficient protection from discriminatory public action. This concluding chapter seeks to explore both theoretical and practical alternatives to the status quo that advance the cause of equality by promoting both antiessentialism and antisubordination.

### *Membership versus Personhood: Cognitive Psychology, Critical Race Theory, and Common Sense*

For the United States, how to properly allocate immigrants' rights is particularly difficult because of two competing values that lie at the core of American legal history and culture: the conception of the United States as

an immigrant nation on the one hand, and the notion of limiting resources and rights to U.S. citizens only on the other. Images of the former
include the Statue of Liberty, Ellis Island, multiculturalism, the melting
pot. In contrast, the latter notion conjures up visions of the Chinese Exclusion Act, World War II internment camps, current anti-Arab and Muslim violence, Proposition 187, welfare reform. Not surprisingly, the U.S.
Supreme Court's jurisprudence in the area of noncitizens' rights demonstrates this dichotomy between the celebration of the personhood of immigrants (*a personhood theory*) on the one hand, and the denial of equal
status for noncitizens as nonmembers (*a membership theory*) on the
other.

This next section will briefly examine the history of three immigrant
groups in America and the competing theories underlying the Supreme
Court's jurisprudence—*personhood* versus *membership*— in an effort to
gain a better understanding of the challenges U.S. citizens face in balancing the need to restrict membership in this society against the interest in
protecting all persons' rights.

## 1. A Historical Perspective: Non-English White, Chinese, and Mexican Immigrants

Throughout U.S. history, our law affecting immigration and noncitizens' rights has reflected a tension between welcoming the immigrant as
a person entitled to the same legal protections and benefits as citizens on
the one hand, and denigrating the immigrant as one outside the circle of
national membership on the other. To illustrate this tension, this section
will briefly discuss how three groups in U.S. history—the non-English
whites, the Chinese, and the Mexicans—have been alternately treated as
insiders and outsiders by the U.S. citizenry. In reviewing this history, two
patterns emerge: where the out-group can be characterized by the majority as possessing attributes similar to the majority's or as helping to further the majority's interests, then discrimination abates; however, where
the out-group is viewed as different and threatening, discrimination esca-
lates.

In early America, there was no federal immigration law as it is currently thought of today. Rather, America was "the New World," free to
be populated by those fleeing religious persecution in Europe. Through
the 1700s, many of the first immigrants were of English or Scottish descent, many of whom were members of dissenting Protestant sects.[1] Tied

by a bond of common culture and purpose, many of these new settlers came to prefer things English[2] and likely felt no need to discourage the immigration of others like themselves. However, with the influx of other Europeans—the non-English, the poor, the Catholics, the Jews—the first wave of immigrants began to resent the newcomers' intrusion and, indeed, did not make them feel welcome.[3]

Interestingly, early "immigration law" restricted entry into the various states rather than into America itself, although these state-imposed rules differed from modern federal immigration law in that the former applied to other states' citizens as well as to foreigners and were often ostensibly concerned with specific social ills, such as regulating the spread of disease or crime,[4] rather than with excluding undesirable non-English Europeans. Similarly, the first federal immigration laws enacted in the late 1800s appeared to be racially and ethnically neutral,[5] although anti-Catholic sentiment was rampant.[6]

Over time, however, the English settlers began to accept the non-English because of their shared "whiteness."[7] Thus, despite the initial classification of the non-English as the other, ultimately, the Europeans' shared "whiteness" constituted a sufficient basis for constructing a unified community. Congress might have foreseen this eventual merger of the English and non-English whites when in 1790 it restricted naturalization to "white persons," thus creating a common bond between the two groups.[8]

Like the non-English whites, the Chinese in America have also experienced being members of both the in-group and out-group. Initially brought to California to work on the railways, Chinese laborers outlived their usefulness in the eyes of the European Americans once the transcontinental railroad was completed, and, in the ensuing Panic of 1873, drought, and depression of 1877, the Chinese became easy targets of anti-immigrant sentiment.[9] In the 1880s, Congress passed the "Chinese Exclusion Laws," so-called because they were designed to prohibit Chinese immigration.[10] To add insult to injury, in *Chae Chan Ping v. United States*,[11] the U.S. Supreme Court held that Congress possessed plenary constitutional power over immigration and, therefore, could exclude noncitizens on the basis of race, as we learned in chapter 1. With this decision, the so-called "plenary power" doctrine was born, and it has been a resilient, important organizing principle of immigration law ever since.[12] Justice Field chillingly captured the nativists' view of the Chinese as "outsiders" during that time:

The differences of race added greatly to the difficulties of the situation. . . . [T]hey remained strangers in the land, residing apart by themselves, and adhering to the customs and usages of their own country. It seemed impossible for them to assimilate with our people or to make any change in their habits or modes of living. As they grew in numbers each year the people of the coast saw, or believed they saw, in the facility of immigration, and in the crowded millions of China, where population presses upon the means of subsistence, great danger that at no distant day that portion of our country would be overrun by them. . . .

If, therefore, the government of the United States, through its legislative department, considers the presence of foreigners of a different race in this country, who will not assimilate with us, to be dangerous to its peace and security, their exclusion is not to be stayed because at the time there are no actual hostilities with the nation of which the foreigners are subjects.[13]

Like the non-English whites before them, the Chinese were viewed as outsiders who chose not to assimilate and who therefore posed a threat to the security of the majority. Reading between the lines, there were only two ways in which the perceived threat of "invasion" could be abated: through assimilation (the route traversed by the non-English whites) or through exclusion. Viewing the Chinese as incapable of assimilating to the white culture, the dominant majority chose exclusion instead.[14] Just as the English settlers used facially objective laws to keep social "undesirables" out of the colonies, the white majority utilized the fiction of sovereign power to justify its overtly racist policies.[15]

Despite the continued prejudice and violence against Chinese Americans today, the dominant society has come to view the Chinese as having assimilated in some areas of American life. For example, Chinese and other East Asians often do very well on college entrance examinations and are viewed as "model minority" groups that succeed by virtue of traditional "American" values such as industry and loyalty.[16] Thus, just as the non-English whites have been able to assimilate into the dominant culture, the Chinese have been accepted in areas in which they have been able to reflect values that the larger society holds dear.

Mexican laborers, like the Chinese coolies before them, have also been welcomed and shunned at different times by the larger American society, based on their perceived usefulness to the United States. While the Chinese were imported to build railroads, the Mexicans were tasked with agricultural work, mostly in the southwestern United States.[17] Based on economic demand for their services, the Mexicans were alternately recruited (both through formal and informal immigration arrangements)[18] and rejected by American agricultural businesses.

U.S. immigration policy has frequently reflected business demand for Mexican labor. For example, World War II created an increased need for agricultural workers. Accordingly, the United States negotiated a treaty with Mexico, popularly known as the "Bracero Program," under which Mexican citizens would be allowed temporary entry into the United States to work on agricultural lands.[19] However, once the U.S. government realized that it could not control its businesses' continued recruitment of cheaper, undocumented non-Bracero labor, the INS initiated "Operation Wetback" in 1954 to expel over a million undocumented Mexican workers.[20] Thus, rather than design a coherent immigration policy that punished its businesses for hiring undocumented immigrants, the federal government instead made the workers bear the ignominy of deportation.[21] It was not until 1986—some thirty years after "Operation Wetback"—that Congress decided to amend the Immigration and Nationality Act to include employer sanctions for hiring undocumented persons.[22] Rather than value and respect the industry of these Mexican workers, many of whom toil in jobs rejected by the citizenry, the United States has often reaffirmed the primacy of one's legal immigration status over one's desire to put in an honest day's work.

Even the most cursory review of the immigration histories of the non-English whites, the Chinese, and the Mexicans in the United States reveals that their acceptance by the dominant culture, both inside and outside the law, depended greatly on their perceived similarity or usefulness to the larger society. The non-English whites shared their skin color with the original English settlers; the Chinese were able to excel scholastically; the Mexicans provided vital, inexpensive agricultural labor. Just as each immigrant group has achieved varying degrees of acceptance, U.S. immigration policies toward group members has run hot and cold depending on the citizenry's ability to recognize in the noncitizens values the dominant American culture holds dear.

This section has examined the historical tension between the acceptance and rejection of the foreigner by the citizen; the next section will examine how the Supreme Court's alienage jurisprudence reflects this tension. Specifically, the next section describes two competing paradigms in

Supreme Court precedent to explain the Court's opinions about noncitizens: the membership and personhood paradigms.

## 2. A Legal-Theoretical Perspective:
## Membership versus Personhood

Two important law review articles succinctly summarize the Supreme
Court's jurisprudence regarding the membership and personhood status
of immigrants in American society. In the first piece, "Membership,
Equality, and the Difference That Alienage Makes,"[23] legal scholar Linda
Bosniak contends that the Court's alienage decisions may best be understood through the prisms of "separation" and "convergence." Borrowing
these terms from political scientist Michael Walzer,[24] Bosniak describes
the "separation" model[25] as one that assumes that the government's plenary power[26] over immigration—that is, the admission and exclusion of
noncitizens—is separate from its limited power over the immigrant's personal rights. Therefore, a government that has the power to deny a noncitizen admission to this country does not have the power to beat a confes-
sion out of an immigrant accused of committing a crime. The "convergence" model asserts the converse: The government's power over
immigration converges with its power over the immigrant's rights.[27] For
example, the government may fairly restrict the right to vote to citizens
only, while denying the franchise to foreigners.

Despite these distinctions, Bosniak acknowledges that the boundaries
between these two models is not, at the margin, clearly delineated: "The
defining question in the current politics of [noncitizen] status is just how
far the government's power to regulate immigration legitimately extends."[28] In other words, does the government's power to deny a foreigner entry into the United States also include the power to deny the
noncitizen access to public benefits once in the United States? Ultimately,
Bosniak chooses not to predict how courts will respond to the ever-in-
creasing number of rights claims by noncitizens in the current anti-immigrant climate, but she is satisfied that, for now, her two models provide a
useful framework from which to evaluate these claims. (In a more recent
article, Bosniak argues that while she personally favors more universal
and inclusive conceptions of citizenship, she recognizes the nationalist
normative assumptions embedded in our Constitution that arguably limit
rights claims by noncitizen outsiders.)[29]

In the second article, "Partial Membership: Aliens and the Constitutional Community,"[30] immigrant rights expert Michael Scaperlanda picks up where Bosniak leaves off. Using the term "personhood" in place of "separation" and "membership" in lieu of "convergence," Scaperlanda contends that the Supreme Court favors "membership" over "personhood."[31] In reviewing a noncitizen's rights claim, the Court will first ask whether membership issues are present. If so, then the noncitizen's claim will be summarily denied, and the Court will defer to the political arm which has chosen to differentiate between citizen and foreigner.[32] For instance, in *Mathews v. Diaz*, the Court held that Congress's plenary power over immigration extended into the realm of the distribution of Medicare benefits.[33] Accordingly, the Court upheld the statutory scheme that made a noncitizen's length of continued residence in the United States a condition for participation in a federal medical insurance program.[34] Because Diaz was not a citizen, Congress could legitimately exercise its immigration power over him to deny him certain federal benefits.[35] His claim to personhood did not matter in the face of his status as a foreigner.

However, if membership is not an issue, then the Court more closely scrutinizes the discriminatory governmental conduct, often validating the noncitizen's claim to equal personhood.[36] In another benefits case, *Graham v. Richardson*,[37] the Court invalidated an Arizona statute that deprived noncitizens of certain welfare benefits, stating that "classifications based on alienage, like those based on nationality or race, are inherently suspect and subject to close judicial scrutiny."[38] Here, national membership was not an issue; therefore, Arizona, which unlike Congress possesses no plenary power over immigration, could not deny noncitizens their rights to equal personhood absent a compelling reason. Equal personhood trumps governmental claims where national membership is a nonissue.

Given the Court's preference for the membership model, Scaperlanda argues for a redefinition of the debate over membership from one that pits the plenary power of the government against the noncitizen's claim to equal rights, to one that weighs the rights of the citizenry "to create a constitutional community" against the rights of the noncitizen to equal personhood. Scaperlanda cites the Court's so-called "political function" cases in support of his theory.[39] In these cases, the Court found that a state's right to define who is part of its community overrides any personhood claims the noncitizen might have.[40] For example, in *Cabell v.*

*Chavez-Salido,* in which the Court sustained a California requirement that all "peace officers" be citizens,[41] the Court stated that the "exclusion of [noncitizens] from basic governmental processes is not a deficiency in the democratic system but a necessary consequence of the community's process of political self-definition. Self-government . . . begins by defining the scope of the community and thus the governors as well: [Noncitizens] are by definition those outside of this community."

Scaperlanda specifically cites this passage in *Cabell* to emphasize that the Court should justify its preference for membership over personhood only when membership involves the citizenry's attempt at self-definition in accordance with constitutional mandates. Thus, the current plenary power or "inherent sovereign power" paradigm is essentially un-bounded, Scaperlanda maintains. His alternative—a model that requires that communal formation be tempered by the Constitution and then weighed against the noncitizen's personhood claim—forces the government to recognize that it is one of limited power. The primacy of the Constitution prevents the government from playing the membership card to trump personhood. Scaperlanda concludes by calling for a constitutional dialogue among "We the People." While he questions whether the political branches will act to protect the rights of noncitizens, he hopes that the process of engaging in a frank discussion about citizenship and personal rights will help shape our view of the "noncitizen in our polity."[42]

Notably, Scaperlanda's call to vigilantly safeguard personhood against the dominant membership paradigm promotes the twin equality norms of antiessentialism and antisubordination. The personhood theory fosters antiessentialism by ensuring that the status of noncitizen does not become a proxy for perpetuating other disabilities relating to socioeconomic standing, race, gender, or other classifications. Antiessentialism reminds us that not all noncitizens are alike just because they share the formal status of noncitizen; and further, antiessentialism eschews broad classifications for their own sake, especially when used to further subordination. The personhood paradigm furthers antiessentialism by ensuring that we recognize the individual person behind the category of non-U.S. citizen. Likewise, the personhood theory promotes antisubordination by forcing policymakers to pay heed to the reality that foreign citizenship automatically subjects an entire class of people to second-class status (indeed, that is the idea behind the membership paradigm). Thus, by focusing on each noncitizen's personhood, policymakers will be more closely attuned to the ways in which their status-based decisions adversely affect individuals whose foreign citizenship already marks them as outside the boundaries of some legal protections.

### 3. "Membership" and "Personhood" Applied: The Promise Enforcement Cases

Each of the three cases described below highlights the tensions between Scaperlanda's membership and personhood paradigms in a judicial milieu that generally favors membership over personhood.

### A. THE PERSONHOOD PARADIGM APPLIED: *Thomas v. Immigration and Naturalization Service*

Clive Charles Thomas arrived in the United States in 1954 and was admitted as a lawful permanent resident. In 1983, Thomas, still a noncitizen, pled guilty to conspiracy to possess cocaine for sale; he was sentenced to seven years' imprisonment. By cooperating with the government in a major narcotics investigation, Thomas was released after serving only two years of his sentence. As part of his deal with the government, Thomas entered into a written cooperation agreement in which he agreed to turn over a sworn statement about his drug trafficking and to serve as a prosecution witness for two years. In exchange, the government promised to advise Thomas's parole board of his cooperation and agreed not to oppose motions made by Thomas's attorney for reduction of sentence or relief from deportation.

After his conviction, the INS issued an order for Thomas to show cause why he should not be deported. Thomas's attorney moved for discretionary relief under Section 212(c) of the Immigration and Naturalization Act (INA). Notwithstanding the government's express promise not to do so, the INS opposed the request for relief, calling two witnesses at the immigration court hearing who testified to Thomas's criminal activities. Despite Thomas's testimony about his reformed behavior and his cooperation with the government, the immigration judge denied Thomas's request; Thomas also lost his appeal before the Board of Immigration Appeals (BIA).

Thomas then brought his case before the Ninth Circuit Court of Appeals, claiming that the government had violated his due process rights by reneging on its promise not to contest his motion for relief from deportation. In a 2-to-1 decision, the Ninth Circuit panel agreed with Thomas and remanded the case to the immigration judge for a new Section 212(c) proceeding for discretionary relief from deportation.

Citing well-known and long-standing Supreme Court precedent, the Ninth Circuit began the heart of its opinion strongly in Thomas's favor: "It has long been the law that the government's failure to keep a commitment which induces a guilty plea requires that the judgment be vacated and the case remanded." Noting that a cooperation agreement is analogous to a plea agreement, the court stated that the government would be held to the literal terms of the agreement and would ordinarily bear responsibility for any lack of clarity. However, to enforce the agreement, the promisee must detrimentally rely on the promise and the person making the promise must be authorized.

The INS offered two arguments in opposition to Thomas's appeal. First, it contended that the INS was neither a party to the agreement, nor bound by it, nor did the agreement specify that it would not oppose Thomas's request. Second, it argued that the U.S. Attorney lacked authority to enter into the cooperation agreement on the INS's behalf.

The court rejected the first argument outright regarding the INS's alleged nonparticipation in the agreement negotiations. Although acknowledging the reasonableness of the INS's wish not to be bound by an agreement crafted without its consultation, the court nonetheless focused on the harm to Thomas caused by the U.S. Attorney's gaffe: "Thomas was entitled to the performance by the government of its promise." Moreover, the text of the agreement clearly spoke to the issue of deportation and expressly bound the INS:

> In the first paragraph, the agreement says that "Government," designated as the promisor, "includes its departments, officers, agents, and agencies." . . . The eighth paragraph bound "[t]he Government," so defined, not to oppose motions for "relief from deportation to the . . . U.S. Immigration Service." . . . Motions for relief from deportation are made and heard before the INS, and opposed by INS lawyers, so this particular promise, to mean anything, had to mean that the INS would not oppose such a motion.

The court spent considerably more time analyzing the INS's second argument that the U.S. Attorney lacked authority to bind the INS. Applying common law agency principles, the court stated that an agent may bind the principal only if it had actual authority—express or implied—to do so: "Therefore, the United States Attorney's promise that the government would not oppose Thomas's § 212(c) application is binding on the INS if the United States Attorney had either an express grant of authority to make such a promise, or his authority for making the promise is incidental to some other express grant of authority."

Examining the duties of U.S. attorneys, the court noted that Congress expressly confers upon them the power to "prosecute for all offenses against the United States." However, Congress specifically delegated to the Attorney General the power to administer and enforce the INA. In turn, the Attorney General has delegated much of this power to officials of the INS, leading the court to conclude that "[s]o far as we have found in the Code of Federal Regulations, no delegation of that authority has been made to United States Attorneys."

After finding no *express* delegation, the court next considered whether the U.S. Attorney's congressionally sanctioned power to prosecute gives her *implied* authority to prevent the government, including the INS, from opposing motions for relief from deportation. The court ruled that the U.S. Attorney has such implied authority. Again citing common law agency principles, the court held that the power to enter a cooperation agreement and bind the government in the process is an incident of the same prosecutorial power that gives U.S. attorneys the implied authority to negotiate plea bargains. The court specified three reasons for its holding:

> First, deportation commonly arises from the context of criminal prosecution. It is likely to be a central issue in many criminal cases involving [noncitizens]. Second, the terms of a plea or cooperation agreement will commonly affect deportation. The attorneys will negotiate the offenses of conviction and sentences partly by considering the effects of these determinations on deportation. Third, there is no reason why, in the absence of regulations or orders to the contrary, we should doubt that Congress implied this grant of authority.[43]

This holding does not mean that the INS is without a remedy, albeit late in coming: the court noted that the Attorney General, if she wished, could limit the authority of the U.S. attorneys through an appropriate section in the Code of Federal Regulations, but she has chosen not to.

This case is a marvelous example of the personhood theory of noncitizens' rights at work. More specifically, this case demonstrates three characteristics of the personhood paradigm: (1) the paradigm's focus is on constraining government power rather than determining the extent to which the noncitizen may enjoy the rights of the citizen; (2) the paradigm sees the government as a unified entity rather than separate branches in instances where it seeks to limit a noncitizen's rights; and (3) the paradigm recognizes the reality that noncitizens should be accorded more protection in some instances, especially since the threat of deportation is a constant in noncitizens' lives. Let us examine these lessons in turn.

First, the court did not analyze the due process problem by looking at the noncitizenship of Thomas in order to determine what process was due. Instead, it focused on the government's failure to satisfy its end of the bargain, noting that this failure caused a direct harm to Thomas. While it sympathized with the INS's plight owing to the agency's nonparticipation in the cooperation agreement talks, the court stressed that, ultimately, it was Thomas who was "entitled to performance by the government"—whether that obligation was fulfilled by the U.S. Attorney or the INS. Thomas's personhood and, therefore, his claim against the government, was not diminished by his noncitizenship; in the court's eyes, he was entitled to the same process due citizens subject to prosecution by the government and its myriad entities.

In addition, the personhood paradigm is especially applicable here because membership issues are of secondary concern in the "promise enforcement" scenario. The primary object of the cooperation agreement between the government and the noncitizen is to facilitate the prosecution of a criminal case, not to affect immigration law. Put another way, in cooperation agreements, the government cares more about acquiring the defendant's cooperation than about affecting the defendant's citizenship. While the government's breach adversely impacts Thomas's immigration status, this is a tangential concern. The court properly kept its focus on the government's ability to live up to its promises rather than be distracted by the irrelevance of the defendant's citizenship status.

Second, this case is instructive because the court correctly comprehended that, in the noncitizen's eyes, the government is monolithic. When the government purports to negotiate with any person, noncitizens included, it should not be allowed to feign ignorance when one of its branches fails to communicate with another branch. Thus, drawing an artificial boundary between the government's immigration arm and its criminal prosecutorial arm means little to the noncitizen who attempts to negotiate in good faith for a result fair to both sides. Viewing the government as monolithic makes perfect sense, especially when the government's negotiating arm seeks to acquire from the noncitizen cooperation that benefits the general public. If the government wants to reap the benefits of its negotiated deal, it must also, as one entity, be willing to accept the accompanying burdens.

At one level, this distaste of the monolithic government also mirrors the general sentiment held by some scholars that there should be little difference between state and federal discrimination against noncitizens. Commentators have long recognized that plenary power over immigration effectively immunizes the federal government from equal protection scrutiny when it decides to treat noncitizens worse than citizens, while state governments engaging in the same discriminatory conduct are generally subject to heightened scrutiny. This federal-state dichotomy in alienage jurisprudence has led some to call for the dismantling of the plenary power doctrine, while others have suggested that at the very least some congruence be sought between the levels of scrutiny currently used to examine federal versus state action. From the noncitizen's perspective, the view of the government is the same in the *Thomas* case as in the plenary power debate: all the noncitizen knows is that she is being confronted by an American government seeking to restrict her liberty in some way.

Third and finally, the court correctly observed that, as a practical matter, cooperation agreements in criminal law proceedings bear more greatly on noncitizens than citizens because of the "everpresent threat of deportation."[44] Perhaps second only to the inability to vote, the constant threat of deportation divides the noncitizen from the citizen community. And because noncitizens cannot exercise the franchise, they are unable to vote for procedural safeguards to temper prosecutorial zeal in deportation hearings. Therefore, courts must pay attention to the double threat facing a noncitizen charged with a crime: criminal prosecution and deportation. The *Thomas* court did just that; it acknowledged that, when a noncitizen is a criminal defendant, deportation must be considered, and therefore any plea or cooperation agreement could very well involve deportation considerations.

In sum, the *Thomas* decision captures what is best about the personhood paradigm: the belief that due process rights require the government to act fairly in its dealings with both citizens and noncitizens.

## B. THE MEMBERSHIP PARADIGM APPLIED:
### *San Pedro v. United States*

This next subsection examines a case whose facts, though similar to those in *Thomas,* led the presiding court to deny the noncitizen protection and implicitly, though likely unintentionally, to assert the primacy of the membership theory of noncitizens' rights.

Alberto San Pedro is a Cuban citizen, but he has been a lawful permanent resident of the United States for over forty years. He was indicted for bribing, and for entering into a conspiracy to bribe, a federal public official. After entering into a plea agreement with the U.S. Attorney's Office, San Pedro pled guilty to the conspiracy charge in exchange for transactional immunity. In addition, the government promised not to prosecute San Pedro for any other offenses based upon any evidence revealed during the investigation leading to the bribery charges.

It is at this point that San Pedro's and Thomas's stories converge. As in *Thomas,* the INS issued an order for San Pedro to show cause why he should not be deported because of his conviction. San Pedro responded by filing a Petition for Writ of Mandamus in federal district court, contending, as did Thomas, that the government's promise in the plea agreement prevented the INS from deporting him. The government filed a motion to dismiss, arguing, as did the government in *Thomas,* that it never promised San Pedro nondeportation, and even if it did, the promise did not bind the INS because the U.S. Attorney did not have the authority to make such a promise.

Converting the motion to one for summary judgment, the court ruled that although there was a factual issue as to whether the government made the nondeportation promise, the crucial legal issue was whether the U.S. Attorney "had the authority to promise not to deport a criminal defendant as a condition of a plea bargain." The court held that neither the U.S. Attorney's Manual nor the INA vested the U.S. Attorney with the power to bind the INS through a nondeportation clause; accordingly, the court granted summary judgment in the government's favor.

On appeal, the Eleventh Circuit grappled with the same issues that *Thomas* did, and indeed cited *Thomas* as prior authority. While it agreed with the *Thomas* court that Congress did not expressly grant the U.S. Attorney power to bind the INS or any other governmental agency, the Eleventh Circuit disagreed with the former's interpretation of the controlling law:

We believe *Thomas* incorrectly harmonized the statutes that empower the United States attorneys and the attorney general, and failed to consider that *the express authority to enforce immigration law is concentrated solely in the attorney general*. It is unclear to this court, as it was to the district court, why Congress would have granted United States attorneys the authority to enter into agreements with criminal defendants that bind the INS while simultaneously granting the authority to enforce the specific provisions of the immigration laws to the attorney general in the INA. We therefore follow the principle, upheld by the Supreme Court on numerous occasions, that a specific statute takes precedence over a more general one.[45]

Unlike the Ninth Circuit's affirmation of Thomas's personhood, the Eleventh Circuit implicitly upholds the theory of membership by emphasizing the separate, unique status of immigration law enforcement. By extension, the *San Pedro* court also highlights the practical disadvantage separate immigration enforcement creates for noncitizens like San Pedro who cannot rely on a monolithic government to abide by its promises, but instead must specifically adhere to the INS's rules and requirements regardless of what other agencies might guarantee.

The *San Pedro* decision reminds us of two other important points that appear in the Supreme Court's alienage jurisprudence about membership. First, the court was quick to rely on a seemingly neutral rule—that specific statutes take precedence over more general ones—without examining the adverse consequences to San Pedro. In a similar way, the Supreme Court in *Mathews v. Diaz* invoked another neutral rule—the plenary power doctrine—to deny Medicare benefits to certain noncitizens[46] when, arguably, the distribution of public benefits has little to do with the admission or expulsion of people, which is the basic province of immigration law. Invoking the plenary power doctrine is even more frustrating when the Supreme Court in *Graham v. Richardson* held that alienage is a suspect classification like race and that states may not discriminate against noncitizens in the distribution of public benefits.[47] The plenary power doctrine, like the "specific statute" rule used in *San Pedro,* provides the court with an apparently legitimate and neutral way to discriminate against noncitizens but simultaneously ignores the real hardship such a rule inflicts.

Second, the court characterized the government as being multidimensional rather than monolithic by emphasizing the differences between the immigration and prosecutorial powers of the federal government: the immigration power focuses on the admission and expulsion issue, while the prosecutorial power examines the criminal liability of those subject to U.S. law. In contrast, the *Mathews* court chose not to separate the immigration question (should a noncitizen be admitted or expelled) from the immigrant's rights question (should a noncitizen be entitled to public benefits) and instead invoked the plenary power doctrine to assert a united government's power over immigrants as long as they are in the United States. This example illustrates how courts can manipulate their characterization of the government from a singular entity to a fragmented structure to avoid government responsibility for noncitizens' welfare. In the end, the result is the same, whether intended or not: the failure to focus on the personhood of the noncitizen tightens the circle of membership, excluding those who are not full citizens.

## C. Membership "Trumps" Personhood: *Ramallo v. Reno*

As a final illustration of the workings of the personhood-membership dichotomy in recent lower court decisions, this section examines the curious case of *Ramallo v. Reno* in which Congress intervened to reestablish the primacy of the membership theory after the lower court had implicitly endorsed the idea of personhood.

Marlena Ramallo is a Bolivian citizen who entered the United States in 1972; she became a permanent resident in 1978. In August 1986, she pled guilty to the charge of conspiracy to import cocaine. Three months after Ramallo's conviction, the INS initiated deportation proceedings against her. During the course of these proceedings, the government entered into an agreement with Ramallo in which she promised to assist in prosecuting other drug traffickers.[48] In return, the government, with the approval of the Assistant U.S. Attorney, the Drug Enforcement Agent, and the INS District Director,[49] agreed not to deport Ramallo and to restore her status as a lawful permanent resident. Pursuant to her understanding of the agreement, Ramallo withdrew her objection to deportability in the INS proceedings. In apparent violation of the agreement, an immigration judge subsequently issued a deportation order.[50] When the government later attempted to enforce the order, Ramallo filed suit in federal district court, claiming the violation of her due process rights[51] and seeking to enforce the cooperation agreement to restore her to permanent resident status.[52]

After several rounds of briefing, the parties filed cross-motions for summary judgment. Ramallo claimed that the government had violated her constitutional rights by breaching its agreement and that, therefore, it was promissorily and equitably barred from deporting her. In response, the government argued that, among other things,[53] the government representatives who dealt with Ramallo did not have the authority to bind the government—the same argument the government raised before the *Thomas* and *San Pedro* courts.

On the issue of agency, the court cited its approval of *Thomas*[54] and its rejection of *San Pedro*, but ultimately decided that it did not need to definitively choose between these conflicting precedents because an INS agent was directly involved in the negotiations along with the U.S. Attorney. If anyone has authority to bind the INS, the INS attorney "whose job is to represent the INS . . . in matters of deportation proceedings" must have that power.[55] Soon thereafter,[56] the court granted judgment in Ramallo's favor, ruling that fundamental due process concerns required the government to restore Ramallo's status as a lawful permanent resident.[57]

At first blush, *Ramallo* appears to be a much easier case than either *Thomas* or *San Pedro*. The *Ramallo* district court did not have to choose between the conflicting theories of *Thomas*'s personhood paradigm and monolithic government, on the one hand, and *San Pedro*'s membership paradigm and divided government, on the other. The D.C. district court simply applied general principles of agency law to hold that an INS agent who promises a noncitizen that she will not be deported binds the INS by that promise—a rather uncontroversial statement.

However, this obvious truth would not hold sway for long. The government took an appeal of this case to the District of Columbia Circuit Court of Appeals on the grounds that the lower court lacked jurisdiction when it found for the plaintiff. In a May 27, 1997 decision, the appellate court agreed with the government.[58] After the district court heard the case, Congress enacted the Illegal Immigration Reform and Immigrant Responsibility Act (IIRAIRA),[59] which amended the INA to deprive federal courts of jurisdiction to decide cases like *Ramallo*. Section 306(a) of the IIRAIRA amends section 242 of the INA[60] by depriving federal courts of jurisdiction over noncitizens' claims that arise out of proceedings brought against the noncitizens by the Attorney General. Because Ramallo's case was a claim arising out of the INS's efforts to deport her, the IIRAIRA barred the federal courts from entertaining her claim.[61]

What happened here? What started out as a decision closely tracking the "personhood" paradigm was transformed into a "membership" case by congressional fiat! Indeed, *Ramallo* was not even a controversial case at the outset. Just as a citizen should be able to insist that a prosecutor's promise bind the prosecuting office, so should a noncitizen be able to surmise that an INS agent's word will obligate the INS. Unfortunately, Congress, with its plenary power over immigration, invoked the membership paradigm to quash any claims to equal personhood Ramallo could have made.[62]

As the prior chapters suggest, *Ramallo* is but one other recent example of the U.S. government using its power over immigration and naturalization to deny even the most basic due process rights to noncitizens—here, the right to be able to rely on a government promise given during good faith plea negotiations. As long as the government continues to value the membership paradigm (and its enforcer, the plenary power doctrine) over equal personhood for noncitizens, the circle of membership will continue to tighten. And what does that mean for people like Marlena Ramallo and Alberto San Pedro? Even if they fulfill their promises to the U.S. government and bring their coconspirators to justice, they face almost certain retaliation upon return to their home countries.[63]

## 4. Reasserting the Importance of Personhood

The previous sections demonstrate the prominence of the membership paradigm in both Supreme Court jurisprudence and in recent "promise enforcement" cases brought before the lower federal courts. Scaperlanda's challenge still must be met, as the paramount question remains: "What can be done to redefine and expand the circle of membership?" The work of critical race theorist Jody Armour and recent social psychology research on attitudes about immigrants may help effect a paradigm shift: If we can all acknowledge the stereotypes we have about others—immigrants included—we may begin to dismantle those stereotypes, debunk those myths, and ultimately welcome and value the equal personhood of those who are different.

### A. Armour on Stereotype Reduction in Judicial Decision Making

Much like psychologist Gordon Allport's conception of prejudice described in chapter 2, Armour's work on effective legal decision making provides us with a framework for understanding our views about "the other." Armour has challenged the approach adopted by most courts and advocated by many commentators, which leaves descriptions of race, gender, and sexual orientation out of the courtroom because doing so appeals to the prejudices of the jury. Indeed, defense lawyer Johnnie Cochran was criticized time and again in the press for "playing the race card" during the O. J. Simpson trial.[64] When Cochran sought to paint Mark Fuhrman as racist, critics viewed the accusation as irrelevant to whether Simpson was guilty of double murder and asserted that it would make the black jurors empathize with Simpson. Rather than seeing the acquittal as a reflection of reasonable doubt in the jurors' minds, some thought the *Simpson* verdict was the product of black people acting prejudicially in favor of a fellow black, ignoring what in critics' minds was overwhelming evidence of Simpson's guilt.[65]

Armour challenges conventional wisdom by drawing distinctions between constructive and destructive uses of stereotypes about social outgroups to enhance the legal decision-making process. Borrowing from recent social psychology theory, Armour distinguishes between prejudice and stereotype: "Stereotypes consist of well-learned sets of associations among groups and traits established in children's memories at an early age, before they have the cognitive skills to decide rationally upon the personal acceptability of the stereotypes."[66] For example, a three-year-old child, upon seeing a black infant, might describe the infant as a "baby maid," demonstrating a recognition of the social stereotype without having the cognitive wherewithal to approve or disapprove of the ascription.[67] "In contrast, prejudice consists of derogatory *personal beliefs,*" those that "people endorse and accept as being true."[68] Thus, the three-year-old in our hypothetical who grows up to reject the stereotype of the black maid is not "prejudiced" under this definition.[69]

Aside from highlighting the distinction between "stereotype" and "prejudice," Armour notes that social psychologists also differentiate between "low prejudiced individuals" (those who have personally rejected cultural stereotypes as inappropriate) and "high prejudiced individuals" (those who know and endorse cultural stereotypes).[70] He argues that people commonly err by labeling "low prejudiced individuals" who exhibit stereotype-congruent responses as "racist" when, as social psychologists point out, "nonprejudiced beliefs and stereotype congruent thoughts and feelings may coexist within the same individual."[71] For example, some Southerners, despite rejecting prejudice against blacks, have expressed feeling squeamish when shaking African Americans' hands—a product of residual feelings from their childhood, social scientists say.[72]

Armour next points to empirical evidence that suggests that unless they monitor their behavior, low prejudiced people may fall easily into stereotype-congruent responses and habits because negative cultural stereotypes are well established in our environment and are reinforced by the mass media. Thus, prejudice-like responses that are sometimes labeled "racist" may simply be the product of a bad habit rather than a personal belief in the inferiority of a given race.

Armour uses this research to argue against the tendency of many courts to disallow arguments to the jury relating to race, gender, sexual orientation, or other group characteristics on the grounds that such evidence engenders prejudice. He contends that legal decision makers should be reminded of their nonprejudiced personal beliefs so that they may guard against unconscious discrimination. Armour cites the example of a 1920s case in which Clarence Darrow effectively utilized this strategy in his defense of a black doctor, the doctor's relatives, and friends accused of murdering a white man. Two days after Dr. Ossian Sweet and his family moved into a white Detroit neighborhood in 1925, an angry white mob gathered outside their home, shouting racial epithets and throwing rocks. As the mayhem intensified, the police officers dispatched to keep the peace did nothing. After seeing a big rock crash through an upstairs window and the crowd make a sudden movement, Dr. Sweet and his brother fired a warning shot over the mob's heads; one of the crowd's members was killed, and all eleven household members were charged with murder.[73]

In his summation before an all-white jury, Darrow challenged them to resist giving in to their racial prejudices:

> I haven't any doubt but that every one of you is prejudiced against colored people. I want you to guard against it. I want you to do all you can to be fair in this case, and I believe you will. . . .
> . . . Here were eleven colored men, penned up in the house. Put yourselves in their place. Make yourselves colored for a little while. It won't hurt, you can wash it off. They can't, but you can; just make yourself black for a little while; long enough, gentlemen, to judge them, and before any of you would want to be judged, you would want your juror to put himself in your place. That is all I ask in this case, gentlemen.[74]

The jury acquitted Dr. Sweet, and the prosecution dropped the charges against the remaining defendants.

Darrow's triumph provides an inspiring narrative of the power of social psychology. His decision to remind the jury members—all white males—of their unconscious proclivity for prejudice forced them to suppress this irrational emotion in favor of a just verdict. More importantly, Armour's research serves as a useful starting point for engaging in a better informed dialogue about citizenship and membership in the U.S. polity along the lines envisioned by Scaperlanda: If social psychologists are correct, U.S. citizens can train themselves to guard against any lingering stereotypes they may have against immigrant groups—such as those maintained against non-English whites, Chinese, and Mexicans—and reject the primacy of membership in cases where the bond of personhood should prevail, as in the "promise enforcement" cases discussed above. When the government makes a promise in a criminal proceeding and the promisee upholds her side of the bargain, it should not matter whether the promisee is a citizen or a foreigner. Because the IIRAIRA currently permits the assertion of this difference, citizens should act to ensure that noncitizens receive the same bargain from the government by calling for the repeal of the Act's court-stripping provisions.

The next section examines recent social psychology scholarship that explores a citizenry's reactions to new immigrant groups, with an eye toward learning how to reassert the importance of personhood in our own constitutional dialogue.

## B. Maio et al.'s Research on Attitudes toward New Immigrant Groups

Strong parallels may be drawn between Armour's citations of race prejudice and the anti-immigrant sentiment in the United States today. First, just as deep-seated historical biases and the media have helped to contribute to the image of the black male as hostile or prone to violence,[75] the media have also contributed to the perception of the "illegal alien" as a young, unskilled Mexican male, although a January 2004 study estimates that Mexicans comprise only 57 percent of all undocumented immigrants.[76] Second, despite the persistence of these racial and immigrant stereotypes, most people are low-prejudiced individuals. A 1997 poll of 1,314 whites, blacks, and Latino/as, all citizens or residents of the United States since 1980, revealed that while the respondents were divided on the issue of whether immigrants benefit or burden the nation overall, only one in three respondents offered negative views toward individual immigrant groups.[77] In an interesting commentary on how alienage serves as a proxy for race, the respondents viewed European immigrants in the most favorable light, while Mexicans, Middle Easterners, and people from the Caribbean were perceived most unfavorably.[78] And third, given this intersection of race and alienage, Armour's research may prove useful in identifying and confronting racial prejudice masquerading as politically more palatable anti-immigrant sentiment.[79] Thus, Armour's work may help inform Scaperlanda's constitutional dialogue about membership by forcing U.S. citizens to confront any stereotypes they may have regarding immigrant groups, knowing that some of these stereotypes may have their roots in racial bias.

But Armour's work is just the beginning; two useful social psychology articles specifically address the issue of people's attitudes toward new immigrant groups and may help advance Scaperlanda's proposed constitutional dialogue. The first is a study conducted by psychologists Gregory R. Maio et al. to examine how indirect information regarding a new immigrant group affects people's attitudes toward that group.[80] This experiment started with the premise that many people first receive their information about a new group indirectly—say, through the media—rather than through direct person-to-person contact. In the study, over two hundred residents of Ontario, Canada, were asked their views regarding the impending arrival of a fictitious group of new immigrants, the "Camarians," who were fleeing to various countries because of natural disasters in their nation. The subjects were told that the Canadian Statistics on Immigration agency expected seven thousand Camarians to arrive in Canada within seven months. To examine the extent to which the subjects' views might be influenced by the perceived impact the impending immigration might have on their lives, some subjects were told the Camarians would immigrate to Ontario (high personal relevance), while others believed the immigrants would settle in British Columbia (low personal relevance). The subjects were also told that, because the Camarians might cause a shift in provincial employment and economic conditions, the experimenters were interested in the subjects' views.

Finally, the subjects received tables that contained fictitious information regarding the emotions Camarians elicit from others, their personality traits, and their values;[81] the respondents were told that these tables were taken from a survey of perceptions of Camarians in England and the southwestern United States. Each subject was randomly given either uniformly positive information regarding these three characteristics, uniformly negative information, or a mixture of both positive and negative information. After reviewing the fictitious survey information, the subjects were asked to indicate their attitudes toward Camarians using an attitude thermometer with a scale from 0° (extremely unfavorable) to 100° (extremely favorable).

The study revealed that people formed more favorable attitudes toward new immigrant groups when they were provided uniformly positive consensus information about the emotions elicited by the group's members, their personality traits, and their values. Thus, those who received uniformly positive information about the Camarians were, not surprisingly, most receptive to their immigration. However, people who believed that they would be most affected by the Camarians' immigration acted less favorably—but still positively—to the uniformly positive information than those for whom the immigration was less relevant.[82] For example, the Ontarian subjects who were told that the Camarians would settle in Ontario favored the immigration, but did so at a lower attitude reading than those who believed the Camarians would settle in British Columbia, even though both groups received uniformly positive information regarding the Camarians. Despite its moderating effect on the perception of uniformly positive information, personal relevance had no noticeable effect on subjects' views toward the Camarians based on the immigrants' fictitious values. Maio et al. hypothesize that the subjects may have perceived the emotions elicited by Camarians and their personality traits as having had a more immediate, personal effect on the respondents' lives than the more abstract notion of "values."

In constructing our dialogue about membership, we should consider Maio et al.'s findings to better inform our discussion. Their study teaches us that while imparting positive consensus information is important in fostering favorable attitudes toward new immigrants, it is even more important to recognize the bias played by the role of personal relevance. To convince citizens of the value of the personhood of immigrants, one must find a way to convey positive images of "the immigrant as person" that will resonate with the citizen so that the native becomes personally vested in the immigrant's plight. This "connection" between in-group and out-group members is what Darrow successfully accomplished in obtaining Dr. Sweet's acquittal, and this is the challenge faced by those seeking to restore personhood's importance in the debate over immigrants' rights.

But how do we achieve this "connection" in our constitutional dialogue? A 1996 study by Maio et al. provides support for Armour's position that better informing decision makers of their inherent biases may enhance their evaluative processes. As mentioned earlier, psychological research has shown that while most people do not subscribe to racial discrimination, they unconsciously retain certain negative stereotypes about many out-groups. Other research has shown that some people may hold positive and negative views of an out-group. For example, while some white Americans may hold negative views toward blacks, they may simultaneously sympathize with their plight.[83] As a follow-up to the earlier study, Maio et al. decided to test the effect this kind of ambivalence might have on the way people process persuasive messages about certain immigrant groups.[84] Like many of the studies Armour cites, Maio et al.'s experiment addressed the issue of how information is processed by people with conflicting attitudes.

This study was conducted in two parts: First, over 113 psychology undergraduates were evaluated on the ambivalence of their attitudes toward "Oriental" people, defined by the researchers as persons from China, Japan, and Hong Kong. Next, each subject was given either a "strong" or "weak" persuasive message in favor of immigration from Hong Kong: the strong message described a strong tendency for Hong Kong residents to elicit positive emotions from people, possess positive personality traits, and favor positive values; the weak message described a weak, but still positive, tendency. The researchers then examined the effect of these messages on the subjects' agreement with immigration from Hong Kong, favorability toward Hong Kong residents, and the immigration-related thoughts the subjects listed in response to the messages.

The study demonstrated that those people who possessed ambivalent attitudes toward the immigrants were more likely to systematically process persuasive messages about the group than those people who held nonambivalent beliefs. Thus, the ambivalent participants given the strong positive message about immigration from Hong Kong favored this immigration more than those who received the weak positive message; however, nonambivalent respondents were not affected differentially by the strong and weak messages. Maio et al. posited that because they had conflicting views of the out-group, ambivalent persons would be more motivated to pay attention to new information about that group and also be better able to process such new information.[85]

It is at this point that Armour's and Maio et al.'s theories complement each other. If both theories are correct in assuming that most people are, to varying degrees, ambivalent about out-group members, but that ambivalent people are more effective than nonambivalent people in processing information about the out-group, it behooves us all to develop strategies to communicate positive messages about personhood to citizens acting to define membership in this polity.

For example, throughout history, many U.S. businesses have been ambivalent about employing Mexican undocumented immigrant workers.[86] On the one hand, the industries enjoy the fruits of cheap labor; on the other, the businesses do not want to encourage undocumented immigration. So when an undocumented worker is sexually harassed by her employer and reports the abuse to the authorities, should she be subject to deportation because of her status? Should the immigrant's lack of membership in the polity preempt her personal claim to protection from abuse? What is more important: discouraging "illegal" immigration or preventing employer abuse? For the many ambivalent citizens employed by the businesses pondering an answer to this problem, additional information regarding the significance of one's immigration status might be helpful. The average citizen holds little sympathy for the stereotype of the "illegal alien" as the unskilled, dark-skinned Mexican laborer sneaking into the United States. But here, the citizen decision maker must fight against that stereotype by considering three additional points: first, regardless of how one feels about undocumented immigration, the immigrant in this case is a person who suffered sexual abuse. Second, by deporting the immigrant, the United States sends the message that it discourages the reporting of similar incidents of abuse. Third, and perhaps most importantly, the definition of whether one is a "legal" or "illegal alien" may depend upon the country from which one hails, a point also made in chapter 4. For instance, a Mexican citizen who enters the United States without the proper documents is automatically an "illegal alien," while many Western European citizens may remain in the United States for up to ninety days without a visa.

With this new information, the ambivalent citizen, aware that she is influenced by the media-driven image of the "illegal alien" stereotype, might be able to effectively process this positive data to reach a decision valuing personhood over membership. One good example of a citizen who decided to reassert the importance of personhood on this issue is Rudolph Giuliani, the Republican former mayor of New York City. Giuliani, who was sometimes criticized for being unsympathetic to minority concerns,[87] believed that it was more important to encourage the reporting of abuse suffered by immigrants than to worry about the "illegal" presence of an undocumented person—hence his position supporting the nondeportation of undocumented persons who sought basic municipal services, such as police protection.[88]

By adopting the strategies outlined by Armour and Maio et al., "we the people" might be in a better position to reach decisions on immigrants' rights matters unfettered by the stereotypes that might cause us to discount the value of equal personhood. This in turn should lead to legislative action consistent with these ideals. The next section applies the social psychology research outlined here to articulate a model for reinjecting personhood into the discussion of the "promise enforcement" cases discussed above.

## C. APPLICATION OF SOCIAL PSYCHOLOGY RESEARCH TO THE "PROMISE ENFORCEMENT" CASES

Like the question of undocumented immigrant employment, the "promise enforcement" cases raise the issue of balancing membership and personhood concerns by a largely ambivalent citizenry. In the "promise enforcement" cases, the question is whether a noncitizen should be precluded from receiving the benefit of her bargain with the government simply because of her foreign status; put another way, does her foreign, nonmembership status preempt her personal right to enforce her claim that the government promised not to deport her in exchange for her cooperation?

Assuming that the federal courts have abdicated the membership decision to the citizenry, as Scaperlanda suggests, how does the social psychology research cited here help "we the people" value personhood in the midst of a discussion about membership? First, citizens must, as Armour's research indicates, acknowledge their deep-rooted, media-influenced biases, which include anti-immigrant sentiment as well as the United States' long and sordid history of alienating newcomers. Related to this first point, citizens must reflect whether any anti-immigrant stereotypes they harbor have roots in racial bias. Second, citizens must, as Darrow suggested in his defense of Dr. Sweet, put themselves in the shoes of the noncitizen; after all, many of their ancestors were once noncitizens. Would not citizens expect that a government will abide by its promises? And third, citizens must ask themselves whether the primary purpose of due process as it relates to the "promise enforcement" cases is to restrain government action against citizen and noncitizen alike or to ensure the primacy of a citizen's rights over those of a noncitizen. Because Maio et al.'s work reveals that ambivalent people are better at processing new information than nonambivalent persons, and current data suggests that most Americans are ambivalent about immigration and immigrants, adopting the social psychology techniques outlined here may lead to a more self-aware citizenry better able to engage in a dialogue about membership without forgetting the importance of personhood.

But unlike Armour's application of such research to judicial decision makers, this chapter advocates that U.S. citizens use these techniques to help construct fair alienage policies that value equal personhood, especially in terms of promoting the twin norms of antiessentialism and antisubordination. Hopefully, a reflective and thoughtful citizenry will call for the repeal of the court-stripping provisions of the IIRAIRA, and will ensure that, at a minimum, the U.S. government abides by its promises to all, citizen and noncitizen alike.

## Protecting Immigrant Rights in the Real World: Using City Hall and the State Assembly in Addition to Congress and the Courts

The last section's prescription was quite conventional—have the citizenry use the political process to get Congress to repeal the court-stripping provisions of the IIRAIRA. In practical terms, this is what most immigration lawyers and advocates would suggest to anyone seeking to advance the cause of immigrants' rights, whether under the rubric of "personhood" or under the egalitarian norms of antiessentialism and antisubordination. Recall this theme first developed in chapter 1: because the Supreme Court has granted Congress plenary power over immigration law (and, for the most part, immigrants' rights), advocates have long believed that any significant, positive change in immigrants' rights law will have to be written by the federal legislature. Indeed, aside from my call for the repeal of IIRAIRA, I have endorsed several federal bills and initiatives throughout this book—the Border Commuter Student Act of 2002 in chapter 2 and the Child Citizenship Act of 2000 in chapter 3, to give but two examples.

Yet to rely exclusively on a single strategy of federal immigration law reform misses out on other initiatives at both the federal and state-local governmental levels to improve on the condition of noncitizens. At the federal level, seeking change in the enforcement of the law and questioning the law's validity in court are certainly two other alternatives to legislative reform initiatives. The executive's decision to phase out the mandatory registration of citizens from primarily Arab and Muslim nations came on the heels of intense lobbying and litigation efforts by many concerned advocacy groups, which led in turn to the adoption and implementation of the US VISIT system described in chapter 2. Similarly, the chapter 6 discussion regarding the selective deportation of foreign same-gender partners of U.S. citizens analyzed the constitutional due process and equal protection implications of a federal court strategy to challenge such a practice.

But the most interesting (and perhaps least obvious) aspect of immigrant rights advocacy is the use of state and local governments to gain greater protections for noncitizens. While many first-year law students learn that their individual states can choose to provide greater protections under their own state laws and constitutions than the U.S. Supreme Court might deem appropriate under the federal Constitution, few learn about the advantages that might be gained by non-U.S. citizens, *including undocumented persons,* from favorable state and local laws. For example, as described in chapter 5, the movement to provide undocumented students access to financial aid for college tuition has proven effective among many immigrant-rich states, in contrast with the federal government's more cautious immigration policy post-9/11.

This final section of the book, then, examines three issues pertinent to the idea of how to enhance immigrant rights through effective advocacy in the state and local government milieu. First, as a practical matter, might there be benefits to certain other disadvantaged groups—racial minorities and gays and lesbians, say—from a devolution of immigration power from the federal government to the states? Second, why might some state and local initiatives be easier to pass, and therefore be more effective in securing immigrants' rights than proimmigrant congressional legislation? And third, are there examples of state and local initiatives that are worth emulating and that can be replicated elsewhere irrespective of the particular conservative or liberal leanings of the local polity?

As I describe in detail below, states and localities that decide to provide more protection to noncitizens than their federal counterparts might do so because they aim to uplift a disadvantaged minority group; for example, if Massachusetts had more control over immigration policy, it would be able to provide a sanctuary for binational gay and lesbian couples who choose to marry and settle there. In addition, because they involve decision-making bodies that are closer to the people they affect, state and local initiatives are more likely to take into consideration the fact that federal anti-immigrant laws will affect people *qua* people, that there are individual persons who might benefit from ameliorative laws passed by their own communities. Finally, as examples, immigrant advocates should look to the local anti–PATRIOT Act resolutions passed by over three hundred communities, including three states, vowing not to enforce this federal law's provisions against vulnerable noncitizens, as well as the nationwide movement to recognize Mexican matrícula consular cards as valid identification for undocumented persons.

## 1. Devolution and Discrimination: More State Control over Immigration Law?

Despite calls among many to dismantle them, Congress's plenary power over immigration and the executive's concomitant authority to enforce it are likely here to stay, as most recently evidenced by the flurry of immigration-related bills post–September 11. And while one may quibble over whether Congress has too much power over immigration, there is appeal to the notion that the federal government should have primary control over immigration rather than the states. After all, from the average American's perspective, foreigners immigrate to, and citizens hold passports from, the United States and not Rhode Island.

Yet the first formal federal immigration law was not enacted until 1875[89] despite the fact that the U.S. Constitution had created the national government close to a century earlier, in 1787. Moreover, historian Roger Daniels tells us that many early immigrants from Europe focused less on coming to America than on moving, for example, from one German enclave in the old to the new world, which led, in one instance, to the founding of Germantown, Pennsylvania.[90] As the national government grew in prominence, federal immigration regulation evolved, shifting power away from the states. Today, the Immigration and Nationality Act is a labyrinth, rivaling the tax code in breadth and complexity. Accompanying this evolution has been a corresponding shift in attitude among more recent migrants. No longer will a Mexican agricultural worker limit himself to tilling the lands of border states like California, Texas, and Arizona; Ohio[91] and Oregon[92] also have substantial numbers of seasonal and long-term Mexican laborers.

Notwithstanding the federalization of immigration law since the nation's founding, the states have continued to play a prominent role, with high-immigration states often seeking to exert the most influence.[93] While the Constitution's equal protection clause strictly scrutinizes state laws that discriminate on the basis of alienage, thereby limiting state power,[94] Congress has found ways to allow the individual states to indirectly control the influx of noncitizens into the United States, which in turn indirectly affects their numbers in these states. If, for example, California was able to influence immigration from the Philippines, it would likely be able to affect Filipino populations in Los Angeles and Honolulu, the two largest Filipino communities in the United States.[95]

Recently, Congress has, wittingly or unwittingly, contributed to the devolution of immigration law. First, the 1996 Welfare Reform Act has made it difficult for many poorer immigrants to remain in the country by allowing states to preclude them from receiving state benefits.[96] And second, states have de facto control over immigration through federal laws that have tied deportation consequences to state criminal laws involving moral turpitude crimes, aggravated felonies, and controlled substances offenses.[97] (In chapter 3, we examined one consequence of this shift which has led to the deportation of foreign-born adoptees of U.S. citizens.) Thus, states today have effectively been given the license to experiment with their laws, systematically disadvantaging certain groups.

Federal welfare reform and crime legislation that have a devolutionary effect on immigration law harm not only noncitizens generally, but particularly vulnerable noncitizens specifically. Worse off than the U.S. citizen have-nots who occupy the next-to-the-last rung of the societal ladder are those similarly situated foreigners whose additional burdens of noncitizenship relegate them to the very bottom step. Whatever else might befall them, U.S. citizens cannot be deported, while noncitizens can. Notwithstanding the grave socioeconomic obstacles created by state laws affecting welfare or criminal law enforcement, serious status-based disabilities like race and sexual orientation often bear the unintended and disproportionate burden of policies that heighten societal inequities based on (non)citizenship.

Although distinct, race and immigration have been inextricably intertwined since the nation's founding. As legal scholars Ian Haney López[98] and Michael Olivas[99] have demonstrated, immigration policy has long reflected prevailing racial tastes with newer immigrants subjected to de jure or de facto burdens placed on them by prior arrivals. Hence, as described in more detail earlier in this chapter, the English picked on the Irish, the Irish on the Chinese, the Chinese on the Mexicans.[100] In addition, critical race theorists Neil Gotanda[101] and Natsu Taylor Saito[102] remind us that, in the United States, one's citizenship is often presumed based on one's color. Whites and blacks are presumptively American; browns (Latino/as) and yellows (Asians) are presumptively foreign.[103]

Indeed, given the racially tinged origins of congressional plenary power in the Chinese exclusion-deportation cases and their progeny, one might suppose that devolution to the states of some immigration authority may be desirable. By ridding ourselves of the racist vestiges of the plenary power doctrine, so the argument goes, we might be able to start afresh, creating new immigration policy free and clear of racism. However, inside and outside of immigration law, critical race theorists assert that racism persisted in the past and persists today in both state and federal institutions despite efforts by one to check the other.[104]

As a sterling example of the federal judiciary curbing racist state legislatures, one need only recall the 1954 Supreme Court's bold statement in *Brown v. Board of Education*[105] outlawing segregated schools despite the southern states' fervent opposition. Without *Brown*, the southern states likely would have continued their racist ways, and although de jure segregation might have eventually been eradicated, it is unlikely that the end would have come as quickly absent the Court's intervention. Inside immigration law, Congress may have not been as effective a check. Because deportations will often be triggered by criminal activity, and because criminal law is traditionally left to the states, many states might enforce race-neutral laws in a racially discriminatory manner, sweeping up scores of noncitizens of color along the way.

Race and immigration scholar Kevin Johnson has written extensively about the intersection between race and immigration,[106] arguing vigilance on the part of both federal and state government actors not to conflate the two, in what has in recent years been labeled "racial profiling."[107] Just as African American U.S. citizens worry about being charged with "Driving While Black," Latino/as guard against claims of "Driving While Mexican," while Middle Easterners eschew the label "Flying While Arab" (as we had explored earlier in chapter 2). Thus, the bottom line appears to be this sad fact: if racism within immigration law and policy is systemic, then devolution will not cure the problem. Put simply, both federal and state governments are just as likely to employ racist policies.

One response to this gloomy prediction might be that devolution could lead to proimmigrant policies in some progressive, high-immigration states. Because such states value the cultural and ethnic diversity immigration brings, their governments might be more willing to pass proimmigrant legislation than their federal counterparts. However, recent reality belies this hypothesis. California, long a bastion of immigration, reached its tipping point in the early 1990s when its voters approved Proposition 187, the state initiative curtailing public services for certain undocumented residents.[108] Indeed, a substantial number of citizens of color voted to approve the measure, to the detriment of their noncitizen brethren.[109] Although Proposition 187 was eventually struck down in federal court as unconstitutional,[110] its passage serves as a cautionary tale to those who argue that state control over immigration might lead to more protection for noncitizens of color.

There are, however, situations today where some minority groups might benefit from immigration devolution. Let's take the case of same-gender partners, for example. As I described in chapter 6, under the Immigration and Nationality Act as interpreted by the Ninth Circuit in *Adams v. Howerton,* same-gender binational couples married under a valid state law may not avail themselves of immigration benefits even though the code typically allows a U.S. citizen to petition her other-gender foreign "spouse" so that he may eventually apply for U.S. citizenship based on their marriage. In addition, Congress in 1996 passed the Defense of Marriage Act, which not only prevented same-gender couples from receiving federal benefits afforded heterosexual married couples, but also permitted states not to recognize same-gender unions performed in other states.

It seems to me that immigration devolution would work wonders for U.S.-based same-gender binational couples, who, as of this writing, may be married under the laws of Massachusetts only. If, as has happened in welfare reform and in criminal law enforcement, federal law permitted the states' marriage and domestic partnership laws to influence immigration law, then we would probably see many more same-gender binational marriages in Massachusetts followed by applications to the USCIS for the adjustment of status of the foreign partner. Like welfare and criminal laws, marriage, civil union, and domestic partnership laws vary from state to state, and yet the federal authorities have not viewed that lack of uniformity as problematic in either the welfare or criminal law contexts. Allowing the state of Massachusetts to influence immigration law by conferring marriage upon same-gender couples would go far toward uniting families, a goal long valued by our federal immigration policy.

While the lack of uniformity that accompanies immigration law devolution might lead to undesirable results in welfare reform and criminal law enforcement and would likely not stem the tide of racism, it might lead to the opening of opportunities for gay Americans to petition their binational partners for immigration benefits. Such a development would turn the state of Massachusetts and possibly a few other states in the near future into safe havens for binational same-gender marriages, thereby improving upon the federal immigration code's desire to keep families together by extending the breadth of its reach to include others usually excluded. Devolution in that case would lead to more protection for immigrants than what is currently available under the status quo.

## 2. Keeping It in the Family: Why State and Local Initiatives Might Work

As sociologists Robert Bellah et al. have observed, for most Americans, "the bond to spouse and children is our most fundamental social tie."[111] As we enter larger and larger social organizations, our ties to other members seem less strong than those we have to our family, leading us to feel increasingly less obligated to act benignly toward nonfamily members. Political philosopher Michael Walzer observes: "Favoritism begins in the family—as when Joseph is singled out from his brothers—and is only then extended into politics and religion, into schools, markets, and workplaces."[112] Indeed, cognitive scientist Steven Pinker posits an anthropological reason for nepotism: "Relatives are natural allies, and before the invention of agriculture and cities, societies were organized around clans of them."[113] The smaller the workplace, therefore, the more likely we are to treat our coworkers "like family" (indeed, family-owned businesses are just that); consequently, the larger the office, the less family-friendly, the more corporate the environment becomes.

The same principles apply to legislative advocacy. It might be easier to get favorable legislation passed in a local community where people know and like each other than at a national level where stock (not to mention essentialist and oppressive) conceptions of the "illegal alien" from Mexico or the "terrorist" from the Middle East or the "shrewd and inscrutable businessman" from Japan and/or China might influence voters. So, even if states no longer have the de facto power to grant U.S. citizenship as they did during the early days of the Republic, they can exert a tremendous amount of influence in bettering the lives of those noncitizens whose presence they value and want to keep in their communities.

The concluding section of this chapter illustrates the power of state and local advocacy by providing two important examples of recent proimmigrant initiatives: the rise of anti–PATRIOT Act resolutions around the country and the nationwide movement to accept the Mexican government's matrícula consular cards as valid identification for some government and business purposes.

### 3. Anti-PATRIOT Backlash and the Matrícula Consular: States and Municipalities Thwarting the Feds

On January 7, 2002, a scant four months after 9/11, the city of Ann Arbor, Michigan, passed the nation's first anti–PATRIOT Act resolution, decrying portions of the Act as undue incursions upon civil liberty and directing its citizens, in their private and public capacities, not to enforce it.[114] Aside from being a strong antifederalist statement, such resolutions will have the effect of diverting resources away from the federal government if states and local governments refuse to cooperate in federal investigations pursuant to the PATRIOT Act.

Since January 2002, over three hundred communities—including the states of Hawaii, Alaska, and Vermont—have passed similar resolutions. Indeed, the American Civil Liberties Union (ACLU) has begun an initiative to help other communities pass similar laws, drafting a model resolution for cities and states to adopt as they see fit. Aside from declaring their distrust of the PATRIOT Act, communities that adopt the model resolution effectively deprive the federal government of state and local resources that could be deployed in assisting initiatives pursuant to the Act.

While many of the provisions of the model resolution are concerned with the expanded powers of law enforcement officers to invade the privacy of Americans in the guise of enhancing national security, quite a few focus specifically on the rights of noncitizens. Thus, the model resolution:[115]

- "AFFIRMS [the City's] strong support for the rights of immigrants and opposes measures that single out individuals for legal scrutiny or enforcement activity based on their country of origin."
- "DIRECTS the [City's] Police Department to: (a) refrain from participating in the enforcement of federal immigration laws";
- "(d) refrain from racial profiling. The police department shall not utilize race, religion, ethnicity, or national origin as a factor in selecting which individuals to subject to investigatory activities except when

seeking to apprehend a specific suspect whose race, religion, ethnicity or national origin is part of the description of the suspect."

PATRIOT Act Section 507 permits the federal government to disclose student educational records pursuant to a terrorism investigation without notice to the student. If one is a foreign student, such an investigation could lead to deportation, as we learned in chapter 2. The ACLU's model resolution directs public schools and colleges to provide notice to the student—both citizen and noncitizen—pursuant to basic notions of due process and fair play. In response, Attorney General Ashcroft began a nationwide tour of cities and communities in 2003, ostensibly in an effort to stem the movement and, according to the ACLU, to promote future initiatives such as PATRIOT Act II, deemed by some to be even more restrictive of civil liberties.[116]

While it might be tempting to dismiss this backlash as the product of liberal communities like Ann Arbor, Michigan, cities as diverse—and as conservative—as Castle Valley, Utah, and Carrboro, North Carolina, have also joined the fray.[117] This antiessentialist (i.e., liberal and conservative), antisubordination coalition has proven that states and localities can be effectively mobilized even after a horrifying event such as 9/11 to stand up for immigrant (and citizen) rights.

This nationwide, nonpartisan response to the PATRIOT Act demonstrates how grassroots movements in communities should not be overlooked by noncitizens residing in the United States. To pick one example, should local law enforcement officers effectively be inhibited from attempting to enforce the federal immigration laws, that would help minimize the risk that untrained state and local police might rely on racial and ethnic stereotypes as proxies for immigration status. Such protection would be of particular concern to cities with large Arab and Muslim communities such as Detroit, Michigan, which passed its own resolution on December 6, 2002.[118]

Aside from supporting anti–PATRIOT Act movements, many state and municipal governments have also frustrated the federal crackdown on immigration by recognizing the "matrícula consular." For many years now, the Mexican government has issued these cards to identify its nationals living in the United States.[119] Recently, the matrícula consular has found a second use as identification for undocumented Mexicans in their dealings with private and public organizations in their U.S. communities.

While only a handful of entities recognized their validity as of March 2002, the *New York Times* reports that now "more than 100 cities, 900 police departments, 100 financial institutions and 13 states, including Indiana, New Mexico and Utah, accept the cards."[120] For undocumented Mexican immigrants, the matrícula consular opens the door to many private and public goods, including library and bank accounts, and public water and electric utility services. It also allows them to board aircraft, wire money to relatives, and provide identification to police departments.

The card's growing acceptance by state and local authorities has been spurred by the concern among both private and public entities that, post-9/11, it is important to be able to identify and track who lives in the community. Because undocumented immigrants are often rendered invisible by their status, state and local governments are beginning to welcome the matrícula consular cards as a reasonably secure and reliable method of identification. Further, because the cards do not change the holders' deficient immigration status, many public and private entities do not believe that they unduly impede the federal government's efforts to clamp down on undocumented immigration.

Not that there aren't any detractors. Aside from those who believe that the cards condone "illegal" immigration, there are others who are wary of an identification card not issued by the U.S. government, arguing that it might easily be appropriated by terrorists, thereby compromising national security. Indeed, several members of Congress are considering a nationwide ban on the cards.

Not long after 9/11, a student of mine and her husband traveled by air to a conference in another city. When her flight was called, my student noticed that a foreign family who appeared to look Arab or Middle Eastern was pulled out of line and inspected three times before boarding the flight. No other passenger was subjected to such scrutiny. The two young girls of the family asked their parents why they had to take off their shoes not once but three times. My student noticed that other passengers eyed the family with suspicion. Once on board the plane, several passengers seated next to the family asked to be reseated elsewhere. At one point during their travels, my student and her husband had an opportunity to chat with the man of the family, discovering that they were en route to the same conference. Instead of expressing anger at how he was treated, he said that he understood the situation but felt bad that his family had to endure this indignity, especially since he had enticed his wife to accompany him with the promise that Americans valued liberty and freedom.

I am certain that no offense was meant toward this visiting family; the officers who screened them three times, the people who viewed them with distrust, and the seatmates who asked to be reassigned, just wanted to make sure that the flight would be safe. After all, the 9/11 terrorists looked like these people. Since the family was not detained and were allowed to board the flight, no one was harmed. Just as a black motorist who is stopped should not worry because he was not charged with a crime, this Arab-looking family should not fret because they were allowed on board the plane like everyone else.

However, what impact might such an incident have had on the two little girls in that family? Might they have said to themselves, "We thought we were going on a fun trip to America with mother and father. Why did these persons go through our luggage and clothing three times when, at most, some other passengers were screened only once? Why did the other passengers look at us with suspicion and distrust? Why wouldn't they sit next to us? We thought America treated everyone as individuals, so why did they assume that we were terrorists?"

We should listen to the little girls' pleas, just as we should listen to the minority motorist's lament, because while racial and immigrant profiling might make people *feel* more secure, it does not necessarily *make* them more secure. As we learned in chapter 2, even the federal government's General Accounting Office found in its study of the U.S. Customs Service that status profiling is likely to be less efficient than nonprofiling. Citizens and noncitizens are individuals first and group members second; embracing equality as a fundamental norm within constitutional immigration law and policy provides us a baseline from which to gauge our treatment of everyone within our borders.

# Notes

Notes to the Introduction

1. Two issues are worth clarifying here: first, I do not plan to draw technical legal distinctions between noncitizens at a U.S. port of entry or border (e.g., airport, wharf, or San Diego-Tijuana), nor do I plan to draw precise, lawyerly distinctions between legal permanent residents, temporary visitors (like students or tourists), and undocumented migrants based on factors such as the person's intent to remain in the United States permanently or the person's length of residence in the United States, legal or illegal. Second, while interesting, I choose not to weigh in on several other important constitutional immigration law issues, such as the applicability of international norms to protect non-U.S. citizens or the extraterritorial application of the U.S. Constitution. For more on the former, see, e.g., Yasemin Nuhoğlu Soysal, *Limits of Citizenship: Migrants and Postnational Membership in Europe* (Chicago: University of Chicago Press, 1994); for more on the latter, see, e.g., Gerald L. Neuman, *Strangers to the Constitution: Immigrants, Borders, and Fundamental Law* (Princeton: Princeton University Press, 1996).

2. Hap Palmer, *Baby Songs: ABC, 123, Colors and Shapes* (Backyard Enterprises, 1999).

3. Philip Gleason, "American Identity and Americanization," in *Concepts of Ethnicity*, ed. William Petersen, Michael Novak, and Philip Gleason (Cambridge, MA: Harvard University Press, 1982), 62.

4. See, e.g., Ian F. Haney López, *White by Law: The Legal Construction of Race* (New York: NYU Press, 1996). Haney López outlines in great detail the extent to which "whiteness" was, and is, a social construction as a means to preserve privilege.

5. Act of May 26, 1924, ch. 190, *U.S. Statutes at Large* 43 (1924): 153.

6. *U.S. Code* 8 (2003) § 1153(c) (describing diversity visa program).

7. *Korematsu v. United States,* 323 U.S. 214 (1944).

8. Peter Irons, *The Courage of Their Convictions: Sixteen Americans Who Fought Their Way to the Supreme Court* (New York: Free Press, 1988; reprint, Penguin, 1990), 42. Citations are to the Penguin edition.

9. Neil Gotanda, "Asian American Rights and the 'Miss Saigon Syndrome,'" in *Asian Americans and the Supreme Court: A Documentary History*, ed. Hyung-Chan Kim (Westport, CT: Greenwood Press, 1992), 1098. See also Neil Gotanda, Book Review: "Other Non-Whites" in American Legal History: A Review of *Justice at War*, *Columbia Law Review* 85 (1985): 1190–92 (discussing Korematsu and other wartime "camp cases").

10. See, e.g., Frank Valdes, Jerome McCristal Culp, and Angela P. Harris, eds., *Crossroads, Directions, and a New Critical Race Theory* (Philadelphia: Temple University Press, 2002).

11. See, e.g., Kevin R. Johnson, ed., *Mixed Race America and the Law* (New York: NYU Press, 2002).

12. Legal scholars Alex Aleinikoff and Gerald Neuman cover similar ground in their respective works. T. Alexander Aleinikoff, *Semblances of Sovereignty: The Constitution, the State, and American Citizenship* (Cambridge, MA: Harvard University Press, 2002); Neuman, *Strangers to the Constitution*.

13. See, e.g., Paul Brest et al., *Processes of Constitutional Adjudication*, 4th ed. (Boston: Aspen, 2000).

NOTES TO CHAPTER 1

1. The closest term to "immigration" is the word "migration," which appears in article I, section 9, clause 1, but apparently refers to the slave trade. See U.S. Constitution, art. 1, sec. 9, cl. 1; Ira J. Kurzban, *Kurzban's Immigration Law Sourcebook*, 8th ed. (Washington, DC: American Immigration Law Foundation, 2002–03), 16.

2. U.S. Const., art. I, § 8, cl. 4.

3. U.S. Const., art. I, § 8, cl. 3.

4. U.S. Const., art. I, § 8, cl. 11.

5. See, e.g., Head Money Cases, 112 U.S. 580 (1884); Passenger Cases, 48 U.S. (7 How.) 283, 509–10 (1849) (Daniel, J., dissenting). See also Stephen H. Legomsky, *Immigration and Refugee Law and Policy*, 3d ed. (New York: Foundation Press, 2002), 10–13.

6. See, e.g., *McCulloch v. Maryland*, 17 U.S. (4 Wheat.) 316 (1819).

7. Legomsky, *Immigration and Refugee Law and Policy*, 10.

8. 130 U.S. 581 (1889).

9. 149 U.S. 698 (1893).

10. 338 U.S. 537 (1950).

11. 342 U.S. 580 (1952).

12. 345 U.S. 206 (1953).

13. 525 U.S. 471 (1999).

14. 130 U.S. 581 (1889).

15. Ibid., 609.

16. Ibid., 606.

17. 118 U.S. 356 (1886).

18. 149 U.S. 698 (1893).

19. One of the most frustrating and fascinating aspects of the case is that Fong Yue Ting was required to present a non-Chinese witness to attest to his lawful presence in this country for the noncitizen registration certificate to be issued. Because Fong Yue Ting presented a Chinese witness, the collector of internal revenue deemed the witness not credible and refused to issue him the certificate. Ibid., 703.

20. *Fong Yue Ting,* 149 U.S. at 724.

21. The abolition of the National Origins Quota system did not occur until 1965, although there was a steady decline in race-based exclusionary law from about 1934 forward, when the Chinese Exclusion Act was repealed. See Gabriel J. Chin, "The Civil Rights Revolution Comes to Immigration Law: A New Look at the Immigration and Nationality Act of 1965," *North Carolina Law Review* 75 (1996): 273–345.

22. 338 U.S. 537 (1950).

23. Ibid., 544.

24. Legomsky, *Immigration and Refugee Law and Policy,* 50 n.8.

25. 342 U.S. 580 (1952).

26. 345 U.S. 206 (1953).

27. As found in IIRAIRA, "removal" has replaced "deportation" as the term of art, although "deportation" is more commonly found in the literature. Illegal Immigration Reform and Immigrant Responsibility Act of 1996, 110 *Stat.* § 3009 (1996).

28. *Harisiades v. Shaughnessy,* 342 U.S. 580, 583–84 (1952).

29. Ibid., 591.

30. 345 U.S. at 206.

31. Ibid., 209.

32. See Michael A. Scaperlanda, "Are We That Far Gone? Due Process and Secret Deportation Hearings," *Stanford Law and Policy Review* 7 (1996): 23–25.

33. 345 U.S. at 210 (citing *Chae Chan Ping, Fong Yue Ting, Knauff,* and *Harisiades*).

34. Ibid., 212.

35. Ibid. (citing *Knauff,* 338 U.S. at 544).

36. 345 U.S. at 217 (Black, J., dissenting); ibid., 227 (Jackson, J., dissenting).

37. 344 U.S. 590 (1953).

38. *Mezei,* 345 U.S. at 214.

39. See, e.g., Gabriel J. Chin, "Segregation's Last Stronghold: Race Discrimination and the Constitutional Law of Immigration," *UCLA Law Review* 46 (1995): 12–13.

40. 525 U.S. 471 (1999).

41. Ibid., 488.

42. Ibid., 491.

43. See, e.g., David G. Savage, "Terrorism War Arrives at High Court: A Trio of Cases Could Determine How the Government Probes Security Threats," *American Bar Association Journal*, December 2002, 28–30.

44. Michelle Malkin, *Invasion: How America Welcomes Terrorists, Criminals, and Other Foreign Menaces to Our Shores* (Washington, DC: Regnery Publishing, 2002).

45. Ibid., xiv.

46. In *Bolling v. Sharpe*, 347 U.S. 497 (1954), the Supreme Court held that the equal protection guarantees of the Fourteenth Amendment apply against the federal government through the Due Process Clause of the Fifth Amendment.

47. See *United States v. Carolene Products*, 304 U.S. 144, 152 n.4 (1938).

48. In truth, the reverse is true: U.S. school officials generally dislike playing immigration police. See infra chapter 5.

49. In *Olsen v. Albright*, 990 F. Supp. 31 (D.D.C. 1997), the court found in favor of a Consular Officer who sued after being fired for refusing to comply with the Sao Paulo, Brazil, office's practice of using racial and economic profiles in adjudicating visa applications. See also Legomsky, *Immigration and Refugee Law and Policy*, at 437.

50. Dinesh D'Souza, *The End of Racism* (New York: Free Press, 1995), 259.

51. Ibid.

52. Ibid.

53. Peter H. Schuck, *Citizens, Strangers, and In-Betweens* (Boulder, CO: Westview Press, 1998), 442 n.22 (noting that half of all immigrants from Africa are white). Further, although sometimes the terms "race" and "ethnicity" are used interchangeably, Schuck notes that "race" "connotes a close phenotypical affinity among people" while "ethnicity" "connotes a cultural affinity." Ibid., 441 n.14.

54. Michael Lind, "The Beige and the Black," *New York Times Magazine*, August 16, 1998, 38–39.

55. Much has been written about the perpetual foreignness of Asians and Latino/as who immigrate to the United States and become citizens. See, e.g., Natsu Taylor Saito, "Alien and Non-Alien Alike: Citizenship, 'Foreignness,' and Racial Hierarchy in American Law," *Oregon Law Review* 76 (1997): 261–345; Gotanda, "Asian American Rights," 1087–103.

56. "'La migra' is a well-known southwestern colloquialism among Spanish-speaking Chicanas/os and Mexicanas/os referring to the INS." Elvia R. Arriola, "LatCrit Theory, International Human Rights, Popular Culture, and the Faces of Despair in INS Raids," *University of Miami Inter-American Law Review* 28 (1997): 258 n.41.

57. See, e.g., *Orhorhaghe v. INS*, 38 F.3d 488 (9th Cir. 1994) (holding that arrest of noncitizen based solely on his foreign-sounding name was an egregious violation of Fourth Amendment); Joseph J. Migas, "Exclusionary Remedy Available in Civil Deportation Proceedings for Egregious Fourth Amendment Violations," *Georgetown Immigration Law Journal* 9 (1995): 207–11.

58. Angela Dillard, *Guess Who's Coming to Dinner* Now? (New York: NYU Press, 2001).

59. See, e.g., Kevin R. Johnson, "An Essay on Immigration Politics, Popular Democracy, and California's Proposition 187: The Political Relevance and Legal Irrelevance of Race," *Washington Law Review* 70 (1995): 658–59.

60. I borrow this term from the title of Hiroshi Motomura's forthcoming book from Oxford University Press.


NOTES TO CHAPTER 2

1. Steven Brill, *After: How America Confronted the September 12 Era* (New York: Simon & Schuster, 2003), 1–2.

2. David Cole, *Enemy Aliens: Double Standards and Constitutional Freedoms in the War on Terrorism* (New York: New Press, 2003).

3. *The American Heritage Dictionary*, 2d College edition (Boston: Houghton Mifflin, 1985), 745.

4. Among the different technologies currently being developed are advanced explosive and trace metal detection machines, facial recognition systems, and fingerprint identification devices. See Karen Kaplan, "Fighting Terrorism," *Los Angeles Times*, September 20, 2001; see also Guy Gugliotta, "Tech Companies See Market for Detection," *Washington Post*, September 28, 2001. Despite these developments, and recent nontechnological advances aimed at fortifying airport security such as random screenings and covert military presence, flying is still not as safe as it could be. See, e.g., Romesh Ratnesar, "How Safe Now?" *Time*, May 27, 2002, 34–35; Richard Zoglin and Sally B. Donnelly, "Welcome to America's Best-Run Airport (And Why It's Still Not Good Enough)," *Time*, July 15, 2002, 22–29. Perhaps a more important flaw is the government's inability to act quickly and decisively on intelligence. See, e.g., Michael Elliott, "How the U.S. Missed the Clues," *Time*, May 27, 2002, 24–32.

5. See Jessica Mitford, "The Criminal Type," in *The Dilemmas of Corrections*, 3d ed., ed. Kenneth C. Haas and Geoffrey P. Alpert (Prospect Heights, IL: Waveland Press, 1995), 21.

6. Ibid. Lombroso also determined that criminals were a "subspecies." Ibid. See also Louis Menand, *The Metaphysical Club* (New York: Farrar, Straus and Giroux, 2001), 97–116; and Richard J. Herrnstein and Charles Murray, *The Bell Curve* (New York: Simon & Schuster, 1996).

7. Mitford, 21. Mitford indicates, however, that not everyone found Lombroso's work convincing. Ibid., 22.

8. Ibid.

9. Ibid., 23.

10. Ibid., 23–24. Mitford further notes that in the past the criminal type that filled the nation's prisons included poor Native Americans as well as Irish and Italian immigrants. Ibid., 24.

11. Ibid., 25–26.

12. Ibid., 26.

13. Ibid., 27–28.

14. Ibid., 28.

15. Ironically, pre–September 11, there was a growing distaste for racial profiling; among others, President Bush and Attorney General Ashcroft spoke out against the practice. Susan Akram and Kevin R. Johnson, "Race, Civil Rights, and Immigration Law after September 11, 2001: The Targeting of Muslims and Arabs," *NYU Annual Survey of American Law* 58 (2002): 295–355. "9/11" quickly reversed that trend with persons of apparent Arab or Muslim background questioned, and as described below, detained for possible links to terrorism. Ibid., 352–55. See also Susan Sachs, "Five Passengers Say Airlines Discriminated by Looks," *New York Times,* June 5, 2002, B4; "Lawsuits Accuse 4 Airlines of Bias," *Washington Post,* June 5, 2002, A01; Leti Volpp, "The Citizen and the Terrorist," *UCLA Law Review* 49 (2002): 1575–99; Natsu Taylor Saito, "Symbolism under Siege: Japanese American Redress and the 'Racing' of Arab Americans as 'Terrorists,'" *Asian Law Journal* 8 (2001): 1–29; Adrien K. Wing, "Reno v. American-Arab Anti-Discrimination Committee: A Critical Race Perspective," *Columbia Human Rights Law Review* 31 (2000): 561–95; Michael J. Whidden, "Unequal Justice: Arabs in America and United States Antiterrorism Legislation," *Fordham Law Review* 69 (2001): 2825–88.

16. Daniel Eisenberg, "How Safe Can We Get?" *Time,* September 24, 2001, 85–89.

17. Akram and Johnson, 331–41. See also Somini Sengupta, "Ill-Fated Path to America, Jail and Death," *New York Times,* November 5, 2001, A1.

18. Michael Kinsley, "Discrimination We're Afraid to Be Against," *The Responsive Community* 12 (Winter 2001–02): 64–66; see also Michael Kinsley, "When Is Racial Profiling Okay?" *Washington Post,* September 30, 2001, B7. Cf. Stanley Crouch, "Drawing the Line on Racial Profiling," *New York Daily News,* October 4, 2001, 41; Dorothy Rabinowitz, "Hijacking History," *Wall Street Journal,* December 7, 2001, A18; Ronald J. Sievert, "Meeting the Twenty-First-Century Terrorist Threat within the Scope of Twentieth-Century Constitutional Law," *Houston Law Review* 37 (2000): 1421–64.

19. PBS On-Line Newshour, *Profile of a Terrorist,* September 26, 2001 (avail-

able at http://www.pbs.org/newshour/bb/terrorism/July-dec01/racial_profile .html).

20. *United States v. Korematsu,* 323 U.S. 214 (1944).

21. Ibid., 236 n.2 (1944) (Murphy, J., dissenting).

22. See Akram and Johnson, 331–48.

23. See Peggy C. Davis, "Law as Microaggression," *Yale Law Journal* 98 (1989): 1559–77.

24. Dan B. Dobbs, *The Law of Torts* (St. Paul, MN: West, 2000), 821.

25. See, e.g., Keith Aoki, "'Foreign-Ness' and Asian American Identities: Yellowface, World War II Propaganda, and Bifurcated Racial Stereotypes," *UCLA Asian Pacific American Law Journal* 4 (1996): 1–60; Frank H. Wu, *Yellow: Race in America beyond Black and White* (New York: Basic Books, 2001), 79–129; Kevin R. Johnson, "Public Benefits and Immigration: The Intersection of Immigration Status, Ethnicity, Gender, and Class," *UCLA Law Review* 42 (1995): 1509–75.

26. See, e.g., John Derbyshire, "A (Potentially) Useful Tool," *The Responsive Community* 12, no. 1 (Winter 2001–02): 67–70; Stephen J. Singer, "Racial Profiling Also Has a Good Side," *Newsday* (New York), September 25, 2001, A38; Editorial, "Profiling Debate Resumes," *Denver Post,* October 3, 2001, B6.

27. David A. Harris, *Profiles in Injustice: Why Racial Profiling Cannot Work* (New York: New Press, 2002). See also David Cole, *No Equal Justice: Race and Class in the American Criminal Justice System* (New York: New Press, 1999); Randall Kennedy, *Race, Crime and the Law* (Cambridge, MA: Pantheon, 1997); Albany Law Review Symposium, "Panel I: Racial Profiling," *Albany Law Review* 66 (Spring 2003): 329–71; R. Richard Banks, "Beyond Profiling: Race, Policy, and the Drug War," *Stanford Law Review* 56 (2003): 571–602; Devon W. Carbado, "(E)Racing the Fourth Amendment," *Michigan Law Review* 100 (2002): 946–1044; Peter H. Schuck, "A Case for Profiling," *American Lawyer,* January 2002, 59–61; Kevin R. Johnson, "The Case against Race Profiling in Immigration Enforcement," *Washington University Law Quarterly* 78 (2000): 675–736; Angela J. Davis, "Race, Cops, and Traffic Stops," *University of Miami Law Review* 51 (1997): 425–43; Tracey Maclin, "Race and the Fourth Amendment," *Vanderbilt Law Review* 51 (1998): 333–92; Anthony C. Thompson, "Stopping the Usual Suspects: Race and the Fourth Amendment," *NYU Law Review* 74 (1999): 956–1013; Katheryn K. Russell, "'Driving While Black': Corollary Phenomena and Collateral Consequences," *Boston College Law Review* 40 (1999): 717–31.

28. General Accounting Office, *U.S. Customs Service, Better Targeting of Airline Passengers for Personal Searches Could Produce Better Results* (March 2000); Harris, *Profiles in Injustice,* 215–22.

29. See, e.g., Johanna McGeary, "Next Stop Mindanao," *Time,* January 28, 2002, 36; Richard C. Paddock, "U.S. to Help Philippines Battle Terrorist Threat

in Asia," *Los Angeles Times,* December 16, 2001, A1; Adam Brown, "More U.S. Troops Fly In to Train Filipinos," *Chicago Tribune,* January 25, 2002, 4. Apparently, the joint Philippine-U.S. military offensive against the Abu Sayyaf group has paid dividends, leading to a substantial decrease in its strength. See Foreign Desk, "President Tours Rebel Territory; Philippines: Leader Pays Respects to a Slain Hostage and Lauds Troops for Rescue in a Visit to Underscore Government Control of the Area," *Los Angeles Times,* June 12, 2002, A4.

30. Massimo Calabresi and Romesh Ratnesar, "Can We Stop the Next Attack?" *Time,* March 11, 2002, 24–34.

31. See, e.g., John Riley, "Lindh Admits Guilt," *Newsday* (New York), July 16, 2002, A3; Michael Hodges, "Lindh Faces Court," *Houston Chronicle,* January 25, 2002, 1. More recently, experts have questioned whether even Lindh was as much of a terrorist as the government claims. See Jane Mayer, "Lost in the Jihad," *New Yorker,* March 10, 2003, 50–59.

32. See, e.g., Tim Wise, "We Show Our True Colors in Wake of Tragedy," *St. Louis Post-Dispatch,* March 13, 2001, D9; Donald S. Bustany, "Why Is It Still OK to Defame Arabs?" *Newsday* (New York), May 9, 1995, A35.

33. Even within this context, using race as a factor should not lead to an overreliance on that one trait. In *Brown v. City of Oneonta,* the Second Circuit upheld the questioning of over two hundred persons of color based on victim testimony that the fugitive was African American. See 221 F.3d 329 (2d Cir. 1999), *cert. denied,* 122 S. Ct. 44 (2001). Contrary to the *Brown* case, I believe courts should more strictly scrutinize police tactics to discern whether too much emphasis was placed on race or any other single characteristic. See Kevin R. Johnson, "U.S. Border Enforcement: Drugs, Migrants, and the Rule of Law," *Villanova Law Review* 47 (2002): 897–919.

34. Harris, *Profiles in Injustice,* 49.

35. See Associated Press, "Prosecutor Ties Syria to El Al Bomb Attempt," *Los Angeles Times,* October 6, 1986, 2; Lisa Beyer, "Israel's El Al Airline: Is This What We Really Want?" *Time,* September 24, 2001, 91.

36. Kate Novack, "Let the Airport Scramble Begin," *Time,* June 2, 2003, 20.

37. *The Records of the Federal Convention of 1787,* ed. Max Farrand, rev. ed. (New Haven: Yale University Press, 1966), vol. 2, 116–17 (emphasis added).

38. See U.S. Const., art. II, § 1, cl. 5.

39. Farrand, *Records,* vol. 2, 367. The conventioneers' initial draft provided that "he shall be of the age of thirty five years, and a Citizen of the United States, and shall have been an Inhabitant thereof for Twenty one years." Ibid.

40. Joseph Story, *Commentaries on the Constitution* (1833). 1997. Hilliard, Gray and Company, and Brown, Shattuck and Company, Constitution Society, http://www.constitution.org/js/js_000.htm, vol. 3, § 1473. Story also observed that the exception created for the immigrant Founders was a departure from the

policy exercised by all governments of excluding foreign influence from executive councils and duties. Ibid.

41. See Randall Kennedy, "A Natural Aristocracy?" *Constitutional Commentary* 12 (1995): 175–77; Robert Post, "What Is the Constitution's Worst Provision?" *Constitutional Commentary* 12 (1995): 191–93.

42. See 50 *U.S.C.* § 453 (1994).

43. Gordon W. Allport, *The Nature of Prejudice* (1954; reprint, Reading, MA: Perseus Books, 1979), 46.

44. Ibid.

45. More recent surveys suggest that the number of those favoring *status-based* profiling as opposed to *behavior-based* profiling is on the decline. Although a Fox Broadcasting survey of 900 registered voters conducted in June 2002 revealed that 54 percent would approve of racial profiling to screen Arab male airline passengers, a July 2002 Public Agenda telephone poll of 1,520 people indicated that 92 percent would favor the screening of all persons who take flying lessons, while only 6 percent thought the government should target those from the Middle East only. Compare Fox Broadcasting Co. telephone poll, June 4–5, 2002 with Public Agenda telephone poll, July 10–24, 2002 (available on Polling the Nations Website, http://poll.orspub.com).

46. See, e.g., Wiley A. Hall, "Arab-Americans Assail Rush to Judgment," *Baltimore Evening Sun,* April 25, 1995, 2A; Michael Grunwald, "Muslims Fear Being Made Scapegoats," *Boston Globe,* April 21, 1995, 1. After September 11, the backlash against the Arab and Muslim community was staggering. See, e.g., David Van Biema, "As American as . . . ," *Time,* October 1, 2001, 72–74. In response, the Justice Department stated that it has investigated some 350 reported crimes against people of Middle Eastern or South Asian origin since the terrorist attacks of 2001. See Associated Press, "On Lookout for Retaliation," *Newsday* (New York), June 26, 2002, A17. In an interesting twist post–Oklahoma City, the Southern Poverty Law Center has discovered links between Muslim terrorists and domestic neo-Nazi extremists based on their similar distaste for the U.S. government. Martin A. Lee, "The Swastika and the Crescent," *Intelligence Report (Southern Poverty Law Center)* Spring 2002 http://www.splcenter.org/intel/intelreport/article.jsp?aid=132.

47. See, e.g., Michael D. Lemonick, "Lessons Learned: Anthrax," *Time,* December 31, 2001, 126–28; Martha Kranes, "Anthrax Probe Shifts to Home-grown Hate Groups," *New York Post,* October 25, 2001, 4. But see Peter Slevin, "In Anthrax Probe, Questions of Skill, Motive," *Washington Post,* November 5, 2001, A05.

48. Associated Press, "Deported Man Said to Have Al Qaeda Tie," *Washington Post,* August 11, 2002, A19. An even more depressing example is that Mohammed Atta, one of the key 9/11 hijackers, was arrested for a traffic violation

in Florida in July 2001; he was released when officials failed to uncover a prior warrant for his arrest from a neighboring county. Charlie Weaver and Robert Ulrich, "Mr. Magoo v. the Terrorists," *Washington Times,* August 5, 2002, A17.

49. Counsel at removal hearings appear "at no expense to the Government." Immigration and Nationality Act, 8 *U.S.C.* §§ 1229a(b)(4)(A), 1362. Moreover, although there is no Sixth Amendment right to counsel at removal hearings (because they are not criminal proceedings), Fifth Amendment due process limitations do apply. See Legomsky, *Immigration and Refugee Law and Policy,* 663–64. Federal courts are understandably reluctant to find Fifth Amendment violations absent truly egregious conduct in specific cases, a standard common within constitutional immigration law. See, e.g., *Reno v. Arab-American Anti-Discrimination Committee,* 525 U.S. 471, 491 (1999).

50. A *New York Times*–CBS News poll revealed that, since the 9/11 attacks, many are skeptical of the government's antiterrorism efforts and their effectiveness. See Adam Clymer and Janet Elder, "Poll Finds Unease on Terror Fight and Concerns about War on Iraq," *New York Times,* September 8, 2002, A1.

51. As widely reported in the press, for a time Ashcroft wanted broader powers of investigation generally, hoping that Congress would provide such authorization in the USA-PATRIOT Act. See, e.g., Eric Lichtblau, Ricardo Alonso-Zaldivar, and Nick Anderson, "After the Attack, Security Clampdown," *Los Angeles Times,* September 17, 2001, A9. While not a paragon of restraint, the resulting legislation is less draconian. See USA-PATRIOT Act of 2001, Pub. L. No. 107-56, 115 Stat. 272 (2001).

52. In the *New York Times* poll cited above, two-fifths of the respondents believed that the government had not done enough since 9/11 to protect them against another terrorist attack; one of those polled suggested initiating "things like background checks on people who go in and out of the country" as a means by which such additional security could be achieved. Clymer and Elder, A1.

53. John Walker Lindh and Jose Padilla were Time.com's "Person of the Week," for example, on January 25, 2002 and June 14, 2002, respectively. A scan of CBSnews.com revealed that as of October 17, 2002, that service alone had reported eighty-eight times on John Walker Lindh and twenty-two times on Jose Padilla. For more on Lindh, see Riley, A3; Hodges, 1. For more on Padilla, see Amanda Ripley, "The Case of the Dirty Bomber," *Time,* June 24, 2002, 28–32; Susan Schmidt and Walter Pincus, "Al Muhajir Alleged to Be Scouting Terror Sites; U.S. Says Al Qaeda Had Instructed Suspect," *Washington Post,* June 12, 2002, A01; Caroline Daniel and Jeremy Grant, "Ex-Gang Member Who Went Unnoticed," *Financial Times* (London), June 11, 2002, A1; David G. Savage, "Detention of a Citizen Questioned Law: 'Dirty Bomb' Suspect Was Secretly Held and Hasn't Been Charged," *Los Angeles Times,* June 12, 2002, A1. This is not to suggest that the two *are* in fact terrorists. While Lindh has pled guilty to

terrorist activity, Padilla's lawyers are still fighting his designation as an enemy combatant.

54. See, e.g., Ron Kampeas, "Anthrax Probe Figure to Undergo Blood Test," *Chicago Sun-Times,* August 26, 2002, 5; Susan Schmidt, "Evidence Lacking as Probe of Scientist in Anthrax Scare Intensifies," *Washington Post,* August 15, 2002, A07; Curt Anderson, "Justice Dept. Denies Casting Suspicion on Germ Researcher," *Boston Globe,* December 13, 2002, A51.

55. Of course, this unequal press coverage might be more a reflection of the press's priorities than existing reality.

56. See generally Akram and Johnson; Volpp, 1575–99; Sameer Ashar, "Immigration Enforcement and Subordination: The Consequences of Racial Profiling after September 11," *Connecticut Law Review* 34 (2002): 1185–99; David Cole, "Enemy Aliens," *Stanford Law Review* 54 (2002): 953–1004.

57. See, e.g., Kevin R. Johnson, "Racial Hierarchy, Asian Americans and Latino/as as 'Foreigners,' and Social Change: Is Law the Way to Go?" *Oregon Law Review* 76 (1997): 347–68.

58. See, e.g., Kevin R. Johnson, "Immigration and Latino Identity," *Chicano-Latino Law Review* 19 (1998): 197–211.

59. Peter Katel, "Slamming the Door," *Time,* March 11, 2002, 37.

60. Eric L. Hinton, "Racial Profiling: Is It Ever the Right Thing to Do?" *DiversityInc. Magazine,* November–December 2002, 111, 112.

61. See, e.g., Cole, "Enemy Aliens," 997–98.

62. Ibid., 1003. See also Kevin R. Johnson, "Race, the Immigration Laws, and Domestic Race Relations: A 'Magic Mirror' into the Heart of Darkness," *Indiana Law Journal* 73 (1998): 1111–59; Kevin R. Johnson, "September 11 and Mexican Immigrants: Collateral Damage Comes Home," *DePaul Law Review* 52 (2003): 849–70.

63. See *In re All Matters Submitted to the Foreign Intelligence Surveillance Court,* 21 F. Supp. 2d 611 (2002), *abrogated,* 310 F.3d 717 (2002). See also Raquel Aldana-Pindell, "The 9/11 'National Security' Cases: Three Principles Guiding Judges' Decisionmaking," *Oregon Law Review* 81 (2002): 985–1049; Philip Shenon, "Secret Court Says It Was Misled by FBI," *San Diego Union-Tribune,* August 23, 2002, A01.

64. *Detroit Free Press v. Ashcroft,* 303 F.3d 681 (6th Cir. 2002). Most recently, the Sixth Circuit Court of Appeals declined the Justice Department's invitation to review the panel's decision *en banc. North Jersey Media Group, Inc. v. Ashcroft,* 308 F.3d 198 (3d Cir. 2002). This conflict between the Third and Sixth Circuits led to speculation that the Supreme Court might want to resolve this issue before long. In May 2003, however, the Court declined the ACLU's invitation to review the Third Circuit's decision, leaving the apparent conflict unresolved. See Edward Walsh, "High Court Stays Out of Secrecy Fray; Dispute Centers on Closed Deportation," *Washington Post,* May 28, 2003, A04.

65. *Rasul v. Bush, 124 S. Ct. 2686 (2004).*

66. Alternatives to aggressive immigration enforcement in combating terrorism include the development of better technologies that do not unduly trample individual privacy rights and better utilization of security policies designed to thwart terrorist activity, such as bag-matching at airports. See, e.g., Kaplan, T1; Gugliotta, A08; John Hughes, "New Baggage Screening Raises Concerns," *Chicago Sun-Times,* December 31, 2002, 50.

67. It is conceivable that we deport suspected terrorists to an ally that engages in torture so as to extract valuable information from the suspects without having to ourselves violate human rights law. Our decision to leave terror suspect Mohammed Heidar Zammar in the hands of the Syrian government rather than taking custody ourselves was allegedly motivated by similar goals. See Mitch Frank, "Help from an Unlikely Ally," *Time,* July 1, 2002, 28.

68. Dena Bunis, "Security a Focal Point of Immigration Policy," *Orange County Register* (California), September 9, 2002.

69. Nicholas D. Kristof, "Security and Freedom," *New York Times,* September 10, 2002, A25.

70. See, e.g., Akram and Johnson; Volpp; Ashar.

71. Similar to Section 507 is 508, which allows the government access to student information from the National Center for Education Statistics, pursuant again to an *ex parte* court order. While this might implicate foreign nationals, it has yet to come into play.

72. 20 *U.S.C.* § 1232g.

73. If the student is under eighteen. See generally Recent Amendments to FERPA relating to Anti-Terrorism Activities (LeRoy Rooker, Director, Family Compliance Office, U.S. Dept. of Education, April 12, 2002), 1 [hereinafter Rooker Letter].

74. 34 *C.F.R.* §§ 99.31(a)(10), 99.36 (FERPA regulations relating to health and safety emergencies).

75. USA-PATRIOT Act of 2001, § 507 (amending 20 *U.S.C.* § 1232g).

76. Ibid.

77. The information regarding the FBI's recent interactions with universities and public reaction to this comes from Dan Eggen, "FBI Seeks Data on Foreign Students," *Washington Post,* December 25, 2002, A1.

78. The international reaction to the FBI's actions comes from "Malaysia's Biggest Student Association Slams U.S. 'Phobia.'" *IRNA On-Line,* December 27, 2002, http://www.irna.com/en/head/021227125633.ehe.shtml.

79. Scott Carlson and Andrea L. Foster, "Colleges Fear Anti-Terrorism Law Could Turn Them into Big Brother," *Chronicle of Higher Education,* March 1, 2002, A31–32.

80. Ibid.

81. Homeland Security: Information Sharing Responsibilities, Challenges, and Key Management Issues (U.S. General Accounting Office, May 8, 2003).

82. Rooker Letter.

83. Ibid.

84. Illegal Immigration Reform and Immigrant Responsibility Act of 1996 (IIRAIRA) § 641, 8 *U.S.C.* § 1372.

85. Legomsky, *Immigration and Refugee Law and Policy,* 352 (discussing IIRAIRA § 641).

86. Ibid.

87. See, e.g., Kurzban, 11.

88. INS, "Fact Sheet: Student and Exchange Visitor Information System (SEVIS)—Final Rule Implementing SEVIS," December 11, 2002, http://www.immigration.gov/graphics/publicaffairs/factsheets/02.

89. As of March 1, 2003, the Immigration and Naturalization Service, or INS, ceased to exist. Its enforcement and visa processing functions have been divided among three bureaus within the new Department of Homeland Security—U.S. Customs and Border Protection, U.S. Immigration and Customs Enforcement, and U.S. Citizenship and Immigration Service. See U.S. Dept. of Homeland Security, *Immigration and Borders.* http://www.dhs.gov/dhspublic/theme_home4.jsp.

The immigration enforcement functions I refer to here now come within the purview of Investigation and Customs Enforcement, although U.S. Citizenship and Immigration Service administers SEVIS. To simplify matters and because many of the reported abuses are alleged against the INS, I will use the designation "INS" in this section.

90. INS, "Fact Sheet."

91. Ellen H. Badger, "SEVIS: The U.S. INS's New Tracking System for International Students and Exchange Visitors," *ILW.COM,* September 5, 2002, http://www.ilw.com/lawyers/immigdaily/digest/2002,0905.shtm.

92. For instance, schools must keep the following information for F-1 and M-1 students: name, date and place of birth, country of citizenship, current address where the student and his or her dependents reside; the student's current academic status; date of commencement of studies; degree program and field of study; whether the student has been certified for practical training, and the beginning and end dates of certification; termination date and reason, if known; the documents referred to in paragraph (k) of this section; the number of credits completed each semester; and a photocopy of the student's I-20 ID Copy. 8 *C.F.R.* § 214.3(g)(1).

93. INS, "Fact Sheet."

94. Dave Curtin, "6 Mideast Students Jailed for Cutting Course Hours," *Denver Post,* December 26, 2002, A01.

95. Ibid. See also INS, *Special Registration,* http://www.immigration.gov
/graphics/shared/lawenfor/specialreg/index.htm.

96. Associated Press, "Students' Arrests Prompt a New Class," *Los Angeles
Times,* December 29, 2002, A25.

97. "Rights Groups Sue Due to Arrests of NSEERS Registrants," *Interpreter
Releases* 80 (January 13, 2003): 41–43 (describing class action lawsuit entitled
*ADC v. Ashcroft,* No. 8:02cv01200 (C.D. Cal., December 24, 2002).

98. December 23, 2002, Letter from Feingold et al. to Ashcroft, *Interpreter
Releases* 80 (January 13, 2003): 55–58.

99. Office of the Press Secretary, "First 100 Days of Homeland Security,"
April 29, 2003, http://www.whitehouse.gov/news/releases/2003/04/20030429-
7.html.

100. Ibid.

101. 8 *C.F.R.* § 214.2(f)(18) modifies the requirements of 8 *C.F.R.* § 214.1 for
Mexican and Canadian commuters who are enrolled in a full course of study on
a part-time basis.

102. "Part-Time Commuter Students Will No Longer Be Admitted to Schools
in U.S.," *Interpreter Releases* 79 (June 3, 2002): 872–73; Associated Press, "Visiting Part-Time Students Barred," *Washington Post,* May 30, 2002, A26.

103. Mike Mrkvicka, "Hutchison Backs Part-Time Foreign Students," *El
Paso Times* (El Paso, TX), July 2, 2002, 01.

104. Ibid.

105. *Congressional Record* E1906–01 (daily ed., October 15, 2002) (statement of Representative Ciro Rodriguez).

106. Erik Lords, "Part-Time Students to Return to U.S.," *Detroit Free Press,*
August 27, 2002.

107. Pub. L. No. 107-274, 116 Stat. 1923 (2002).

108. Ibid.

NOTES TO CHAPTER 3

1. Congressman Barney Frank raised this example in his statement in favor of
the proposed Family Reunification Act of 2002. Family Reunification Act,
HR1452, 107th Cong., 1st sess. (2002).

2. See generally U.S. Congress, *Senate Subcommittee on Immigration and
Claims.* Testimony of Cecilia Muñoz, April 2001, http://www.senate.gov/~judi-
ciary/te040401cm.htm; and U.S. Congress, *Senate Subcommittee on Immigration and Claims.* Testimony of Karen Narasaki, April 2001, http://www.senate
.gov/~judiciary/te040401kn.htm.

3. No less than 226,000 immigrant visas shall be allocated to the four family
preference categories per fiscal year. 8 *U.S.C.* § 1151(c)(1)(B)(ii). In addition,

there is no limit to the number of "immediate relative" visas that may be issued per year. 8 *U.S.C.* § 1151(b)(2).

4. T. Alexander Aleinikoff, David A. Martin, and Hiroshi Motomura, *Immigration and Citizenship* (St. Paul, MN: West, 2000), 319.

5. See McCarran-Walter Act, U.S. Code 8 (1952) §§ 1101 *et seq.* For more on family immigration, see generally Sarah B. Ignatius and Elisabeth S. Stickney, *Immigration Law and the Family* (St. Paul, MN: West, 2003).

6. Family Reunification Act, HR1452, 107th Cong., 1st sess. (2002).

7. *Congressional Record* H7774 (2000) (statement of Rep. Jackson-Lee).

8. See Child Citizenship Act of 2000: Hearing on H.R. 2883 before the House Committee on the Judiciary Subcommittee on Immigration and Claims, 106th Cong., 146 Cong. Rec. S 10491 (2000) (testimony of Maureen Evans, Joint Council on International Children's Services).

9. The 2003 version seeks the same discretionary power for the Secretary of Homeland Security, now that DHS has jurisdiction over immigration matters since the INS was dissolved in March 2003.

10. Public Law 104-132, 110 *U.S. Statutes at Large* 1214 (April 24, 1996).

11. Nancy Morawetz, "Understanding the Impact of the 1996 Deportation Laws and the Limited Scope of Proposed Reforms," *Harvard Law Review* 113 (2000): 1940–41. For more of these stories, see also Terry Coonan, "Dolphins Caught in Congressional Fishnets — Immigration Law's New Aggravated Felons," *Georgetown Immigration Law Journal* 12 (1998): 589–619.

12. *Congressional Record* H7774 (2000) (statement of Rep. Jackson-Lee; statement of Rep. Gejdenson).

13. Family Reunification Act, HR1452, 107th Cong., 1st sess. (2002).

14. Ibid.

15. For similar stories, see Susan Levine, "On the Verge of Exile: For Children Adopted from Abroad," *Washington Post,* March 5, 2000, A01.

16. Susan Taylor Martin, "Despite Adversity, Deportee Now Has New Life," *St. Petersburg Times,* August 28, 2000, A4; Associated Press, "Bill Eases Citizenship for Adopted Children," *Charleston Gazette* (Charleston, SC), February 18, 2000.

17. Associated Press, "Deported Brazilian Left on Unfamiliar Ground," *Houston Chronicle,* November 30, 2000, 34; Terry Oblander, "Clemency Proposal Rejected by Taft; Man Faced Deportation on Drug Sale Charge," *Plain Dealer* (Cleveland, OH), August 26, 2000, 1B.

18. Press Release, *House of Representatives Passes Delahunt Child Citizenship Bill.* 2001, http://www.holtintl.org/update091900bpr.html.

19. Ibid.

20. See Elizabeth Bartholet, "Where Do Black Children Belong? The Politics of Race Matching in Adoption," *University of Pennsylvania Law Review* 139

(1991): 1166–67; Burton Z. Sokoloff, "Antecedents of American Adoption," *The Future of Children: Adoption* 3, no. 1, Spring 1993, http://www.future ofchildren.org/information2826/information_show.htm?doc_id=77441; Andrew R. Silverman, "Outcomes of Transracial Adoption,". *The Future of Children: Adoption* 3, no. 1, Spring 1993, http://www.futureofchildren.org/usr_doc /vol3no1ART7%2EPDF.

21. "The 106th Congress include[d] among its 535 voting members 37 African Americans, 18 Hispanics, and three Asians and Pacific Islanders in the U.S. House of Representatives; and two Asians and Pacific Islanders and one American Indian in the U.S. Senate." Kelvin M. Pollard and William P. O'Hare, "America's Racial and Ethnic Minorities," *Population Bulletin* 54, no. 3, September 1999, http://www.prb.org/Content/NavigationMenu/PRB/AboutPRB/ Population_Bulletin2/Americas_Racial_and_Ethnic_Minorities.htm. More specifically, the racial makeup of the 106th Congress was as follows:

    1. Total members—535 (435 H.R., 100 Senate)

    2. Black—37 (6.91 percent) (37 H.R., 0 Senate)

    3. Hispanic—18 (3.36 percent) (18 H.R., 0 Senate)

    4. Asian/Pacific Islander—5 (0.9 percent) (3 H.R., 2 Senate)

    5. American Indian—1 (0.2 percent) (0 H.R., 1 Senate)

    22. See *Congressional Record* H7774 (2000).

    23. Ibid.

    24. Ibid.

    25. Diane Schmidley, *The Foreign Born Population in the United States: March 2002.* February 2003, http://www.census.gov/prod/2003pubs/p20-539.pdf.

    26. Ibid.

    27. Ibid.

    28. Irma D. Herrera, *Hispanic Attitudes toward Adoption,* http://www.pacta-dopt.org/press/articles/hispanic.html; see also Sokoloff, 23.

    29. See Kathy S. Stolley, "Statistics on Adoption in the United States," *Adoption* 3, no. 1, Spring 1993, http://www.futureofchildren.org/usr_doc /vol3no1ART2%2EPDF.

    30. Ironically, despite the epidemic of school shootings in suburban and rural America, committed primarily by young white males, we do not concoct the same racial profile of the would-be school assassin. See Tim Wise, "School Shootings and White Denial," *Alternet.Org,* March 6, 2001, http://www.alter-net.org/story.html?StrotyID=10560.

    31. Family Reunification Act, HR1452, 107th Cong., 1st sess. (2002).

    32. See Michael Fix and Wendy Zimmerman, *All under One Roof: Mixed Status Families in an Era of Reform,* June 1999, Urban Institute Website, http://www.urban.org/immig/all_under.html.

    33. Ibid.

34. Family Reunification Act, HR1452, 107th Cong., 1st sess. (2002).

35. Schmidley.

36. Fortunately, Collado was released after much public outrage; this does not mean, however, that the INS was not acting within its congressionally delegated power. See Mae M. Cheng and Margaret Ramirez, "After Outcry, INS Releases Man Held for Old Crime," *Newsday* (New York), October 25, 1997, A19. For more on Collado, see, e.g., Editorial, "No Justice for Immigrants," *Progressive* (Madison), November 1, 1997, 8–9; Vincent J. Schodolski, "Immigrants Face Deportation for Old Crimes under New Laws: Reform Snares Legal Residents," *Chicago Tribune,* October 12, 1997, 3; Mae M. Cheng, "New INS Guidelines Soften '96 Laws," *Newsday* (New York), November 26, 2000, A48.

37. See, e.g., Gabriel J. Chin, Victor C. Romero, and Michael A. Scaperlanda, eds., *Immigration and the Constitution,* vol. 2 (New York: Garland Publishing, 2000); Kif Augustine-Adams, "Gendered States: A Comparative Construction of Citizenship and Nation," *Virginia Journal of International Law* 41 (2000): 93–139; Kevin R. Johnson, *The "Huddled Masses" Myth: Immigration and Civil Rights* (Philadelphia: Temple University Press, 2004).

38. See, e.g., Matter of Magallanes-Garcia, Int. Decisions 3341 (BIA 1998).

39. Proposed Family Reunification Act, HR1452, 107th Cong., 1st sess. (2001).

40. See, e.g., *INA* §§ 216(c)(4)(A), 212(i), 212(a)(9)(B)(v). See also Family Unity Program, 8 *C.F.R.* § 236.10.

41. Legomsky, *Immigration and Refugee Law and Policy,* 1111 (citing Jeffrey S. Passel, Recent Efforts to Control Illegal Immigration to the United States 3 (unpublished paper, presented to the OECD Working Party on Migration, Paris, June 13–14, 1996)).

NOTES TO CHAPTER 4

1. See, e.g., Michael A. Scaperlanda, "The Domestic Fourth Amendment Rights of Aliens: To What Extent Do They Survive United States v. Verdugo-Urquidez?" *Missouri Law Review* 56 (1991): 213–43; James G. Connell III and René G. Valladares, "Search and Seizure Protections for Undocumented Aliens: The Territoriality and Voluntary Presences Principles in Fourth Amendment Law," *American Criminal Law Review* 34 (1997): 1293–352; Victor C. Romero, "Whatever Happened to the Fourth Amendment? Undocumented Immigrants' Rights after INS v. Lopez-Mendoza and United States v. Verdugo-Urquidez," *Southern California Law Review* 65 (1992): 999–1034.

2. 265 F. Supp. 2d 1254 (N.D. Utah 2003). As this book goes to press, there appears to be no forthcoming appellate ruling on this issue. Even if there were, that should not detract from the legal theory here—namely, that noncitizens in

the United States charged with crimes should not be stripped of constitutional Fourth Amendment protections simply because they are undocumented.

3. Ibid., 1256.

4. Ibid.

5. *United States v. Verdugo-Urquidez*, 494 U.S. 259, 262–63 (1990).

6. See *United States v. Barona*, 56 F.3d 1087, 1093–94 (9th Cir. 1995); *United States v. Guitterez*, No. CR 96-40075 SBA, 1997 U.S. Dist. LEXIS 16446, at *16–17 (N.D. Cal. October 14, 1997); *Esparza-Mendoza*, 265 F. Supp. 2d 1254.

7. *Verdugo-Urquidez*, 265.

8. Ibid. Rehnquist noted that the term "people" appears in the Preamble and the First, Second, Ninth, and Tenth amendments. Ibid.

9. *Verdugo-Urquidez*, 272–73.

10. These different terms were used at various places within the majority opinion. Compare "sufficient connection" with "significant voluntary connection" *and* "substantial connection." Ibid., 265, 271.

11. *Esparza-Mendoza*, 1267.

12. Ibid., 1271.

13. Tourists typically need to apply for B-1 visitors' visas for entry into the United States for a temporary period. *INA* § 101(a)(15)(B) (1998).

14. Even after the successful passage of the North American Free Trade Agreement in 1992, the United States still requires a visa or other immigration documentation from temporary business visitors from Mexico but not from Canadian ones. Harry J. Joe, "Temporary Entry of Business Persons to the United States under the North American Free Trade Agreement," *Georgetown Immigration Law Journal* 8 (1994): 399–400; Gerald A. Wunsch, "Why NAFTA's Immigration Provisions Discriminate against Mexican Nationals," *Indiana International and Comparative Law Review* 5 (1994): 127–42; Kevin R. Johnson, "Free Trade and Closed Borders: NAFTA and Mexican Immigration to the United States," *University of California at Davis Law Review* 27 (1994): 937–78.

15. *Immigration Reform and Control Act 1986,* Public Law 99-603 (November 6, 1986). See also Maurice A. Roberts and Stephen Yale-Loehr, *Understanding the 1986 Immigration Law* (Washington, DC: Federal Publications, 1987), chapter 3.

16. Indeed, the current Immigration and Naturalization Act provides for the cancellation of removal (previously, deportation) of a lawful permanent resident who has resided continuously in the United States, whether or not the noncitizen has been in the country lawfully. *INA* § 240A(a)(2). Hence, a nonimmigrant who overstays her visa prior to adjusting her status to legal permanent residence may arguably count the period of her unlawful residence in the United States toward the seven–year period as long as her stay was continuous. Thus, to the extent that the immigration code specifically allows noncitizens to count their years

of unlawful presence to qualify for Section 240A relief, they should also be able to count such unlawful presence in situations where Fourth Amendment standing is at stake.

17. "What a person knowingly exposes to the public, even in his own home or office, is not a subject of Fourth Amendment protection." *Katz v. United States,* 387 U.S. 347, 351 (1967). See also Charles H. Whitebread II and Christopher Slobogin, *Criminal Procedure* (New York: Foundation Press, 4th ed., 2000).

18. See generally Lisa Kloppenberg, *Playing It Safe: How the Supreme Court Sidesteps Hard Cases and Stunts the Development of Law* (New York: NYU Press, 2001).

19. *Chavez v. Martinez,* 123 S. Ct. 1994 (2003).

20. *Mathews v. Diaz,* 426 U.S. 67 (1976); *Mendoza v. I.N.S.,* 559 F. Supp. 842 (W.D. Tex., May 17, 1982) ("No evidence presented even suggested that the INS and EPPD formulated their plan for the area control operation for the purpose of denying any Mexican-American equal protection of the laws. Discriminatory intent must be shown to recover for denial of equal protection. See *Washington v. Davis,* 426 U.S. 229, 96 S. Ct. 2040, 48 L. Ed. 2d 597 (1976). Discriminatory intent has not been shown; therefore, Plaintiffs are not likely to succeed in the merits of their equal protection claim.").

21. *Allegheny Pittsburgh Coal Co. v. County Comm'n,* 488 U.S. 336 (1984); *City of Cleburne v. Cleburne Living Center,* 473 U.S. 432 (1985); *Romer v. Evans,* 517 U.S. 620 (1996).

22. *FCC v. Beach Communications, Inc.,* 508 U.S. 307, 313 (1993).

23. See Appendix in my original article for survey of the governing premises liability law standards in the fifty states and the District of Columbia. Victor C. Romero, "The Domestic Fourth Amendment Rights of Undocumented Immigrants: On Guitterez and the Tort Law-Immigration Law Parallel," *Harvard Civil Rights–Civil Liberties Law Review* 35 (2000): 57–101.

24. "The occupier is not an insurer of the safety of invitees, and his duty is only to exercise reasonable care for their protection." W. Page Keeton et al., *Prosser and Keeton on the Law of Torts* (St. Paul, MN: West, 5th ed., 1984), 425 and n.89.

25. Ibid., 412.

26. Ibid., 393.

27. See, e.g., *Gladon v. Greater Cleveland Regional Transit Auth.,* 662 N.E.2d 287, 293 (Ohio 1996). Keeton et al., however, note that generally an entrant gains more protection as her status improves from "trespasser" to "licensee" to "invitee." Keeton et al., 393.

28. *Rowland v. Christian,* 443 P.2d 561 (Cal. 1968).

29. *Basso v. Miller,* 352 N.E.2d 868 (N.Y. 1976); *Scurti v. City of New York,* 354 N.E.2d 794 (1976).

30. See Appendix in my original article for list of all Model 3 jurisdictions. Romero, "The Domestic Fourth Amendment Rights of Undocumented Immigrants."

31. See Vitauts M. Gulbis, "Modern Status of Rules Conditioning Landowner's Liability upon Status of Injured Party as Invitee, Licensee, or Trespasser," *American Law Reports, 4th* 22 (1981): 294–314.

32. While the distinction between the "invitee" and "licensee" can sometimes be a tenuous one, much of the distinction turns on whether the landowner benefits from the entry—that is, licensees confer no benefit on the landowner and are on the land solely for their own purposes, while invitees confer a benefit on the landowner. See Dan B. Dobbs and Paul T. Hayden, *Torts and Compensation* (St. Paul, MN: West, 3d ed., 1997), 307–08 nn.2(a) and 3.

From this benefits analysis, the legal permanent resident (like the invitee) confers long-term benefits upon the United States through her labor and purchasing power, while the legal nonimmigrant (like the licensee) benefits largely herself, conferring only incidental benefits on the United States during her temporary visit.

33. *Rowland,* 562.

34. Ibid., 561, 569.

35. Ibid., 565 (citing *Oettinger v. Stewart,* 24 Cal. 2d 133, 138–39 (1944)).

36. Ibid., 566 (citing *Kermarec v. Compagnie Generale,* 358 U.S. 625, 630–31 (1959)).

37. Ibid.

38. See, e.g., *Basso,* 873; *Scurti,* 798. In *Basso,* the New York Court of Appeals followed California's lead by abolishing the traditional land entrant classifications in favor of a unitary due care standard. *Basso,* 872. *Scurti,* which was decided the same day as *Basso,* added to the analysis by specifying that the traditional classes would be relevant to, but not determinative of, landowner liability. *Scurti,* 798. In assessing the reasonableness of a landowner's conduct, the court specifically listed three factors that would carry continued significance: (1) whether the injury occurred on the defendant's property; (2) whether the plaintiff entered the land with the defendant's permission; and (3) the age of the plaintiff. Ibid., 796–99. Thus, in abolishing the traditional system, the New York court simply incorporated the entrant's status as a factor in assessing reasonableness.

39. 457 U.S. 202 (1982); see also *Yick Wo v. Hopkins,* 118 U.S. 356 (1886).

40. *Kwong Hai Chew v. Colding,* 344 U.S. 590 (1953); *Bridges v. Wixon,* 326 U.S. 135 (1945).

41. See Whitebread and Slobogin, 18.

42. *Mathews v. Diaz,* 426 U.S. 67 (1976).

43. *Verdugo-Urquidez,* 284–85 (Brennan, J., dissenting). See also Neuman, *Strangers to the Constitution,* 107–17.

44. *Verdugo-Urquidez,* 284–85.

45. In *American Federation of Labor v. American Sash & Door Co.,* 335 U.S. 538, 549 n.5 (1948), Justice Frankfurter invoked Article 20(2) of the Universal Declaration in his concurrence supporting the Court's decision to uphold a state law designed to protect nonunion members. Article 12 of the Universal Declaration provides that "[n]o one shall be subjected to arbitrary interference with his privacy, family, home or correspondence, nor to attacks upon his honor and reputation. Everyone has the right to protection of the law against such interference or attacks." "Universal Declaration of Human Rights," translated by U.N. Doc. A/810, *G.A. Res. 217A(III)* (1948), 71, art. 12.

46. Johnson, "Public Benefits and Immigration," 1545–46.

47. See, e.g., Gotanda, "Asian American Rights," 1098. As the United States becomes more and more racially diverse, perhaps this concern about who is most likely to be an undocumented immigrant is waning. However, following the passage of Proposition 187 in November 1994, people across California appointed themselves "immigration police" and would report any Latino/as in the area to the INS because they allegedly fit the profile of the undocumented immigrant. See, e.g., Demetria Martinez, "Hatred Rumbles Along New Fault Line Called Proposition 187," *National Catholic Reporter* (Kansas City), February 10, 1995, 18.

48. See, e.g., *Orhorhaghe v. INS,* 38 F.3d 488 (9th Cir. 1994).

49. Wayne R. LaFave, *Search and Seizure: A Treatise on the Fourth Amendment* (St. Paul, MN: West, 3d ed., 1996), § 1.2(b) and (c).

50. Twenty-eight states continue to follow the tripartite Model 1 classification scheme. Nineteen states considered but rejected arguments to switch to a Model 2 or Model 3 system; however, nine of the twenty-eight Model 1 states have yet to consider the change. Nine states have abolished traditional entrant classifications and fall under Model 2. Thirteen states and the District of Columbia have adopted Model 3. See Romero, "The Domestic Fourth Amendment Rights of Undocumented Immigrants," 93–101.

51. This information on Cassell derives heavily from Edward Cohn, "Paul Cassell and the Goblet of Fire," *American Prospect* (Princeton), August 28, 2000, 32–36.

52. Ibid.

NOTES TO CHAPTER 5

1. The "positive"/"negative" rights distinction is usually attributed to Isaiah Berlin. See Isaiah Berlin, *Two Concepts of Liberty: An Inaugural Lecture Delivered before the University of Oxford, on 31 October 1958* (Oxford: Clarendon Press, 1958). See also John Denvir, *Democracy's Constitution: Claiming the Privileges and Immunities of American Citizenship* (Champaign-Urbana, IL:

University of Illinois Press, 2001) (arguing that positive rights to work and education emanate from the Constitution).

2. Personal Responsibility and Work Opportunity Reconciliation Act, Public Law 104-193, §§ 400–51 (1996), codified as amended at 8 *U.S.C.* §§1601–46 (2000) [hereinafter PRWORA].

3. See, e.g., Antiterrorism and Effective Death Penalty Act of 1996, Public Law 104-132, §§ 401–43 (1996) [hereinafter AEDPA]; Illegal Immigration Reform and Immigrant Responsibility Act of 1996, Public Law 104-208, § 306 (1996), codified as amended at 8 *U.S.C.* § 1252(g) (2000) [hereinafter IIRAIRA]; Uniting and Strengthening America by Providing Appropriate Tools Required to Intercept and Obstruct Terrorism Act of 2001, Public Law 107-56, 115 *U.S. Statutes at Large* 272 (October 26, 2001) [hereinafter USA PATRIOT ACT].

4. 8 *U.S.C.* § 1623 (2000). There is a second provision that deprives undocumented immigrants of certain state and local benefits, although it permits states to override this provision through subsequent legislation. See Stanley Mailman and Stephen Yale-Loehr, "College for Undocumented Immigrants after All?" *New York Law Journal,* June 25, 2001, 3.

5. Michael A. Olivas, "Storytelling out of School: Undocumented College Residency, Race, and Reaction," *Hastings Constitutional Law Quarterly* 22 (1995): 1033. Olivas's latest article on college residency policies is scheduled to be published in the *Journal of College and University Law* 30.

6. Ibid., 1034.

7. Compare Howard F. Chang, "Migration as International Trade: The Economic Gains from the Liberalized Movement of Labor," *UCLA Journal of International Law and Foreign Affairs* 3 (1998): 371–414 with Rebecca L. Clark, et al., "Fiscal Impacts of Undocumented Immigrants," *Government Finance Review* 11, no. 1 (February 1995): 20–22.

8. Olivas, "Storytelling out of School," 1055.

9. As of 1996, the top state of residence for undocumented persons was California. *1999 Statistical Yearbook of Immigration and Naturalization Service,* § VII, tbl. I (1999) (listing Texas, New York, Florida, and Illinois as four other top states of residence).

10. See James A. Ferg-Cadima, Legislative Analyst, *MALDEF Survey of Recent State Law and Legislation during the 2003–04 Legislative Term Aimed at Facilitating Undocumented Student Access to State Universities,* Mexican-American Legal Defense Fund (May 18, 2003). These states are Texas, California, Utah, New York, Washington, Oklahoma, and Illinois. Although close to twenty others are considering similar legislation, the number has remained at seven for close to a year, from May 2003 to January 2004. See National Immigration Law Center, Chart of In-State Tuition Bills (January 22, 2004) (on file with author).

11. See Ferg-Cadima.

12. Ibid. See also *INA* §§ 101(a)(15)(F), (J), (M), 8 *U.S.C.* §§ 1101(a)(15)(F),

(J), (M) (2000). The foreign student exemption might be a response to the criticism that some Asian families have sent their children to private schools in the United States on student visas, only to have them transfer to public schools upon their arrival, thus earning the pejorative moniker "parachute kids." Action Alert, *Wisconsin Governor Scott McCollum Veto's [Sic] Illegal Alien Tuition Provision.* September 17, 2001, http://www.fairus.org/html/07382109.htm.

13. See Joseph Treviño, "Degrees of Inequality." August 24–30, 2001, *Los Angeles Weekly,* http://www.laweekly.com/ink/01/40/news-trevino.shtml.

14. See Ferg-Cadima, 2. These states are Alaska, Mississippi, and Virginia.

15. While the federal law excusing from removal those undocumented persons who had information about the terrorist attacks might be viewed as "proimmigrant," it appears to be of a different magnitude, driven in part by the necessity to gather as much information as possible about September 11. *INA* § 101(a)(15)(S), 8 *U.S.C.* § 1101(a)(15)(S) (2000).

16. The 2003 version of the SAA is apparently identical to the first, with the exception of technical changes owing to the dissolution of the INS and the assignment of its immigration functions to the Department of Homeland Security. See Student Adjustment Act of 2003, HR 1684, 108th Cong., 1st sess. (2003); E-mail from Josh Bernstein to Student-Adjustment@yahoo.groups.com, April 9, 2003).

17. Office of Congressman Chris Cannon, *Press Release, Cannon Introduces the Student Adjustment Act, Designed to Help Children of Illegal Immigrants Gain Access to Higher-Ed.* June 7, 2001, http://www.house.gov/cannon /press2001/jun07.htm.

18. Ibid.

19. 457 U.S. 202 (1982).

20. Ibid. (quoting *Trimble v. Gordon,* 430 U.S. 762, 770 (1977)) (emphasis in original).

21. Ibid., 222–23 (quoting *Wisconsin v. Yoder,* 406 U.S. 205, 221 (1972)).

22. Action Alert, *Wisconsin Governor.*

23. Ibid. The term "parachute kids" refers to children from Asia who come to the United States on nonimmigrant student visas and then enter the public school system once here. See ibid.

24. Ibid.

25. Interview with Carmen Medina, Exec. Dir. of Adams County Delinquency Prevention Program, October 1, 2001.

26. Olivas, "Storytelling out of School," 1085.

27. Action Alert, *Wisconsin Governor.*

28. PRWORA, former President Clinton's so-called "welfare-to-work" initiative, provides that some forms of education can be considered work. Therefore, one might still receive welfare benefits while pursuing an education. However, it appears that postsecondary education does not meet this expansive definition of

work, suggesting that Congress intended an educational floor, not a ceiling. See Matthew Diller, "Working without a Job: The Social Messages of the New Workfare," *Stanford Law and Policy Review* 9 (1998): 19–32.

29. The recent efforts of graduate students to unionize based on their "work" suggests a further blurring of the education-work dichotomy. Cf. *Brown University and International Union,* 342 N.L.R.B. No. 42, 2004 NLRB LEXIS 385 (July 13, 2004).

30. *INA* § 201(a), 8 *U.S.C.* § 1151(a); *INA* § 207(a), 8 *U.S.C.* § 1157(a).

31. See, e.g., *Little v. Little,* 193 Ariz. 518, 975 P.2d 108 (1999), citing *Rubenstein v. Rubenstein,* 655 So. 2d 1050, 1052 (Ala. Civ. App. 1995).

32. See, e.g., *Dailey v. Chater,* 1995 U.S. Dist. LEXIS 13192 (D. Kan. 1995); *Alexander v. Shalala,* Unempl. Ins. Rep. (CCH) ¶ 14612B (W.D. Mo. 1994).

33. See Student Adjustment Act of 2001, HR 1918, 107th Cong., 1st sess., § 3(a)(2) (May 2001).

NOTES TO CHAPTER 6

1. See *In re Opinions of the Justices to the Senate,* 440 Mass. 1201 (2004) (holding that only state-sanctioned marriage, and not civil unions, between gay partners will satisfy the Massachusetts equal protection requirement).

2. In the long run, it is also possible that same-gender marriages may not even be legal in Massachusetts should the Commonwealth decide to amend its constitution to limit marriage to the union between a man and a woman. However, until it does so, I would suspect not a few same-gender couples will be rushing to Town Hall to take advantage of the Supreme Judicial Court's favorable ruling.

3. Vermont Civil Union Review Commission, "Report of the Vermont Civil Union Review Commission," January 2001, http://www.leg.state.vt.us/baker /cureport.htm, Finding 2.

4. See INS 2001 *Statistical Yearbook,* table 37 (note that the 741,000 figure cited by the INS includes spouses and the children of some F and M visa students); Paul Grondahl, "Visas in Hand, Foreign Students Fill Employers' Needs," *Times Union* (Albany, NY), July 27, 2003, E1.

5. Robin Toner, "Opposition to Gay Marriage Is Declining, Study Finds," *New York Times,* July 25, 2003, A16.

6. Amanda Paulson, "Debate on Gay Unions Splits among Generations," *Christian Science Monitor* (Boston), July 7, 2003, 01.

7. By mentioning marriages and civil unions in the same sentence, I do not mean to trivialize the significant differences between the way Vermont views same-gender civil unions and heterosexual marriages. Indeed, the "civil union" in Vermont was a political compromise born of the fact that state legislators did not want to recognize same-gender marriages as being equal to heterosexual marriages. While recognizing that civil unions are a first step toward true parity

between same-gender and heterosexual marriages, I agree with the Massachusetts court that anything short of true parity is not true equality.

8. 673 F.2d 1036 (9th Cir. 1982).

9. Ibid., 1042.

10. Joyce Murdoch and Deb Price, *Courting Justice: Gay Men and Lesbians v. the Supreme Court* (New York: Basic Books, 2001), 224.

11. Public Law No. 104-199 (1996) (codified at 1 *U.S.C.* § 7). On DOMA, see generally Andrew Koppelman, "Dumb and DOMA: Why the Defense of Marriage Act Is Unconstitutional," *Iowa Law Review* 83 (1997): 1–33.

12. See Victor C. Romero, "The Selective Deportation of Same-Gender Partners: In Search of the Rara Avis," *University of Miami Law Review* 56 (2002): 540 n.18.

13. See Permanent Partners Immigration Act, HR832, 108th Cong., 1st sess. (2003).

14. LGIRTF, *PPIA Gains Landmark Political Support,* July 14, 2003, http://www.lgirtf.org/ppiapress.html.

15. Andrew Sullivan, "Beware the Straight Backlash," *Time,* August 11, 2003, 35.

16. Michael McGuire, "Vatican Assaults Same-Sex Marriages," *Chicago Tribune,* August 1, 2003, 1.

17. See, e.g., Alan Simpson, "Missing the Point on Gays," *Washington Post,* September 5, 2003, A21.

18. 525 U.S. 471 (1999).

19. For a thorough discussion of this case and other issues involving the targeting of so-called "terrorists" because of their political affiliations, see David Cole and James X. Dempsey, *Terrorism and the Constitution: Sacrificing Civil Liberties in the Name of National Security* (New York: New Press, 2d ed., 2002).

20. *AADC,* 488.

21. Ibid., 491.

22. The protection of the heterosexual public from homosexuals is a resonant theme in American legal history both within and outside immigration law. See generally William N. Eskridge Jr., "No Promo Homo: The Sedimentation of Antigay Discourse and the Channeling Effect of Judicial Review," *NYU Law Review* 75 (2000): 1328–29; William N. Eskridge Jr., *Gaylaw: Challenging the Apartheid of the Closet* (Cambridge, MA: Harvard University Press, 1999), 35–36, 69–70, 132–34, 383–84.

23. Memorandum from Doris Meissner, Commissioner, Immigration and Naturalization Service, to INS Regional Directors et al., at 4 (November 17, 2000). Post–September 11, 2001, Attorney General John Ashcroft's zeal in combating terrorism has led to the concern among many that the Department of Justice, which houses the INS, has become the "Department of Anti-Terrorism,"

leading some to speculate that the protection of civil liberties, another one of the office's functions, might be compromised. See, e.g., John Cloud, "General on the March," *Time,* November 19, 2001, at 63.

24. See Editorial, "Tom Tancredo Meet Inspector Javert: An Unseemly Resolve to Deport an Honor Student," *Rocky Mountain News* (Denver, CO), September 17, 2002, 38A.

25. See Juliet Eilperin, "Immigration Critic on the Defensive," *Washington Post,* September 21, 2002, A04.

26. *Romer v. Evans,* 517 U.S. 620 (1996).

27. *Boy Scouts of America v. Dale,* 530 U.S. 640 (2000).

28. *Bowers v. Hardwick,* 478 U.S. 186 (1986), overruled by *Lawrence v. Texas,* 123 S. Ct. 2472 (2003).

29. 123 S. Ct. 2472 (2003).

30. 123 S. Ct. 1708 (2003).

31. *Lawrence,* 2484.

32. Ibid.

33. Ibid., 2483.

34. *Kim,* 1708.

35. Justice Stevens did not join the majority opinion, but filed a concurrence agreeing with Scalia's constitutional "outrageous" test in *AADC.* See *AADC,* 501 (Stevens, J., concurring).

36. Ibid., 491.

37. Cole and Dempsey, 37.

38. *AADC,* 488.

39. Ibid., 491.

40. Ibid.

41. Ibid., 501 (Stevens, J., concurring).

42. Ibid., 497 (Ginsburg, J., concurring).

43. Ibid., 511 (Souter, J., dissenting).

44. Gerald L. Neuman, "Terrorism, Selective Deportation and the First Amendment after Reno v. AADC," *Georgetown Immigration Law Journal* 14 (2000): 345; David Cole, "Damage Control? A Comment on Professor Neuman's Reading of Reno v. AADC," *Georgetown Immigration Law Journal* 14 (2000): 359; David A. Martin, "On Counterintuitive Consequences and Choosing the Right Control Group: A Defense of Reno v. AADC," *Georgetown Immigration Law Journal* 14 (2000): 365. For a broader analysis of the First Amendment implications of *AADC,* see Maryann Kamali Miyamoto, "The First Amendment after Reno v. American-Arab Anti-Discrimination Committee: A Different Bill of Rights for Aliens?" *Harvard Civil Rights–Civil Liberties Law Review* 35 (2000): 183–223.

45. Neuman, "Terrorism," 345.

46. Cole, "Damage Control," 348.

47. See John C. Jeffries, Jr., *Justice Lewis F. Powell, Jr.* (New York: C. Scribner's Sons, 1994), 513–14. For a discussion of the facts from Michael Hardwick's perspective, see Irons, 392–403.

48. *Bowers v. Hardwick,* 478 U.S. 186 (1986).

49. Ibid., 203–08 (Blackmun, J., dissenting), 216–18 (Stevens, J., dissenting).

50. See *Hardwick,* 197–98 (Powell, J., concurring).

51. See Jeffries, 530.

52. Ibid.

53. Ibid., 518.

54. *Romer v. Evans,* 517 U.S. 620, 623–24 (1996).

55. See Evan Gerstmann, *The Constitutional Underclass: Gays, Lesbians, and the Failure of Class-Based Equal Protection* (Chicago: University of Chicago Press, 1999). For more on the *Evans* decision, see generally, Symposium, "Romer v. Evans," *William and Mary Bill of Rights Journal* 6 (Winter 1997): 89–259; Symposium, "Gay Rights and the Courts: The Amendment 2 Controversy," *University of Colorado Law Review* 68 (Spring 1997): 287–452.

56. Gerstmann, 105.

57. Ibid., 99–102.

58. *Evans,* 632.

59. Ibid., 636 (Scalia, J., dissenting).

60. Ibid., 641 (emphasis in original).

61. Eskridge, *Gaylaw,* 172.

62. *Lawrence,* 2478.

63. Ibid., 2487 (O'Connor, J., concurring).

64. Ibid. (citing *Railway Express Agency v. New York,* 336 U.S. 106, 112–13 (1949) (Jackson, J., concurring)).

65. *Lawrence,* 2490 (Scalia, J., dissenting). Justice Thomas filed a brief dissent, noting that while he believed the Texas law to be "uncommonly silly," he could not, as a federal judge, read into it the protection for gays and lesbians that the majority wanted to extend here. Ibid., 2498 (Thomas, J., dissenting).

66. *Hardwick,* 219–20.

67. *Lawrence,* 2486 (O'Connor, J., concurring).

68. See Del Dickson, *The Supreme Court in Conference (1940–1985)* (New York: Oxford University Press, 2001), 824.

69. *Hurley v. Irish-American Gay, Lesbian, and Bisexual Group of Boston,* 515 U.S. 557, 560–66 (1995).

70. Ibid., 575.

71. Ibid., 579.

72. *Dale,* 643–48.

73. Ibid., 654.

74. Ibid., 695 (Stevens, J., dissenting).

75. Ibid., 696.

76. Ibid., 701 (Souter, J., dissenting).

77. Ibid., 660.

78. See *Whren v. United States,* 517 U.S. 806, 813 (1996).

79. The portions of the text describing *Miller* were taken in large measure from my previous work, Victor C. Romero, "On Élian and Aliens: A Political Solution to the Plenary Power Problem," NYU *Journal of Legislation and Public Policy* 4 (2000–01): 357–59.

80. *Nguyen v. INS,* 208 F.3d 528 (5th Cir. 2000), *cert. granted,* 121 S. Ct. 29 (September 26, 2000) (No. 99-2017).

81. John Paul Jones, "Anthony McLeod Kennedy," in *The Supreme Court Justices: A Biographical Dictionary,* ed. Melvin I. Urofsky (New York: Garland Publishing, 1994), 277. See also Theodore Eisenberg, "Anthony M. Kennedy," in *The Justices of the United States Supreme Court: Their Lives and Major Opinions,* vol. V, ed. Leon Friedman and Fred L. Israel (New York: Chelsea House Publishers, 1997), 1731–57.

82. See, e.g., Sue Davis, "John Paul Stevens," in *The Supreme Court Justices: A Biographical Dictionary,* ed. Melvin I. Urofsky (New York: Garland Publishing, 1994), 409.

83. See *Evans,* 632.

84. The Court has followed a three-tiered system of equal protection analysis, subjecting racial classifications to strict scrutiny, gender classifications to intermediate review, and general economic legislation to a "rational basis" test. See, e.g., John E. Nowak and Ronald D. Rotunda, *Constitutional Law* (St. Paul, MN: West, 6th ed., 2000), 638–44. Justice Stevens, however, explicitly rejected this approach in *Craig v. Boren,* 429 U.S. 190, 212 (1976) (Stevens, J., concurring).

85. *United States v. Carolene Products Co.,* 303 U.S. 144, 153 n.4 (1938).

86. *Nguyen v. INS,* 533 U.S. 53, 121 S. Ct. 2053, 2078 (2001) (O'Connor, J., concurring).

87. See Hiroshi Motomura, "Immigration Law after a Century of Plenary Power: Phantom Constitutional Norms and Statutory Interpretation," *Yale Law Journal* 100 (1990): 560–61; Hiroshi Motomura, "The Curious Evolution of Immigration Law: Procedural Surrogates for Substantive Constitutional Rights," *Columbia Law Review* 92 (1992): 1625–704.

88. See Motomura, "Phantom," 560–61.

89. *Zadvydas v. Ma,* 121 S. Ct. 2491, 2496–97 (2001).

90. U.S. 206 (1953). See Romero, "Élian," 353–54.

91. *Zadvydas,* 2505 (Scalia, J., dissenting).

92. Ibid., 2517 (Kennedy, J., dissenting).

93. *Kim,* 1708.

94. *Lawrence,* 2498 (Thomas, J., dissenting).

95. *Miller,* 471 (Breyer, J., dissenting) (emphasis added).

96. Cass R. Sunstein, *One Case at a Time: Judicial Minimalism on the Supreme Court* (Cambridge, MA: Harvard University Press, 1999), 131.

97. Legomsky, *Immigration and Refugee Law and Policy,* 157.

98. Louis Uchitelle, "I.N.S. Is Looking the Other Way as Illegal Immigrants Fill Jobs: Enforcement Changes in Face of Labor Shortage," *New York Times,* March 9, 2000, C1.

99. See Lesbian and Gay Immigration Rights Task Force, *Anthony Sullivan and Richard Adams, Plaintiffs in 1982 Case against INS, Celebrate 25th Anniversary.* Fall 1996, Task Force Update, http://www.lgirtf.org/newsletters/Fall96/FA96-12.html.

100. *Sullivan v. INS,* 772 F.2d 609 (9th Cir. 1995).

101. Lesbian and Gay Immigration Rights Task Force, *"Oh Canada, Glorious and Free": French/American Binational Couple Immigrates to Begin New Life Together.* Winter 1997, Task Force Update, http://www.lgirtf.org/newsletters/Winter97/W6.html.

102. The fifteen countries that currently provide immigration benefits to same-gender partners are Australia, Belgium, Canada, Denmark, Finland, France, Germany, Iceland, Israel, the Netherlands, Norway, Portugal, South Africa, Sweden, New Zealand, and the United Kingdom. See Susan Hazeldean and Heather Betz, "Years Behind: What the United States Must Learn about Immigration Law and Same-Sex Couples," *Human Rights,* Summer 2003, 17–18.

103. See David Orgon Coolidge and William C. Duncan, "Reaffirming Marriage: A Presidential Priority," *Harvard Journal of Law and Public Policy* 24 (2001): 623–33.

104. Ibid., 633.

105. See, e.g., Christopher Duenas, "Coming to America: The Immigration Obstacle Facing Binational Same-Sex Couples," *Southern California Law Review* 73 (2000): 811–41; Cynthia M. Reed, "When Love, Comity, and Justice Conquer Borders: INS Recognition of Same-Sex Marriage," *Columbia Human Rights Law Review* 28 (1996): 97–134.

106. See, e.g., Jennifer Gerarda Brown, "Competitive Federalism and Legislative Incentives to Recognize Same-Sex Marriage," *Southern California Law Review* 68 (1995): 745–838; Barbara J. Cox, "Same-Sex Marriage and Choice of Law: If We Marry in Hawaii, Are We Still Married When We Return Home?" *Wisconsin Law Review* 1994 (1994): 1033–118; John G. Culhane, "Uprooting the Arguments against Same-Sex Marriage," *Cardozo Law Review* 20 (1999): 1119–211; Larry Catá Backer, "Constructing a 'Homosexual' for Constitutional Theory: Sodomy Narrative, Jurisprudence, and Antipathy in United States and British Courts," *Tulane Law Review* 71 (1996): 529–96; Lynn D. Wardle, "A Critical Analysis of Constitutional Claims for Same-Sex Marriage," *BYU Law Review* 1996 (1996): 1–101.

Notes to Chapter 7

1. Joe R. Feagin, "Old Poison in New Bottles: The Deep Roots of Modern Nativism," in *Immigrants Out!* ed. Juan Perea (New York: NYU Press, 1997), 15.

2. Ibid., 15–16.

3. Ibid., 17.

4. Neuman, *Strangers to the Constitution,* 21–34.

5. Aleinikoff et al., 2. See Act of March 3, 1875, ch. 141, 18 Stat. 477; Act of August 3, 1882, ch. 376, 22 Stat. 214.

6. Feagin, 19, 25.

7. See, e.g., ibid., 25.

8. Act of March 26, 1790, ch. 3, 1 Stat. 103. On the concept of "whiteness" as a social construct, see generally Haney López. Feagin correctly notes, however, that white-on-white ethnic conflict has not completely disappeared from the American scene, citing 1984 vice presidential candidate Geraldine Ferraro's and former New York Governor Mario Cuomo's need to defend themselves against allegations that their Italian heritage suggested Mafia links. Feagin, 27. And, unfortunately, the often white-on-white prejudice of anti-Semitism is alive and well today. Ibid., 27–28.

9. Aleinikoff et al., 2. Authors disagree as to whether the Chinese were consigned to the margins of society from the outset or whether they were gradually resented as their numbers grew. Compare Aleinikoff et al., 3, and Hyung-Chan Kim, *A Legal History of Asian Americans, 1790–1990* (Westport, CT: Greenwood Press, 1994), 47, with Mary Roberts Coolidge, *Chinese Immigration* (New York: Henry Holt and Company, 1909; reprint, Arno Press and the *New York Times,* 1969), 21. For more on the early history of the Chinese in America, see generally Lucy E. Salyer, *Law Harsh as Tigers: Chinese Immigrants and the Shaping of Modern Immigration Law* (Chapel Hill: University of North Carolina Press, 1995); Charles McClain, Jr., "The Chinese Struggle for Civil Rights in Nineteenth-Century America: The First Phase, 1850–1870," *California Law Review* 72 (1984): 529–68.

10. See Aleinikoff et al., 2. See also Kim, 70–91; Chin, "Segregation's Last Stronghold."

11. 130 U.S. 581 (1889).

12. Peter H. Schuck, "The Transformation of Immigration Law," *Columbia Law Review* 84 (1984): 3. Many scholars have called for the dismantling of the plenary power doctrine (see, e.g., Frank H. Wu, "The Limits of Borders: A Moderate Proposal for Immigration Reform," *Stanford Law and Policy Review* 7 (1996): 35–53, but have been disappointed by its continued acceptance. Compare Stephen H. Legomsky, "Immigration Law and the Principle of Plenary Congressional Power," *Supreme Court Review* 1984 (1984): 255–307, with Stephen

H. Legomsky, "Ten More Years of Plenary Power: Immigration, Congress, and the Courts," *Hastings Constitutional Law Quarterly* 22 (1995): 925–37.

13. *Chae Chan Ping*, 595, 606.

14. As noted in the Introduction and chapter 2, Americans of Japanese heritage also suffered the indignity of exclusion and isolation by being interned in camps during World War II, while those of German and Italian descent remained free.

15. Ibrahim J. Wani, "Truth, Strangers, and Fiction: The Illegitimate Uses of Legal Fiction in Immigration Law," *Cardozo Law Review* 11 (1989): 83. By drawing analogies between the experiences of the non-English whites and the Chinese, I do not mean to ignore the role racism played in the subordination of the Chinese. However, I compare these two groups not to determine which has suffered more, but to emphasize the injustice both sets of newcomers endured at the hands of the earlier arrivals, themselves European immigrants.

16. In an interesting twist in group dynamics, some universities have placed ceilings on Asian American admissions to make room for other racial groups. See generally Pat K. Chew, "Asian Americans: The 'Reticent' Majority and Their Paradoxes," *William and Mary Law Review* 36 (1994): 1–94; Grace W. Tsuang, "Assuring Equal Access of Asian Americans to Highly Selective Universities," *Yale Law Journal* 98 (1989): 659–78. Such admissions ceilings have led some Asian Americans to question affirmative action policies as anti-Asian, generating much scholarly commentary. See, e.g., Selena Dong, "Too Many Asians: The Challenge of Fighting Discrimination against Asian Americans and Preserving Affirmative Action," *Stanford Law Review* 47 (1995): 1027–57; Frank H. Wu, "Neither Black Nor White: Asian Americans and Affirmative Action," *Boston College Third World Law Journal* 15 (1995): 225–84.

17. See Michael A. Olivas, "The Chronicles, My Grandfather's Stories, and Immigration Law: The Slave Traders Chronicle as Racial History," *St. Louis Law Journal* 34 (1990): 429.

18. Gerald López asserts that while the evidence is incomplete, many commentaries support his conclusion that "the majority of Mexicans recruited after the 1880s were undocumented." Gerald P. López, "Undocumented Mexican Migration: In Search of a Just Immigration Law and Policy," *UCLA Law Review* 28 (1981): 668.

19. Ibid., 664–67.

20. Ibid., 670; Elizabeth Hull, *Without Justice for All: The Constitutional Rights of Aliens* (Westport, CT: Greenwood Press, 1985), 84–85; Olivas, "The Chronicles," 438–39.

21. López, 707.

22. INA § 274A, 8 *U.S.C.* § 1324a.

23. Linda S. Bosniak, "Membership, Equality, and the Difference That Alienage Makes," *NYU Law Review* 69 (1994): 1047–149.

24. Ibid.

25. Ibid., 1138.

26. *Chae Chan Ping v. United States,* 130 U.S. 581 (1889).

27. Bosniak, 1138.

28. Ibid., 1143.

29. See generally Linda S. Bosniak, "Constitutional Citizenship through the Prism of Alienage," *Ohio State Law Journal* 63 (2002): 1285–325.

30. Michael A. Scaperlanda, "Partial Membership: Aliens and the Constitutional Community," *Iowa Law Review* 81 (1996): 707–73.

31. Ibid., 752.

32. Ibid.

33. *Mathews v. Diaz,* 426 U.S. 67, 80 (1976).

34. Ibid., 83–84.

35. Ibid., 84.

36. Scaperlanda, "Partial Membership," 752.

37. 403 U.S. 365 (1971).

38. Ibid., 372.

39. Scaperlanda, "Partial Membership," 767–71.

40. Ibid., 769.

41. *Cabell,* 454 U.S. at 447.

42. Scaperlanda, "Partial Membership," 708.

43. *Thomas v. INS,* 35 F.3d 1332, 1335–40 (9th Cir. 1994).

44. Michael Walzer, *Spheres of Justice: A Defense of Pluralism and Equality* (New York: Basic Books, 1983), 58.

45. *San Pedro v. United States,* 79 F.3d 1065, 1067, *cert. denied,* 136 L. Ed. 2d 330 (1996) (emphasis added).

46. See *Mathews,* 67.

47. *Graham v. Richardson,* 403 U.S. 365, 372 (1971).

48. *Ramallo v. Reno,* 114 F.3d 1210, 1212 (1997) (*Ramallo I*).

49. *Ramallo v. Reno,* 934 F. Supp. 1,2 (D.D.C. 1996) (*Ramallo II*).

50. *Ramallo I,* 1212.

51. *Ramallo v. Reno,* 931 F. Supp. 884, 887 (D.D.C. 1996) (*Ramallo III*).

52. *Ramallo I,* 1212.

53. Although it did not dispute that a cooperation agreement was reached, the government also claimed that it promised Ramallo only a temporary stay of deportation. Alternatively, the government asserted that Ramallo had modified the original agreement and therefore was barred from receiving equitable relief under the doctrine of "unclean hands." *Ramallo III,* 888.

54. The court also cited *Margalli-Olvera* with approval. *Ramallo III,* 893–94.

55. Ibid., 894.

56. The court denied both sides' motions for summary judgment on the nar-

row factual issue of whether the government promised Ramallo that she would not be deported. Ibid., 892. At the ensuing hearing, the court resolved this factual issue in Ramallo's favor and granted judgment for the plaintiff. *Ramallo II,* 2.

57. Ibid.

58. *Ramallo I,* 1214.

59. Pub. L. No. 104-208 (Sept. 30, 1996), reprinted in 1996 U.S.C.C.A.N. (110 *U.S. Statutes at Large* 3009).

60. Section 242 of the INA deals with the apprehension and deportation of noncitizens. INA § 242, 8 *U.S.C.* § 1252.

61. *Ramallo I,* 1214.

62. In *Ramallo I,* the circuit court noted that Ramallo was not entirely without a remedy; she could file a habeas claim. *Ramallo I,* 1214. But this statement rings hollow. Aside from the difficulty of winning habeas claims, the very fact that this case could turn from an easy, obvious, and just win for the noncitizen into a denial of jurisdiction for what are important constitutional claims sends a very strong message that the government can do whatever it wants to those who are not U.S. citizens. On the difficulty of pursuing habeas relief, see generally Stephen B. Bright, "Is Fairness Irrelevant? The Evisceration of Federal Habeas Corpus Review and Limits on the Ability of State Courts to Protect Fundamental Rights," *Washington and Lee Law Review* 54 (1997): 1, 4.

63. Despite the potentially greater harm to noncitizens from deportation than from incarceration, the Supreme Court has held that deportation is a "purely civil action," and therefore noncitizens at deportation hearings are not given the same constitutional and procedural safeguards as in criminal trials. *INS v. Lopez-Mendoza,* 468 U.S. 1032, 1038 (1984). See also *The Tarnished Golden Door: Civil Rights Issues in Immigration* (Commission on Civil Rights, 1980), 97–101.

64. Steve James, "Warm-Up for O. J. Final Arguments," *Chicago Sun-Times,* September 25, 1995, 16. Indeed, one of Cochran's own critics was cocounsel Robert Shapiro "who berated Cochran for playing the race card 'from the bottom of the deck.'" Lynda Gorov, "Cochran Becomes Celebrity, Draws Criticism regarding the Simpson Verdict," *Boston Globe,* October 5, 1995, 31.

Even Senator Arlen Specter considered probing Cochran's "playing the race card" during closing arguments. Steve Goldstein, "Specter Asks Probe of O. J. Simpson Trial Issues," *Philadelphia Inquirer,* October 11, 1995, A17.

65. See, e.g., Roger Rosenblatt, "A Nation of Pained Hearts," *Time,* October 16, 1995, 40–45; Martin Gottlieb, "The Deep Split in Reactions to the Verdict," *New York Times,* October 4, 1995, A1 and A12.

66. Jody Armour, "Stereotypes and Prejudice: Helping Legal Decisionmakers Break the Prejudice Habit," *California Law Review* 1995, 741. Armour has incorporated many of these arguments in his book. Jody David Armour, *Negrophobia and Reasonable Racism: The Hidden Costs of Being Black in America*

(New York: NYU Press, 1997), 115–53. On the nature of prejudice generally, Gordon Allport's treatise on the subject is a classic.

67. Armour, "Stereotypes and Prejudice," 741.

68. Ibid., 742. Similarly, Allport opines that an adequate definition of prejudice must contain an "*attitude* of favor or disfavor" that must be related to an "overgeneralized (and therefore erroneous) *belief.*" Allport, 13.

69. Armour, "Stereotypes and Prejudice," 742.

70. Ibid.

71. Ibid., 743. This distinction between low- and high-prejudiced individuals might help reduce feelings of defensiveness among those in the white majority who sometimes justifiably feel like scapegoats every time the question of white racism is raised. On the issue of affirmative action, for example, some white males see the issue as one of class rather than race. See, e.g., David Thomas, "Initiative Will Level Playing Field," *Los Angeles Times,* March 10, 1996, B4.

72. Armour, "Stereotypes and Prejudice," 743.

73. Ibid.

74. Ibid., 762–63.

75. Ibid., 753.

76. See Jeffrey S. Passel, Randy Capps, and Michael Fix, *Undocumented Immigration: Facts and Figures.* January 12, 2004, http://www.urban.org/url.cfm?ID=1000587.

77. Associated Press, "Poll: Americans Ease on Immigrants," *1997 WL 4870808,* June 15, 1997 [hereinafter *Poll*]; "New Immigrants Winning Much Wider Acceptance: More Americans Meeting, Learning about Newcomers," *Orlando Sentinel* (Florida), June 15, 1997, A12.

78. *Poll.* Japanese were viewed next most favorably, followed by Chinese and Africans. Ibid.

79. As Karen K. Narasaki, Executive Director of the National Asian Pacific American Legal Consortium, noted in an immigration law symposium at Georgetown University: "My feeling has been that talking about immigrants is really sort of the last acceptable way to talk about race without actually talking about race." Georgetown Immigration Law Journal, "10th Anniversary Symposium—March 6, 1996 Transcript," *Georgetown Immigration Law Journal* 10 (1996): 27.

80. Gregory R. Maio, Victoria M. Esses, and D. W. Bell, "The Formation of Attitudes toward New Immigrant Groups," *Journal of Applied Psychology* 24, no. 19 (1994): 1762–76.

81. The six emotions listed were "comfortable," "curious," "happy," "proud," "relaxed," and "respect." "Friendly," "hardworking," "honest," "intelligent," "loyal," and "polite" were the six personality traits used. The six values included "economic development," "education," "equality," "family,"

"freedom," and "law and order." The fictitious survey reflected the extent to which the Camarians elicited the emotion, possessed the personality trait, or promoted the value listed. Ibid., 1768.

82. Interestingly enough, where mixed positive and negative information was received, the respondents actually had a more favorable response to immigration when they perceived it to be more relevant to their lives, although not as favorable as their response to uniformly positive information. Ibid., 1773.

83. Gregory R. Maio, Victoria M. Esses, and D. W. Bell, "Ambivalence and Persuasion: The Processing of Messages about Immigrant Groups," *Journal of Experimental Psychology* 32 (1996): 514.

84. Ibid.

85. Ibid., 530.

86. See, e.g., López; Linda S. Bosniak, "Exclusion and Membership: The Dual Identity of the Undocumented Worker under United States Law," *Wisconsin Law Review* 1988 (1988): 955–1042.

87. In one infamous incident, Giuliani went head-to-head with the flamboyant Rev. Al Sharpton and his followers over the use of the Brooklyn Bridge for a march to celebrate Rev. Dr. Martin Luther King, Jr.'s birthday. Giuliani prohibited the marchers from using the entire bridge because they would impede the flow of traffic. Sharpton decried Giuliani's decision as racist, citing the City's decision to block off major roads for other events such as the New York City marathon. Kirk Johnson, "On King Holiday, Words of Peace and Protest," *New York Times,* January 16, 1996, B1.

88. Clyde Haberman, "Immigrants: In Plain Sight, But Not Seen," *New York Times,* July 22, 1997, B1.

89. See Act of March 3, 1875, 18 *U.S. Statutes at Large* 477.

90. Roger Daniels, *Coming to America: A History of Immigration and Ethnicity in American Life* (New York: HarperCollins, 1990), 19.

91. The Farm Labor Organizing Committee (FLOC), based in Toledo, Ohio, is a union of migrant and seasonal farmworkers based in the Midwest. Its foreign roots are belied by its flag, which is emblazoned with a Mexican eagle and the words "Hasta la Victoria!" ("Onward to Victory!"). See Farm Labor Organizing Committee, *FLOC Homepage,* http://www.iupui.edu/~floc/home.html.

92. The Latino/a farmworker population is so large in the northwest that a cooperative was formed called the Pineros y Campesinos Unidos del Noroeste (Northwest Treeplanters and Farmworkers United), which represents over forty-five hundred farmworkers in Oregon and is the state's largest Latino/a organization. See Pineros y Campesinos Unidos del Noroeste, *PCUN Homepage,* http://www.pcun.org.

93. When Governor Tom Vilsack of Iowa, a low-immigration state, proposed to remedy the state's labor shortage by encouraging immigration to three "model

234 | Notes to Chapter 7

cities," he was greeted by a backlash in largely white areas, which has been supported by several national anti-immigration organizations. See William Claiborne, "Immigration Foes Find Platform in Iowa," *Washington Post,* August 19, 2001, A03.

94. See generally Victor C. Romero, "The Congruence Principle Applied: Rethinking Equal Protection Review of Federal Alienage Classifications after Adarand Constructors, Inc. v. Peña," *Oregon Law Review* 76 (1997): 425–56.

95. See Bert Eljera, "Filipinos Find Home in Daly City," *Asian Week,* May 3–9, 1996, http://www.asianweek.com/050396/dalycity.html.

96. For two thoughtful pieces on opposite sides of the devolution debate in the context of welfare reform, see Peter Spiro, "Learning to Live with Immigration Federalism," *Connecticut Law Review* 29 (1997): 1627–46; Michael Wishnie, "Laboratories of Bigotry? Devolution of the Immigration Power, Equal Protection, and Federalism," *NYU Law Review* 76 (2001): 493–569.

97. Thus, linking removability to state criminal law has led to deportations for some but not others, despite the commission of the same offense. See also Iris Bennett, "The Unconstitutionality of Nonuniform Immigration Consequences of 'Aggravated Felony' Convictions," *NYU Law Review* 74 (1999): 1696–740.

98. Haney López.

99. See Olivas, "The Chronicles."

100. See Victor C. Romero, "Expanding the Circle of Membership by Reconstructing the 'Alien': Lessons from Social Psychology and the 'Promise Enforcement' Cases," *University of Michigan Journal of Law Reform* 32 (1998): 8–15.

101. See, e.g., Gotanda, "Asian American Rights," 1098.

102. See, e.g., Saito; Johnson, "Racial Hierarchy."

103. See Romero, "Congruence," 446.

104. Race crits posit that "racism is normal, not aberrant, in American society." Richard Delgado, *Critical Race Theory: The Cutting Edge* (Philadelphia: Temple University Press, 1995), xiv.

105. 347 U.S. 483 (1954).

106. See, e.g., Kevin R. Johnson, "Civil Rights and Immigration: Challenges for the Latino Community in the Twentieth Century," *La Raza Law Journal* 8 (1995): 42–89; Johnson, "Race, the Immigration Laws, and Domestic Race Relations," 1111–59; Johnson, "An Essay on Immigration Politics," 629–73.

107. See Johnson, "The Case against Race Profiling," 675–736.

108. See, e.g., Lolita K. Buckner-Inniss, "California's Proposition 187—Does It Mean What It Says? Does It Say What It Means? A Textual and Constitutional Analysis," *Georgetown Immigration Law Journal* 10 (1996): 577–622; Johnson, "An Essay on Immigration Politics"; Gerald L. Neuman, "Aliens as Outlaws: Government Services, Proposition 187, and the Structure of Equal Protection Doctrine," *UCLA Law Review* 42 (1995): 1425–52.

109. See "Times Poll/A Look at the Electorate," *Los Angeles Times*, November 10, 1994, B2.

110. *League of United Latin American Citizens v. Wilson*, 908 F. Supp. 755 (C.D. Cal. 1995).

111. Robert N. Bellah et al., *Habits of the Heart: Individualism and Commitment in American Life* (Berkeley: University of California Press, 1996), 107–08.

112. Walzer, *Spheres of Justice*, 229.

113. Steven Pinker, *How the Mind Works* (New York: W. W. Norton, 1997), 435.

114. American Civil Liberties Union, "Independence Day 2003: Main Street America Fights the Federal Government's Insatiable Appetite for New Powers in the Post 9/11 Era," July 3, 2003, http://www.aclu.org.

115. Ibid., Appendix B (model resolution).

116. American Civil Liberties Union, "Attorney General Ashcroft Goes on the Road to Promote the USA PATRIOT Act," August 21, 2003, http://www.aclu.org.

117. Ibid.

118. ACLU, "Independence Day," 18.

119. See Rachel L. Swarns, "Old ID Card Gives New Status to Mexicans in U.S.," *New York Times*, August 25, 2003; Cecilia M. Vega, "Sonoma Accepts Mexican ID Cards," *The Press-Democrat On-Line*, August 21, 2003, http://www.pressdemocrat.com/local/news/21id_b1cityb.html.

120. Swarns.

# Select Bibliography

Action Alert. *Wisconsin Governor Scott McCollum Veto's [Sic] Illegal Alien Tuition Provision.* Sept. 17, 2001, http://www.fairus.org/html/07382109.htm.

Akram, Susan, and Kevin R. Johnson. "Race, Civil Rights, and Immigration Law after September 11, 2001: The Targeting of Muslims and Arabs." *NYU Annual Survey of American Law* 58 (2002): 295–355.

Albany Law Review Symposium. "Panel I: Racial Profiling." *Albany Law Review* 66 (Spring 2003): 329–71.

Aldana-Pindell, Raquel. "The 9/11 'National Security' Cases: Three Principles Guiding Judges' Decisionmaking." *Oregon Law Review* 81 (2002): 985–1049.

Aleinikoff, T. Alexander. *Semblances of Sovereignty: The Constitution, the State, and American Citizenship.* Cambridge, MA: Harvard University Press, 2002.

Aleinikoff, T. Alexander, David A. Martin, and Hiroshi Motomura. *Immigration and Citizenship.* St. Paul, MN: West, 2000.

Allport, Gordon W. *The Nature of Prejudice.* 1954. Reprint, Reading, MA: Perseus Books, 1979.

American Civil Liberties Union. "Attorney General Ashcroft Goes on the Road to Promote the USA Patriot Act." August 21, 2003, http://www.aclu.org.

———. "Independence Day 2003: Main Street America Fights the Federal Government's Insatiable Appetite for New Powers in the Post-9/11 Era," July 3, 2003.

*American Federation of Labor v. American Sash & Door Co.,* 335 U.S. 538 (1948).

*The American Heritage Dictionary.* 2d College edition. Boston: Houghton Mifflin, 1985.

Amnesty International USA. "Responses to Terrorism." *Amnesty Now,* Summer 2002, 16–17.

Anderson, Curt. "Justice Dept. Denies Casting Suspicion on Germ Researcher." *Boston Globe,* December 13, 2002, A51.

Aoki, Keith. "'Foreign-Ness' and Asian American Identities: Yellowface, World War II Propaganda, and Bifurcated Racial Stereotypes." *UCLA Asian Pacific American Law Journal* 4 (1996): 1–60.

Armour, Jody. "Stereotypes and Prejudice: Helping Legal Decisionmakers Break the Prejudice Habit." *California Law Review* 1995, 733–72.

Armour, Jody David. *Negrophobia and Reasonable Racism: The Hidden Costs of Being Black in America.* New York: NYU Press, 1997.

Arriola, Elvia R. "LatCrit Theory, International Human Rights, Popular Culture, and the Faces of Despair in INS Raids." *University of Miami Inter-American Law Review* 28 (1997): 245–62.

Ashar, Sameer. "Immigration Enforcement and Subordination: The Consequences of Racial Profiling after September 11." *Connecticut Law Review* 34 (2002): 1185–99.

Ashenfelter, David, and Niraj Warikoo. "Court Gives Public Access to Deportation Hearing." *Detroit Free Press,* January 23, 2003, 1.

Associated Press. "Bill Eases Citizenship for Adopted Children." *Charleston Gazette* (Charleston, SC), February 18, 2000.

———. "Deported Brazilian Left on Unfamiliar Ground." *Houston Chronicle,* November 30, 2000, 34.

———. "Deported Man Said to Have Al Qaeda Tie." *Washington Post,* August 11, 2002, A19.

———. "On Lookout for Retaliation." *Newsday* (New York), June 26, 2002, A17.

———. "Poll: Americans Ease on Immigrants." *1997 WL 4870808,* June 15, 1997.

———. "Prosecutor Ties Syria to El Al Bomb Attempt." *Los Angeles Times,* October 6, 1986, 2.

———. "Students' Arrests Prompt a New Class." *Los Angeles Times,* December 29, 2002, A25.

———. "Visiting Part-Time Students Barred." *Washington Post,* May 30, 2002, A26.

Augustine-Adams, Kif. "Gendered States: A Comparative Construction of Citizenship and Nation." *Virginia Journal of International Law* 41 (2000): 93–139.

Backer, Larry Catá. "Constructing a 'Homosexual' for Constitutional Theory: Sodomy Narrative, Jurisprudence, and Antipathy in United States and British Courts." *Tulane Law Review* 71 (1996): 529–96.

Badger, Ellen H. "SEVIS: The U.S. INS's New Tracking System for International Students and Exchange Visitors." In *ILW.COM.,* September 5, 2002, http://www.ilw.com/lawyers/immigdaily/digest/2002,0905.shtm.

Balbin, Remedios C. "Police Prejudice against Muslims." Letter to Editor. *Philippine Daily Inquirer,* June 6, 2002, A8.

Banks, R. Richard. "Beyond Profiling: Race, Policy, and the Drug War." *Stanford Law Review* 56 (2003): 571–602.

Barry, Deborah Barfield. "Lawsuits Target Airlines." *Newsday* (New York), June 5, 2002, A16.

Bartholet, Elizabeth. "Where Do Black Children Belong? The Politics of Race Matching in Adoption." *University of Pennsylvania Law Review* 139 (1991): 1163–256.

Bellah, Robert N., et al. *Habits of the Heart: Individualism and Commitment in American Life*. Berkeley: University of California Press, 1996.

Bennett, Iris. "The Unconstitutionality of Nonuniform Immigration Consequences of 'Aggravated Felony' Convictions." *NYU Law Review* 74 (1999): 1696–740.

Benson, Lenni B. "Back to the Future: Congress Attacks the Right to Judicial Review of Immigration Proceedings." *Connecticut Law Review* 29 (1997): 1411–94.

Berlin, Isaiah. *Two Concepts of Liberty: An Inaugural Lecture Delivered before the University of Oxford, on 31 October 1958*. Oxford: Clarendon Press, 1958.

Beyer, Lisa. "Israel's El Al Airline: Is This What We Really Want?" *Time*, September 24, 2001, 91.

Bosniak, Linda S. "Constitutional Citizenship through the Prism of Alienage." *Ohio State Law Journal* 63 (2002): 1285–325.

———. "Exclusion and Membership: The Dual Identity of the Undocumented Worker under United States Law." *Wisconsin Law Review* 1988 (1988): 955–1042.

———. "Membership, Equality, and the Difference That Alienage Makes." *NYU Law Review* 69 (1994): 1047–149.

Brest, Paul, et al. *Processes of Constitutional Adjudication*. 4th ed. Boston: Aspen, 2000.

Bright, Stephen B. "Is Fairness Irrelevant? The Evisceration of Federal Habeas Corpus Review and Limits on the Ability of State Courts to Protect Fundamental Rights." *Washington and Lee Law Review* 54 (1997): 1–30.

Brill, Steven. *After: How America Confronted the September 12 Era*. New York: Simon & Schuster, 2003.

Brown, Adam. "More U.S. Troops Fly In to Train Filipinos." *Chicago Tribune*, January 25, 2002, 4.

Brown, Jennifer Gerarda. "Competitive Federalism and Legislative Incentives to Recognize Same-Sex Marriage." *Southern California Law Review* 68 (1995): 745–838.

Buckner-Inniss, Lolita K. "California's Proposition 187—Does It Mean What It Says? Does It Say What It Means? A Textual and Constitutional Analysis." *Georgetown Immigration Law Journal* 10 (1996): 577–622.

Bunis, Dena. "Security a Focal Point of Immigration Policy." *Orange County Register* (California), September 9, 2002.

Bustany, Donald S. "Why Is It Still OK to Defame Arabs?" *Newsday* (New York), May 9, 1995, A35.

Calabresi, Massimo, and Romesh Ratnesar. "Can We Stop the Next Attack?" *Time*, March 11, 2002, 24–34.

Calmore, John O. "Race-Conscious Voting Rights and the New Demography in a Multiracing America." *North Carolina Law Review* 79 (2001): 1253–81.

Carbado, Devon W. "(E)Racing the Fourth Amendment." *Michigan Law Review* 100 (2002): 946–1044.

Carlson, Scott, and Andrea L. Foster. "Colleges Fear Anti-Terrorism Law Could Turn Them into Big Brother." *Chronicle of Higher Education*, March 1, 2002, A31–32.

Chamallas, Martha. *Introduction to Feminist Legal Theory.* 2d ed. Boston: Aspen, 1999.

Chang, Howard F. "Migration as International Trade: The Economic Gains from the Liberalized Movement of Labor." *UCLA Journal of International Law and Foreign Affairs* 3 (1998): 371–414.

Chang, Robert S. *Disoriented.* New York: NYU Press, 1999.

———. "A Meditation on Borders." In *Immigrants Out!* ed. Juan F. Perea, 244–53. New York: NYU Press, 1996.

Cheng, Mae M. "New INS Guidelines Soften '96 Laws." *Newsday* (New York), November 26, 2000, A48.

Cheng, Mae M., and Margaret Ramirez. "After Outcry, INS Releases Man Held for Old Crime." *Newsday* (New York), October 25, 1997, A19.

Chew, Pat K. "Asian Americans: The 'Reticent' Majority and Their Paradoxes." *William and Mary Law Review* 36 (1994): 1–94.

Chin, Gabriel J. "The Civil Rights Revolution Comes to Immigration Law: A New Look at the Immigration and Nationality Act of 1965." *North Carolina Law Review* 75 (1996): 273–345.

———. "Segregation's Last Stronghold: Race Discrimination and the Constitutional Law of Immigration." *UCLA Law Review* 46 (1995): 1–74.

Chin, Gabriel J., Victor C. Romero, and Michael A. Scaperlanda, eds. *Immigration and the Constitution.* Vol. 2. New York: Garland Publishing, 2000.

Claiborne, William. "Immigration Foes Find Platform in Iowa." *Washington Post*, August 19, 2001, A03.

Clark, Rebecca L., et al. "Fiscal Impacts of Undocumented Immigrants." *Government Finance Review* 11, no. 1 (February 1995): 20–22.

Cloud, John. "General on the March." *Time*, November 19, 2001, 63.

Clymer, Adam, and Janet Elder. "Poll Finds Unease on Terror Fight and Concerns about War on Iraq." *New York Times*, September 8, 2002, A1.

Cohn, Edward. "Paul Cassell and the Goblet of Fire." *American Prospect* (Princeton), August 28, 2000, 32–36.

Cole, David. "Damage Control? A Comment on Professor Neuman's Reading of Reno v. AADC." *Georgetown Immigration Law Journal* 14 (2000): 347–62.

———. "Enemy Aliens." *Stanford Law Review* 54 (2002): 953–1004.

———. *Enemy Aliens: Double Standards and Constitutional Freedoms in the War on Terrorism.* New York: New Press, 2003.

———. *No Equal Justice: Race and Class in the American Criminal Justice System.* New York: New Press, 1999.

Cole, David, and James X. Dempsey. *Terrorism and the Constitution: Sacrificing Civil Liberties in the Name of National Security.* New York: New Press, 2d ed., 2002.

Connell III, James G., and René G. Valladares. "Search and Seizure Protections for Undocumented Aliens: The Territoriality and Voluntary Presences Principles in Fourth Amendment Law." *American Criminal Law Review* 34 (1997): 1293–352.

Coolidge, David Orgon, and William C. Duncan. "Reaffirming Marriage: A Presidential Priority." *Harvard Journal of Law and Public Policy* 24 (2001): 623–51.

Coolidge, Mary Roberts. *Chinese Immigration.* New York: Henry Holt and Company, 1909; Arno Press and the *New York Times,* 1969.

Coonan, Terry. "Dolphins Caught in Congressional Fishnets—Immigration Law's New Aggravated Felons." *Georgetown Immigration Law Journal* 12 (1998): 589–619.

Cox, Barbara J. "Same-Sex Marriage and Choice of Law: If We Marry in Hawaii, Are We Still Married When We Return Home?" *Wisconsin Law Review* 1994 (1994): 1033–118.

Crouch, Stanley. "Drawing the Line on Racial Profiling." *New York Daily News,* October 4, 2001, 41.

Culhane, John G. "Uprooting the Arguments against Same-Sex Marriage." *Cardozo Law Review* 20 (1999): 1119–211.

Curtin, Dave. "6 Mideast Students Jailed for Cutting Course Hours." *Denver Post,* December 26, 2002, A01.

Daniel, Caroline, and Jeremy Grant. "Ex-Gang Member Who Went Unnoticed." *Financial Times* (London), June 11, 2002, A1.

Daniels, Roger. *Coming to America: A History of Immigration and Ethnicity in American Life.* New York: HarperCollins, 1990.

Davis, Angela J. "Race, Cops, and Traffic Stops." *University of Miami Law Review* 51 (1997): 425–43.

Davis, Peggy C. "Law as Microaggression." *Yale Law Journal* 98 (1989): 1559–77.

Davis, Sue. "John Paul Stevens." In *The Supreme Court Justices: A Biographical Dictionary,* ed. Melvin I. Urofsky, 409–17. New York: Garland Publishing, 1994.

December 23, 2002. Letter from Feingold et al. to Ashcroft. *Interpreter Releases* 80 (January 13, 2003): 55–58.

Delgado, Richard. *Critical Race Theory: The Cutting Edge.* Philadelphia: Temple University Press, 1995.

Delgado, Richard, and Jean Stefancic. *Critical Race Theory: An Introduction.* New York: NYU Press, 2001.

Denvir, John. *Democracy's Constitution: Claiming the Privileges and Immunities of American Citizenship.* Champaign-Urbana, IL: University of Illinois Press, 2001.

Department of Justice, INS. *Memorandum from Commissioner Doris Meissner to INS Regional Directors et al.,* November 17, 2000.

Derbyshire, John. "A (Potentially) Useful Tool." *The Responsive Community* 12, no. 1 (Winter 2001–02): 67–70.

Dickson, Del. *The Supreme Court in Conference (1940–1985).* New York: Oxford University Press, 2001.

Dillard, Angela. *Guess Who's Coming to Dinner* Now? New York: NYU Press, 2001.

Diller, Matthew. "Working without a Job: The Social Messages of the New Workfare." *Stanford Law and Policy Review* 9 (1998): 19–32.

Dobbs, Dan B. *The Law of Torts.* St. Paul, MN: West, 2000.

Dobbs, Dan B., and Paul T. Hayden. *Torts and Compensation.* St. Paul, MN: West, 3d ed., 1997.

Dong, Selena. "Too Many Asians: The Challenge of Fighting Discrimination against Asian Americans and Preserving Affirmative Action." *Stanford Law Review* 47 (1995): 1027–57.

D'Souza, Dinesh. *The End of Racism.* New York: Free Press, 1995.

Duenas, Christopher. "Coming to America: The Immigration Obstacle Facing Binational Same-Sex Couples." *Southern California Law Review* 73 (2000): 811–41.

Editorial. "No Anthrax Answers This Year." *Washington Post,* December 31, 2001, A16.

———. "No Justice for Immigrants." *Progressive* (Madison), November 1, 1997, 8–9.

———. "Profiling Debate Resumes." *Denver Post,* October 3, 2001, B6.

———. "Tom Tancredo Meet Inspector Javert: An Unseemly Resolve to Deport an Honor Student." *Rocky Mountain News* (Denver, CO), September 17, 2002, 38A.

Eggen, Dan. "FBI Seeks Data on Foreign Students." *Washington Post,* December 25, 2002, A1.

Eilperin, Juliet. "Immigration Critic on the Defensive." *Washington Post,* September 21, 2002, A04.

Eisenberg, Daniel. "How Safe Can We Get?" *Time,* September 24, 2001, 85–89.

Eisenberg, Theodore. "Anthony M. Kennedy." In *The Justices of the United States Supreme Court: Their Lives and Major Opinions,* ed. Leon Friedman and Fred L. Israel. Vol. V, 1731–57. New York: Chelsea House Publishers, 1997.

Eljera, Bert. "Filipinos Find Home in Daly City." *Asian Week,* May 3–9, 1996, http://www.asianweek.com/050396/dalycity.html.

Elliott, Michael. "How the U.S. Missed the Clues." *Time,* May 27, 2002, 24–32.

Eskridge Jr., William N. *Gaylaw: Challenging the Apartheid of the Closet.* Cambridge, MA: Harvard University Press, 1999.

———. "No Promo Homo: The Sedimentation of Antigay Discourse and the Channeling Effect of Judicial Review." *NYU Law Review* 75 (2000): 1327–411.

Feagin, Joe R. "Old Poison in New Bottles: The Deep Roots of Modern Nativism." In *Immigrants Out!* ed. Juan Perea, 13–43. New York: NYU Press, 1997.

Ferg-Cadima, James A., Legislative Analyst. *MALDEF Survey of Recent State Law and Legislation during the 2003–04 Legislative Term Aimed at Facilitating Undocumented Student Access to State Universities.* Mexican-American Legal Defense Fund, May 18, 2003.

Fix, Michael, and Wendy Zimmerman. *All under One Roof: Mixed Status Families in an Era of Reform.* June 1999. Urban Institute Website, http://www.urban.org/immig/all_under.html.

"Flurry of Legislative Activity Precedes August Recess." *Interpreter Releases* 78 (Aug. 20, 2001): 1346–47.

Foreign Desk. "President Tours Rebel Territory; Philippines: Leader Pays Respects to a Slain Hostage and Lauds Troops for Rescue in a Visit to Underscore Government Control of the Area." *Los Angeles Times,* June 12, 2002, A4.

Frank, Mitch. "Help from an Unlikely Ally." *Time,* July 1, 2002, 28.

General Accounting Office. *U.S. Customs Service, Better Targeting of Airline Passengers for Personal Searches Could Produce Better Results.* Washington, DC: U.S. Government Printing Office, March 2000.

Georgetown Immigration Law Journal. "10th Anniversary Symposium—March 6, 1996 Transcript." *Georgetown Immigration Law Journal* 10 (1996): 5–28.

Gerstmann, Evan. *The Constitutional Underclass: Gays, Lesbians, and the Failure of Class-Based Equal Protection.* Chicago: University of Chicago Press, 1999.

*Gladon v. Greater Cleveland Regional Transit Authority,* 662 N.E.2d 287 (Ohio Supreme Court 1996).

Gleason, Philip. "American Identity and Americanization." In *Concepts of Ethnicity*, ed. William Petersen, Michael Novak, and Philip Gleason, 57–143. Cambridge, MA: Harvard University Press, 1982.

Goldstein, Steve. "Specter Asks Probe of O. J. Simpson Trial Issues." *Philadelphia Inquirer*, October 11, 1995, A17.

Gorov, Lynda. "Cochran Becomes Celebrity, Draws Criticism regarding the Simpson Verdict." *Boston Globe*, October 5, 1995, 31.

Gotanda, Neil. "Asian American Rights and the 'Miss Saigon Syndrome.'" In *Asian Americans and the Supreme Court: A Documentary History*, ed. Hyung-Chan Kim, 1087–103. Westport, CT: Greenwood Press, 1992.

———. Book Review: "Other Non-Whites" in American Legal History: A Review of Justice at War. *Columbia Law Review* 85 (1985): 1186–92.

Gottlieb, Martin. "The Deep Split in Reactions to the Verdict." *New York Times*, October 4, 1995, A1 and A12.

Grondahl, Paul. "Visas in Hand, Foreign Students Fill Employers' Needs." *Times Union* (Albany, NY), July 27, 2003, E1.

Grunwald, Michael. "Muslims Fear Being Made Scapegoats." *Boston Globe*, April 21, 1995, 1.

Gugliotta, Guy. "Tech Companies See Market for Detection." *Washington Post*, September 28, 2001, A08.

Gulbis, Vitauts M. "Modern Status of Rules Conditioning Landowner's Liability upon Status of Injured Party as Invitee, Licensee, or Trespasser." *American Law Reports, 4th* 22 (1981): 294–314.

Haberman, Clyde. "Immigrants: In Plain Sight, But Not Seen." *New York Times*, July 22, 1997, B1.

Hall, Mary Lee. "Defending the Rights of H-2A Farmworkers." *North Carolina Journal of International Law and Commercial Regulation* 27 (2002): 521–37.

Hall, Wiley A. "Arab-Americans Assail Rush to Judgment." *Baltimore Evening Sun*, April 25, 1995, 2A.

Haney López, Ian F. *White by Law: The Legal Construction of Race*. New York: NYU Press, 1996.

Harris, David A. *Profiles in Injustice: Why Racial Profiling Cannot Work*. New York: New Press, 2002.

———. "The Stories, the Statistics, and the Law." *Minnesota Law Review* 84, no. 265–326 (1999).

Hazeldean, Susan, and Heather Betz. "Years Behind: What the United States Must Learn about Immigration Law and Same-Sex Couples." *Human Rights*, Summer 2003, 17–18.

Herrera, Irma D. *Hispanic Attitudes toward Adoption*, http://www.pactadopt.org/press/articles/hispanic.html.

Herrnstein, Richard J., and Charles Murray. *The Bell Curve.* New York: Simon & Schuster, 1996.

Hinton, Eric L. "Racial Profiling: Is It Ever the Right Thing to Do?" *Diversity-Inc. Magazine,* November–December 2002, 111, 112.

Hodges, Michael. "Lindh Faces Court." *Houston Chronicle,* January 25, 2002, 1.

Holmes, Oliver Wendell. *The Common Law.* Boston: Little, Brown, 1881; Little, Brown, 1938.

Homeland Security: Information Sharing Responsibilities, Challenges, and Key Management Issues (U.S. General Accounting Office, May 8, 2003).

Hughes, John. "New Baggage Screening Raises Concerns." *Chicago Sun-Times,* December 31, 2002, 50.

Hull, Elizabeth. *Without Justice for All: The Constitutional Rights of Aliens.* Westport, CT: Greenwood Press, 1985.

Hurst, Charles E. *Social Inequality: Forms, Causes, and Consequences.* Boston: Allyn and Bacon, 5th ed., 2004.

Ignatius, Sarah B., and Elisabeth S. Stickney. *Immigration Law and the Family.* St. Paul, MN: West, 2003.

INS. "Fact Sheet: Student and Exchange Visitor Information System (SEVIS)— Final Rule Implementing SEVIS." December 11, 2002, http://www.immigration.gov/graphics/publicaffairs/factsheets/02.12FINALRU_FS.htm.

INS. *Special Registration.* http://www.immigration.gov/graphics/shared/lawenfor/specialreg/index.htm.

Irons, Peter. *The Courage of Their Convictions: Sixteen Americans Who Fought Their Way to the Supreme Court.* New York: Free Press, 1988; Penguin, 1990.

James, Steve. "Warm-Up for O. J. Final Arguments." *Chicago Sun-Times,* September 25, 1995, 16.

Jeffries Jr., John C. *Justice Lewis F. Powell, Jr.* New York: C. Scribner's Sons, 1994.

Joe, Harry J. "Temporary Entry of Business Persons to the United States under the North American Free Trade Agreement." *Georgetown Immigration Law Journal* 8 (1994): 391–414.

Johnson, Kevin R. "The Case against Race Profiling in Immigration Enforcement." *Washington University Law Quarterly* 78 (2000): 675–736.

———. "Civil Rights and Immigration: Challenges for the Latino Community in the Twentieth Century." *La Raza Law Journal* 8 (1995): 42–89.

———. "The End of 'Civil Rights' As We Know It? Immigration and Civil Rights in the New Millennium." *UCLA Law Review* 49 (2002): 1481–511.

———. "An Essay on Immigration Politics, Popular Democracy, and California's Proposition 187: The Political Relevance and Legal Irrelevance of Race." *Washington Law Review* 70 (1995): 629–73.

——. "Free Trade and Closed Borders: NAFTA and Mexican Immigration to the United States." *University of California at Davis Law Review* 27 (1994): 937–78.

——. *How Did You Get to Be Mexican?* Philadelphia: Temple University Press, 1998.

——. *The "Huddled Masses" Myth: Immigration and Civil Rights.* Philadelphia: Temple University Press, 2004.

——. "Immigration and Latino Identity." *Chicano-Latino Law Review* 19 (1998): 197–211.

——. "Public Benefits and Immigration: The Intersection of Immigration Status, Ethnicity, Gender, and Class." *UCLA Law Review* 42 (1995): 1509–75.

——. "Race, the Immigration Laws, and Domestic Race Relations: A 'Magic Mirror' into the Heart of Darkness." *Indiana Law Journal* 73 (1998): 1111–59.

——. "Racial Hierarchy, Asian Americans and Latinos as 'Foreigners,' and Social Change: Is Law the Way to Go?" *Oregon Law Review* 76 (1997): 347–68.

——. "September 11 and Mexican Immigrants: Collateral Damage Comes Home." *DePaul Law Review* 52 (2003): 849–70.

——. "U.S. Border Enforcement: Drugs, Migrants, and the Rule of Law." *Villanova Law Review* 47 (2002): 897–919.

Johnson, Kevin R., ed. *Mixed Race America and the Law.* New York: NYU Press, 2002.

Johnson, Kirk. "On King Holiday, Words of Peace and Protest." *New York Times,* January 16, 1996, B1.

Jones, John Paul. "Anthony McLeod Kennedy." In *The Supreme Court Justices: A Biographical Dictionary,* ed. Melvin I. Urofsky, 277–79. New York: Garland Publishing, 1994.

Kampeas, Ron. "Anthrax Probe Figure to Undergo Blood Test." *Chicago Sun-Times,* August 26, 2002, 5.

Kang, Jerry. "Racial Violence against Asian Americans." *Harvard Law Review* 106 (1993): 1926–43.

Kaplan, Karen. "Fighting Terrorism." *Los Angeles Times,* September 20, 2001, T1.

Katel, Peter. "Slamming the Door." *Time,* March 11, 2002, 37.

Keeton et al., W. Page. *Prosser and Keeton on the Law of Torts.* St. Paul, MN: West, 5th ed., 1984.

Kennedy, Duncan. *A Critique of Adjudication.* Cambridge, MA: Harvard University Press, 1997.

Kennedy, Randall. "A Natural Aristocracy?" *Constitutional Commentary* 12 (1995): 175–77.

——. *Race, Crime and the Law.* Cambridge, MA: Pantheon, 1997.

Kershaw, Sarah. "Cabby's Shift Is a Night of Calculating Risks." *New York Times,* May 1, 2000, A1 and A24.

Kim, Hyung-Chan. *A Legal History of Asian Americans, 1790–1990.* Westport, CT: Greenwood Press, 1994.

Kinsley, Michael. "Discrimination We're Afraid to Be Against." *The Responsive Community* 12 (Winter 2001–02): 64–66.

———. "When Is Racial Profiling Okay?" *Washington Post,* September 30, 2001, B7.

Kloppenberg, Lisa. *Playing It Safe: How the Supreme Court Sidesteps Hard Cases and Stunts the Development of Law.* New York: NYU Press, 2001.

Knauff, Ellen Raphael. *The Ellen Knauff Story.* New York: W. W. Norton, 1952.

Koppelman, Andrew. "Dumb and DOMA: Why the Defense of Marriage Act Is Unconstitutional." *Iowa Law Review* 83 (1997): 1–33.

Kranes, Martha. "Anthrax Probe Shifts to Homegrown Hate Groups." *New York Post,* October 25, 2001, 4.

Kristof, Nicholas D. "Security and Freedom." *New York Times,* September 10, 2002, A25.

Kuruvila, Matthai Chakko. "Muslims Allege Customs Intrusions." *San Jose Mercury News* (San Jose, CA), May 29, 2003, 2.

Kurzban, Ira J. *Kurzban's Immigration Law Sourcebook.* 8th ed., 16. Washington, DC: American Immigration Law Foundation, 2002–03.

LaFave, Wayne R. *Search and Seizure: A Treatise on the Fourth Amendment.* St. Paul, MN: West, 3d ed., 1996.

Larrabee, Jennifer A. "'DWB (Driving While Black)' and Equal Protection: The Realities of an Unconstitutional Police Practice." *Journal of Law and Policy* 6 (1997): 291–328.

"Lawsuits Accuse 4 Airlines of Bias." *Washington Post,* June 5, 2002, A01.

Lazarus, Edward. *Closed Chambers: The Rise, Fall, and Future of the Modern Supreme Court.* New York: Times Books, 1998; Penguin, 1999.

Lee, Martin A. "The Swastika and the Crescent." *Intelligence Report (Southern Poverty Law Center)* Spring 2002, http://www.splcenter.org/intel/intelreport/article.jsp?aid=132.

Legomsky, Stephen H. *Immigration and Refugee Law and Policy.* 3d ed. New York: Foundation Press, 2002.

———. "Immigration Law and the Principle of Plenary Congressional Power." *Supreme Court Review* 1984 (1984): 255–307.

———. "Ten More Years of Plenary Power: Immigration, Congress, and the Courts." *Hastings Constitutional Law Quarterly* 22 (1995): 925–37.

Lemonick, Michael D. "Lessons Learned: Anthrax." *Time,* December 31, 2001, 126–28.

Lesbian and Gay Immigration Rights Task Force. *Anthony Sullivan and Richard Adams, Plaintiffs in 1982 Case against INS, Celebrate 25th Anniversary.* Fall

1996. Task Force Update, http://www.lgirtf.org/newsletters/Fall96/FA96-12.html.

———. *"Oh Canada, Glorious and Free": French/American Binational Couple Immigrates to Begin New Life Together.* Winter 1997. Task Force Update, http://www.lgirtf.org/newsletters/Winter97/W6.html.

Levine, Susan. "On the Verge of Exile: For Children Adopted from Abroad." *Washington Post,* March 5, 2000, A01.

LGIRTF. *PPIA Gains Landmark Political Support.* July 14, 2003, http://www.lgirtf.org/ppiapress.html.

Lichtblau, Eric, Ricardo Alonso-Zaldivar, and Nick Anderson. "After the Attack, Security Clampdown." *Los Angeles Times,* September 17, 2001, A9.

Lind, Michael. "The Beige and the Black." *New York Times Magazine,* August 16, 1998, 38–39.

Lords, Erik. "Part-Time Students to Return to U.S." *Detroit Free Press,* August 27, 2002.

López, Gerald P. "Undocumented Mexican Migration: In Search of a Just Immigration Law and Policy." *UCLA Law Review* 28 (1981): 615–714.

Maclin, Tracey. "Race and the Fourth Amendment." *Vanderbilt Law Review* 51 (1998): 333–92.

Mailman, Stanley, and Stephen Yale-Loehr. "College for Undocumented Immigrants after All?" *New York Law Journal,* June 25, 2001, 3.

Maio, Gregory R., Victoria M. Esses, and D. W. Bell. "Ambivalence and Persuasion: The Processing of Messages about Immigrant Groups." *Journal of Experimental Psychology* 32 (1996): 513–36.

———. "The Formation of Attitudes toward New Immigrant Groups." *Journal of Applied Psychology* 24, no. 19 (1994): 1762–76.

"Malaysia's Biggest Student Association Slams U.S. 'Phobia.'" *IRNA On-Line,* December 27, 2002, http://www.irna.com/en/head/021227125633.ehe.shtml.

Malkin, Michelle. *Invasion: How America Welcomes Terrorists, Criminals, and Other Foreign Menaces to Our Shores.* Washington, DC: Regnery Publishing, 2002.

Martin, David A. "On Counterintuitive Consequences and Choosing the Right Control Group: A Defense of Reno v. AADC." *Georgetown Immigration Law Journal* 14 (2000): 363–83.

Martin, Susan Taylor. "Despite Adversity, Deportee Now Has New Life." *St. Petersburg Times,* August 28, 2000, A4.

Martinez, Demetria. "Hatred Rumbles Along New Fault Line Called Proposition 187." *National Catholic Reporter* (Kansas City), February 10, 1995, 18.

Mayer, Jane. "Lost in the Jihad." *New Yorker,* March 10, 2003, 50–59.

McClain Jr., Charles. "The Chinese Struggle for Civil Rights in Nineteenth-Century America: The First Phase, 1850–1870." *California Law Review* 72 (1984): 529–68.

McGeary, Johanna. "Next Stop Mindanao." *Time,* January 28, 2002, 36–38.

McGuire, Michael. "Vatican Assaults Same-Sex Marriages." *Chicago Tribune,* August 1, 2003, 1.

Menand, Louis. *The Metaphysical Club.* New York: Farrar, Straus and Giroux, 2001.

Mitford, Jessica. "The Criminal Type." In *The Dilemmas of Corrections,* 3d ed., ed. Kenneth C. Haas and Geoffrey P. Alpert, 21–28. Prospect Heights, IL: Waveland Press, 1995.

Miyamoto, Maryann Kamali. "The First Amendment after Reno v. American-Arab Anti-Discrimination Committee: A Different Bill of Rights for Aliens?" *Harvard Civil Rights–Civil Liberties Law Review* 35 (2000): 183–223.

Morawetz, Nancy. "Understanding the Impact of the 1996 Deportation Laws and the Limited Scope of Proposed Reforms." *Harvard Law Review* 113 (2000): 1936–62.

Motomura, Hiroshi. "The Curious Evolution of Immigration Law: Procedural Surrogates for Substantive Constitutional Rights." *Columbia Law Review* 92 (1992): 1625–704.

———. "Immigration Law after a Century of Plenary Power: Phantom Constitutional Norms and Statutory Interpretation." *Yale Law Journal* 100 (1990): 545–613.

Mrkvicka, Mike. "Hutchison Backs Part-Time Foreign Students." *El Paso Times* (El Paso, TX), July 2, 2002, 01.

Murdoch, Joyce, and Deb Price. *Courting Justice: Gay Men and Lesbians v. the Supreme Court.* New York: Basic Books, 2001.

Neuman, Gerald L. "Aliens as Outlaws: Government Services, Proposition 187, and the Structure of Equal Protection Doctrine." *UCLA Law Review* 42 (1995): 1425–52.

———. *Strangers to the Constitution: Immigrants, Borders, and Fundamental Law.* Princeton: Princeton University Press, 1996.

———. "Terrorism, Selective Deportation and the First Amendment after Reno v. AADC." *Georgetown Immigration Law Journal* 14 (2000): 313–46.

"New Immigrants Winning Much Wider Acceptance: More Americans Meeting, Learning about Newcomers." *Orlando Sentinel* (Florida), June 15, 1997, A12.

*North Jersey Media Group, Inc. v. Ashcroft,* 308 F.3d 198 (3d Cir. 2002).

Norton-Taylor, Richard. "War on Terror 'Makes World More Perilous'—Amnesty Condemns U.S. and Britain on Human Rights." *Guardian* (London), May 28, 2003, P14.

Novack, Kate. "Let the Airport Scramble Begin." *Time,* June 2, 2003, 20.

Nowak, John E., and Ronald D. Rotunda. *Constitutional Law.* St. Paul, MN: West, 6th ed., 2000.

Oblander, Terry. "Clemency Proposal Rejected by Taft; Man Faced Deportation on Drug Sale Charge." *Plain Dealer* (Cleveland, OH), August 26, 2000, 1B.

Office of Congressman Chris Cannon. *Press Release, Cannon Introduces the Student Adjustment Act, Designed to Help Children of Illegal Immigrants Gain Access to Higher-Ed.* June 7, 2001, http://www.house.gov/cannon /press2001/jun07.htm.

Office of the Press Secretary. "First 100 Days of Homeland Security." April 29, 2003, http://www.whitehouse.gov/news/releases/2003/04/20030429-7.html.

Olivas, Michael A. "The Chronicles, My Grandfather's Stories, and Immigration Law: The Slave Traders Chronicle as Racial History." *St. Louis Law Journal* 34 (1990): 425–41.

———. "Storytelling out of School: Undocumented College Residency, Race, and Reaction." *Hastings Constitutional Law Quarterly* 22 (1995): 1019–86.

Paddock, Richard C. "U.S. to Help Philippines Battle Terrorist Threat in Asia." *Los Angeles Times,* December 16, 2001, A1.

"Part-Time Commuter Students Will No Longer Be Admitted to Schools in U.S." *Interpreter Releases* 79 (June 3, 2002): 872–73.

Passel, Jeffrey S., Randy Capps, and Michael Fix. January 12, 2004. *Undocumented Immigration: Facts and Figures.* http://www.urban.org/url.cfm?ID =1000587.

Passel, Jeffrey S., and Michael Fix. "U.S. Immigration in a Global Context: Past, Present and Future." *Indiana Journal of Global Legal Studies* 2 (1994): 5–19.

Paulson, Amanda. "Debate on Gay Unions Splits among Generations." *Christian Science Monitor* (Boston), July 7, 2003, 01.

PBS On-Line Newshour. "Profile of a Terrorist." September 26, 2001, http://www.pbs.org/newshour/bb/terrorism/July-dec01/racial_profile.html.

Pennsylvania State University Department of Health and Human Services Prevention Research Center for the Promotion of Human Development, Middle Childhood Projects. http:/www.prevention.psu.edu/middle.html.

Pineros y Campesinos Unidos del Noroeste. *PCUN Homepage.* http://www.pcun .org.

Pinker, Steven. *How the Mind Works.* New York: W. W. Norton, 1997.

Polgreen, Lydia. "Bollywood Farce: Indian Actress and Family Are Detained." *New York Times,* July 18, 2002, B1.

Polling the Nations Website. http://poll.orspub.com.

Pollard, Kelvin M., and William P. O'Hare. "America's Racial and Ethnic Minorities." *Population Bulletin* 54, no. 3, September 1999, http://www.prb .org/Content/NavigationMenu/PRB/AboutPRB/Population_Bulletin2/Americas_Racial_and_Ethnic_Minorities.htm.

Post, Robert. "What Is the Constitution's Worst Provision?" *Constitutional Commentary* 12 (1995): 191–93.

Press Release. *House of Representatives Passes Delahunt Child Citizenship Bill.* 2001, http://www.holtintl.org/update091900bpr.html.

Price, Deb. "Parents Join Fight to Let Gays Marry." *The Detroit News,* August 1, 2003, 9A.

Rabinowitz, Dorothy. "Hijacking History." *Wall Street Journal,* December 7, 2001, A18.

Ratnesar, Romesh. "How Safe Now?" *Time,* May 27, 2002, 34–35.

*The Records of the Federal Convention of 1787.* Ed. Max Farrand. Rev. ed. New Haven: Yale University Press, 1966.

Reed, Cynthia M. "When Love, Comity, and Justice Conquer Borders: INS Recognition of Same-Sex Marriage." *Columbia Human Rights Law Review* 28 (1996): 97–134.

"Rights Groups Sue Due to Arrests of NSEERS Registrants." *Interpreter Releases* 80 (January 13, 2003): 41–43.

Riley, John. "Lindh Admits Guilt." *Newsday* (New York), July 16, 2002, A3.

Ripley, Amanda. "The Case of the Dirty Bomber." *Time,* June 24, 2002, 28–32.

Roberts, Maurice A., and Stephen Yale-Loehr. *Understanding the 1986 Immigration Law.* Washington, DC: Federal Publications, 1987.

Romero, Victor C. "Aren't You a Latino? Building Bridges upon Common Misperceptions." *University of California at Davis Law Review* 33 (2000): 837–49.

———. "Broadening Our World: Citizens and Immigrants of Color in America." *Capital University Law Review* 27 (Fall 1998): 13–31.

———. "The Child Citizenship Act and the Family Reunification Act: Valuing the Citizen Child as Well as the Citizen Parent." *Florida Law Review* 55 (January 2003): 489–509.

———. "The Congruence Principle Applied: Rethinking Equal Protection Review of Federal Alienage Classifications after Adarand Constructors, Inc. v. Peña." *Oregon Law Review* 76 (1997): 425–56.

———. "Decoupling 'Terrorist' from 'Immigrant': An Enhanced Role for the Federal Courts Post-9/11." *Journal of Gender, Race and Justice* 7 (Spring 2003): 201–11.

———. "Devolution and Discrimination." *NYU Annual Survey of American Law* 58 (2002): 377–86.

———. "The Domestic Fourth Amendment Rights of Undocumented Immigrants: On Guitterez and the Tort Law-Immigration Law Parallel." *Harvard Civil Rights–Civil Liberties Law Review* 35 (2000): 57–101.

———. "Expanding the Circle of Membership by Reconstructing the 'Alien': Lessons from Social Psychology and the 'Promise Enforcement' Cases." *University of Michigan Journal of Law Reform* 32 (1998): 1–47.

———. "Noncitizen Students and Immigration Policy Post-9/11." *Georgetown Immigration Law Journal* 17 (Spring 2003): 357–66.

———. "On Élian and Aliens: A Political Solution to the Plenary Power Problem." *NYU Journal of Legislation and Public Policy* 4 (2000–01): 343–86.

———. "Postsecondary Education for Undocumented Immigrants: Promises and Pitfalls." *North Carolina Journal of International and Commercial Regulation* 27 (Spring 2002): 393–418.

———. "Proxies for Loyalty in Constitutional Immigration Law: Citizenship and Race after September 11." *DePaul Law Review* 52 (2003): 871–91.

———. "The Selective Deportation of Same-Gender Partners: In Search of the Rara Avis." *University of Miami Law Review* 56 (2002): 537–600.

———. "Whatever Happened to the Fourth Amendment? Undocumented Immigrants' Rights after INS v. Lopez-Mendoza and United States v. Verdugo-Urquidez." *Southern California Law Review* 65 (1992): 999–1034.

Rosenblatt, Roger. "A Nation of Pained Hearts." *Time,* October 16, 1995, 40–45.

Russell, Katheryn K. "'Driving While Black': Corollary Phenomena and Collateral Consequences." *Boston College Law Review* 40 (1999): 717–31.

Sachs, Susan. "Five Passengers Say Airlines Discriminated by Looks." *New York Times,* June 5, 2002, B4.

Saito, Natsu Taylor. "Alien and Non-Alien Alike: Citizenship, 'Foreignness,' and Racial Hierarchy in American Law." *Oregon Law Review* 76 (1997): 261–345.

———. "Symbolism under Siege: Japanese American Redress and the 'Racing' of Arab Americans as 'Terrorists.'" *Asian Law Journal* 8 (2001): 1–29.

Salyer, Lucy E. *Law Harsh as Tigers: Chinese Immigrants and the Shaping of Modern Immigration Law.* Chapel Hill: University of North Carolina Press, 1995.

Savage, David G. "Detention of a Citizen Questioned Law: 'Dirty Bomb' Suspect Was Secretly Held and Hasn't Been Charged." *Los Angeles Times,* June 12, 2002, A1.

———. "Terrorism War Arrives at High Court: A Trio of Cases Could Determine How the Government Probes Security Threats." *American Bar Association Journal,* December 2002, 28–30.

Scaperlanda, Michael A. "Are We That Far Gone? Due Process and Secret Deportation Hearings." *Stanford Law and Policy Review* 7 (1996): 23–30.

———. "The Domestic Fourth Amendment Rights of Aliens: To What Extent Do They Survive United States v. Verdugo-Urquidez?" *Missouri Law Review* 56 (1991): 213–43.

———. "Partial Membership: Aliens and the Constitutional Community." *Iowa Law Review* 81 (1996): 707–73.

Schmidley, Diane. *The Foreign Born Population in the United States: March 2002.* February 2003, http://www.census.gov/prod/2003pubs/p20-539.pdf.

Schmidt, Susan. "Evidence Lacking as Probe of Scientist in Anthrax Scare Intensifies." *Washington Post,* August 15, 2002, A07.

Schmidt, Susan, and Walter Pincus. "Al Muhajir Alleged to Be Scouting Terror Sites; U.S. Says Al Qaeda Had Instructed Suspect." *Washington Post,* June 12, 2002, A01.

Schmitt, Eric. "Ruling Clears Way to Use State Police in Immigration Duty." *New York Times,* April 4, 2002, A19.

Schodolski, Vincent J. "Immigrants Face Deportation for Old Crimes under New Laws: Reform Snares Legal Residents." *Chicago Tribune,* October 12, 1997, 3.

Schuck, Peter H. "A Case for Profiling." *American Lawyer,* January 2002, 59–61.

———. *Citizens, Strangers, and In-Betweens.* Boulder, CO: Westview Press, 1998.

———. "The Transformation of Immigration Law." *Columbia Law Review* 84 (1984): 1–90.

Schulhofer, Stephen J. *The Enemy Within.* New York: Century Foundation Press, 2002.

Sengupta, Somini. "Ill-Fated Path to America, Jail and Death." *New York Times,* November 5, 2001, A1.

Shenon, Philip. "Secret Court Says It Was Misled by FBI." *San Diego Union-Tribune,* August 23, 2002, A01.

Sievert, Ronald J. "Meeting the Twenty-First-Century Terrorist Threat within the Scope of Twentieth-Century Constitutional Law." *Houston Law Review* 37 (2000): 1421–64.

Silverman, Andrew R. "Outcomes of Transracial Adoption." *The Future of Children: Adoption* 3, no. 1, Spring 1993, http://www.futureofchildren.org/usr_doc/vol3no1ART7%2EPDF.

Simpson, Alan. "Missing the Point on Gays." *Washington Post,* September 5, 2003, A21.

Singer, Stephen J. "Racial Profiling Also Has a Good Side." *Newsday,* September 25, 2001, A38.

Slevin, Peter. "In Anthrax Probe, Questions of Skill, Motive." *Washington Post,* November 5, 2001, A05.

Sokoloff, Burton Z. "Antecedents of American Adoption." *The Future of Children: Adoption* 3, no. 1, Spring 1993, http://www.futureofchildren.org/information2826/information_show.htm?doc_id=77441.

Soysal, Yasemin Nuhog̃lu. *Limits of Citizenship: Migrants and Postnational Membership in Europe.* Chicago: University of Chicago Press, 1994.

Spiro, Peter. "Learning to Live with Immigration Federalism." *Connecticut Law Review* 29 (1997): 1627–46.

Steiker, Jordan, Sanford Levinson, and J. M. Balkin. "Taking Text and Structure Really Seriously: Constitutional Interpretation and the Crisis of Presidential Eligibility." *Texas Law Review* 74 (1995): 237–57.

Stern, Jessica. *The Ultimate Terrorists.* Cambridge, MA: Harvard University Press, 1999.

Stevenson, Robert Louis. *Dr. Jekyll and Mr. Hyde.* London: Longmans, Green, 1886; New York: Penguin, 1994.

Stolley, Kathy S. "Statistics on Adoption in the United States." *Adoption* 3, no. 1, Spring 1993, http://www.futureofchildren.org/usr_doc/vol3no1ART2%2EPDF.

Story, Joseph. *Commentaries on the Constitution.* Hilliard, Gray and Company, and Brown, Shattuck and Company: Boston and Cambridge, 1833. 1997, http://www.constitution.org/js/js_000.htm.

———. *Commentaries on the Constitution of the United States.* Boston: Hilliard, Gray, and Company, 1833; New York: Da Capo Press, 1970.

Sullivan, Andrew. "Beware the Straight Backlash." *Time,* August 11, 2003, 35.

Sunstein, Cass R. *One Case at a Time: Judicial Minimalism on the Supreme Court.* Cambridge, MA: Harvard University Press, 1999.

Swarns, Rachel L. "Old ID Card Gives New Status to Mexicans in U.S." *New York Times,* August 25, 2003.

Symposium. "Gay Rights and the Courts: The Amendment 2 Controversy." *University of Colorado Law Review* 68 (Spring 1997): 287–452.

———. "Romer v. Evans." *William and Mary Bill of Rights Journal* 6 (Winter 1997): 89–259.

The Tarnished Golden Door: Civil Rights Issues in Immigration (Commission on Civil Rights, 1980).

Thomas, David. "Initiative Will Level Playing Field." *Los Angeles Times,* March 10, 1996, B4.

Thompson, Anthony C. "Stopping the Usual Suspects: Race and the Fourth Amendment." *NYU Law Review* 74 (1999): 956–1013.

"Times Poll/A Look at the Electorate." *Los Angeles Times,* November 10, 1994, B2.

Toner, Robin. "Opposition to Gay Marriage Is Declining, Study Finds." *New York Times,* July 25, 2003, A16.

Treviño, Joseph. "Degrees of Inequality." August 24–30, 2001. *Los Angeles Weekly,* http://www.laweekly.com/ink/01/40/news-trevino.shtml.

Tsuang, Grace W. "Assuring Equal Access of Asian Americans to Highly Selective Universities." *Yale Law Journal* 98 (1989): 659–78.

Uchitelle, Louis. "I.N.S. Is Looking the Other Way as Illegal Immigrants Fill

Jobs: Enforcement Changes in Face of Labor Shortage." *New York Times,* March 9, 2000, C1.

U.S. Dept. of Homeland Security. "Border Reorganization Fact Sheet." January 30, 2003, http://www.immigration.gov/graphics/publicaffairs/factsheets/bt-sreog.pdf.

U.S. Dept. of Homeland Security. *Immigration and Borders.* http://www.dhs.gov /dhspublic/theme_home4.jsp.

Valdes, Frank, Jerome McCristal Culp, and Angela P. Harris, eds. *Crossroads, Directions, and a New Critical Race Theory.* Philadelphia: Temple University Press, 2002.

Van Biema, David. "As American as . . ." *Time,* October 1, 2001, 72–74.

Vega, Cecilia M. "Sonoma Accepts Mexican ID Cards." *The Press-Democrat On-Line,* August 21, 2003, http://www.pressdemocrat.com/local/news /21id_b1cityb.html.

Vermont Civil Union Review Commission. "Report of the Vermont Civil Union Review Commission." January 2001, http://www.leg.state.vt.us/baker/cure-port.htm.

Volpp, Leti. "The Citizen and the Terrorist." *UCLA Law Review* 49 (2002): 1575–99.

Walsh, Edward. "High Court Stays Out of Secrecy Fray; Dispute Centers on Closed Deportation." *Washington Post,* May 28, 2003, A04.

Walzer, Michael. *Spheres of Justice: A Defense of Pluralism and Equality.* New York: Basic Books, 1983.

Wani, Ibrahim J. "Truth, Strangers, and Fiction: The Illegitimate Uses of Legal Fiction in Immigration Law." *Cardozo Law Review* 11 (1989): 51–118.

Wardle, Lynn D. "A Critical Analysis of Constitutional Claims for Same-Sex Marriage." *BYU Law Review* 1996 (1996): 1–101.

Weaver, Charlie, and Robert Ulrich. "Mr. Magoo v. the Terrorists." *Washington Times,* August 5, 2002, A17.

Weisselberg, Charles D. "The Exclusion and Detention of Aliens: Lessons from the Lives of Ellen Knauff and Ignatz Mezei." *University of Pennsylvania Law Review* 143 (1995): 933–1034.

Whidden, Michael J. "Unequal Justice: Arabs in America and United States Antiterrorism Legislation." *Fordham Law Review* 69 (2001): 2825–88.

Whitebread II, Charles H., and Christopher Slobogin. *Criminal Procedure.* New York: Foundation Press, 4th ed., 2000.

Williams, Gregory Howard. *Life on the Color Line: The True Story of a White Boy Who Discovered He Was Black.* New York: Dutton, 1995; Penguin, 1996.

Wing, Adrien K. "Reno v. American-Arab Anti-Discrimination Committee: A Critical Race Perspective." *Columbia Human Rights Law Review* 31 (2000): 561–95.

Wise, Tim. "School Shootings and White Denial." *Alternet.Org,* March 6, 2001, http://www.alternet.org/story.html?StoryID=10560.

———. "We Show Our True Colors in Wake of Tragedy." *St. Louis Post-Dispatch,* March 13, 2001, D9.

Wishnie, Michael. "Laboratories of Bigotry? Devolution of the Immigration Power, Equal Protection, and Federalism." *NYU Law Review* 76 (2001): 493–569.

Wu, Frank H. "The Limits of Borders: A Moderate Proposal for Immigration Reform." *Stanford Law and Policy Review* 7 (1996): 35–53.

———. "Neither Black Nor White: Asian Americans and Affirmative Action." *Boston College Third World Law Journal* 15 (1995): 225–84.

———. *Yellow: Race in America beyond Black and White.* New York: Basic Books, 2001.

Wunsch, Gerald A. "Why NAFTA's Immigration Provisions Discriminate against Mexican Nationals." *Indiana International and Comparative Law Review* 5 (1994): 127–42.

Zoglin, Richard, and Sally B. Donnelly. "Welcome to America's Best-Run Airport (And Why It's Still Not Good Enough)." *Time,* July 15, 2002, 22–29.

# Index

Adams v. Howerton, 109–11, 153–54, 192

Antiessentialism: after September 11th, 25, 40; and alienage discrimination, 20–22; and the Border Commuter Student Act of 2002, 48; and the Child Citizenship Act of 2000 (CCA), 59–66; the court's role in, 42; as critical race theory, 5, 8; and the Family Reunification Act of 2001 (FRA), 59–66; and the Fourth Amendment, 89–91; and the Illegal Immigration Reform and Immigrant Responsibility Act of 1996 (IIRAIRA) Section 505, 97; and the U.S. Supreme Court justices, 149–51

Antisubordination: after September 11th, 25; and alienage discrimination, 20–22; and the Border Commuter Student Act of 2002, 48; and the Child Citizenship of 2000 (CCA), 59–66; the court's role in, 42; as critical race theory, 5–6, 8; and the Family Reunification Act of 2001 (FRA), 59–66; and fathers as a privileged class, 155; and the Fourth Amendment, 89–91; and the Illegal Immigration Reform and Immigrant Responsibility Act of 1996 (IIRAIRA) Section 505, 97;

and the U.S. Supreme Court justices, 149–51

Bivens v. Six Unknown Named Agents of the Federal Bureau of Narcotics, 88

Border Commuter Student Act of 2002, 48–49

Boy Scouts of America v. Dale, 134–36, 158

Bracero Program, 165

Brown v. Board of Education, 42, 151, 191

Cabell v. Chavez-Salido, 168

Chae Chan Ping v. United States, 10–11, 79, 141, 163–64

Chevron U.S.A., Inc. v. Natural Resources Defense Council, Inc., 154

Child Citizenship Act of 2000 (CCA), 51–57; analysis of, 59–66; compared to the Family Reunification of 2001 (FRA), 52, 54, 57–67

Chinese Exclusion Case. See Chae Chan Ping v. United States

Citizenship: and the Immigrant Founder Exception Clause, 32–33; and the Naturalization Clause, 2; and the Presidential Eligibility Clause, 31–35; as proxy for determining loyalty, 25–31; as proxy

# About the Author

Victor C. Romero is Professor of Law at Pennsylvania State University's Dickinson School of Law.